Web-based Learning : Men & Machines

Web-based Learning : Men & Machines

Proceedings of
The First International Conference
on Web-based Learning
in China (ICWL 2002)

Hong Kong *17–19 August 2002*

Editors

Reggie Kwan
The Open University of Hong Kong

Weijia Jia
City University of Hong Kong

Jimmy Chan
The Open University of Hong Kong

Anthony Fong
City University of Hong Kong

Ronnie Cheung
The Hong Kong Polytechnic University

World Scientific
New Jersey • London • Singapore • Hong Kong

Published by

World Scientific Publishing Co. Pte. Ltd.
5 Toh Tuck Link, Singapore 596224
USA office: 27 Warren Street, Suite 401-402, Hackensack, NJ 07601
UK office: 57 Shelton Street, Covent Garden, London WC2H 9HE

British Library Cataloguing-in-Publication Data
A catalogue record for this book is available from the British Library.

WEB-BASED LEARNING: MEN AND MACHINES
Proceedings of the First International Conference on Web-Based Learning in China (ICWL 2002)

ISBN-13 978-981-238-126-2 (pbk)
ISBN-10 981-238-126-0 (pbk)

Conference Organizer

- *Hong Kong Web Society*

In cooperation with

- *City University of Hong Kong*
- *The Hong Kong Polytechnic University*

Conference Sponsors

- *ACM Hong Kong Chapter*
- *IEEE Hong Kong Chapter*
- *K.C. Wong Education Foundation*
- *Lingnan University*
- *Hong Kong Pei Hua Education Foundation Limited*

Message from the ICWL 2002 Program Co-Chairs

Welcome to Hong Kong and the first ICWL Conference. We hope you don't mind the heat and humidity because there are a lot of exciting things to do in Hong Kong.

At ICWL 2002, we have the privilege and honor to have Prof. Shi Kuo Chang as our keynote speaker. We are thrilled to host this event that brings educators from many disciplines together to share ideas in the context of Web-based learning. We anticipate the three-day events will be energizing and informative.

Though ICWL is only in its first year, members of the Organizing Committee think this is just a beginning of our annual gathering. We look forward to meeting with all of you regarding ideas for the future of ICWL and the Hong Kong Web Society. We hope this conference will keep contributing to the field of Web-based learning.

On behalf of the editors of the conference proceedings, we would like to take this opportunity to thank all the authors for their submissions to the conference. Many of them travel great distance to participate in the conference. The editors are grateful to all reviewers for their efforts in reviewing the many submissions. Thanks also go to the colleagues who take care of all the logistics.

Last but not least we would like to express our gratitude to all of the organizations that support our efforts to bring the conference to fruition. We are grateful to the Hong Kong Web Society for the initiation; to The Pui-Hua Education Foundation, K. C. Wong Foundation, City University of Hong Kong, the Polytechnic University of Hong Kong, and Lingnan University for their sponsorships.

Again – Welcome to ICWL2002 and have fun!

Reggie Kwan
Program Co-chair

Weijia Jia
Program Co-chair

Ronnie Cheung
Program Co-chair

ICWL 2002 Organizing Committee

Honorable Conference Chair	T.Y. Cheung, City University of Hong Kong
Conference Chair	Joseph Fong, City University of Hong Kong
Program Co-chairs	Ronnie Cheung, The Hong Kong Polytechnic University
	Weijia Jia, City University of Hong Kong
	Reggie Kwan, Open University of Hong Kong
Organizing Chair	Keith Chan, The Hong Kong Polytechnic University
Industrial Stream	Anthony Fong, City University of Hong Kong
Treasurer	Qing Li, City University of Hong Kong
Publicity	Jimmy Chan, Open University of Hong Kong
Publication	Philip Tsang, Open University of Hong Kong
Web Master	Hong Va Leong, The Hong Kong Polytechnic University
Tutorial	W.Lok Yeung, Lingnan University
Local Arrangement	Margret Ng, Hong Kong Web Society
Conference Secretary	Cherry Chan, The Hong Kong Polytechnic University

Program Committee Members

Aberer, Karl	GMD-IPSI, Germany
Bressan, Stêphane	National University of Singapore, Singapore
Busseler, Christoph	Oracle Corporation, U.S.A.
Cao, Jiannong	Hong Kong Polytechnic University, Hong Kong
Chan, Daniel	SYSTEK Information Technology Ltd., Hong Kong
Chang, Elizabeth	IPower B2B, Australia
Chen, Arbee	National Tsing Hua University, Taiwan, R.O.C.
Chen, Houn-Gee	National Chung Cheng University, Taiwan , R.O.C.
Chen, Peter	Lousiana State University, U.S.A.
Cheung, David	University of Hong Kong, Hong Kong, China
Chin, Francis	University of Hong Kong, Hong Kong, China
Corkindale, David	University of South Australia, Australia
Dillon, Tharam	LaTrobe University, Australia
Fung Chiwai	Vocation Training Council-IVE, Hong Kong
Halang, Wolfgang	Fernuniversitaet Hagen, Germany
Hou, Wen-Chi	Southern Illionis University at Cardondate, U.S.A
Hughes, John	University of Ulster, Northern Ireland
Huang, Shi-Ming	National Chung Cheng University, Taiwan, R.O.C.
Ip, Horace	City University of Hong Kong, Hong Kong
Jin, Qun	University of Aizu, Japan
Karlapalem, Kamal	Indian Institute of Information Technology, India
Kunii, Tosiyasu	Hosei University, Japan
Lam, Ernest	Hong Kong Baptist University, Hong Kong
Lee, Dik	Hong Kong Uni. of Science&Technology, H. K.
Le Gruenwald, G.	University of Oklahoma, U.S.A.
Li, Guojie	Institute of Computing Technology, China
Liu, Chun Nian	Beijing Polytechnic University, China
Maier, David	Oregon Graduate Institute, Oregon, U.S.A
McLeod, Dennis	University of Southern California, U.S.A
Meersman, Robert	Free University of Brussels, Belgium
Mylopoulos, John	University of Toronto, Canada

Program Committee Members (continued ...)

Navathe, Shamkant	Georgia Institute of Technology, U.S.A
Orlowska, Maria	University of Queensland, Australia
Paul, Ray	Brunel University, U.K.
Smith, Peter	University of Sunderland, U.K
Su, Stanley	University of Florida, U.S.A.
Tang, Changjie	Sichuan University, China
Thalheim, Bernhard	Technical University Cottbus, Germany
Thiel Ulrich	Fraunhofer IPSI, Germany
Tjoa, A Min	Vienna University of Technology, Austria
Wong, Tat-Meng	Open University of Hong Kong, Hong Kong
Wei, Sun	Florida International University, U.S.A
Wong, Kam-Fai	Chinese University of Hong Kong, Hong Kong
Wu, Simon	Merrill Lynch, U.S.A
Zhao, Wei	Texas A & M University, Texas, U.S.A.
Zhou, Wanlei	Deakin University, Australia
Zhuang, Yueting	Zhejiang University, China

Contents

PART TWO Models

PART THREE Tools

PART ONE Applications

A Web-Based Computer-Aided Learning Package on Pipe Flow

P.K. Yu[1] and K.W. Chau[1]

[1]Department of Civil and Structural Engineering, Hong Kong Polytechnic University, Hunghom, Kowloon, Hong Kong
cekwchau@polyu.edu.hk

Abstract. Recent development in information technology establishes a new education paradigm, for which self-directed learning is a foundation strategy. Nowadays, web-based learning, which has the potential to effect fundamental changes in the design of learning processes and the education system, has been gaining momentum with an irreversible trend. In this paper, the development and implementation of a web-based interactive computer-aided learning package on pipe flow is delineated. Several up-to-date expert system shell and web production software including Visual Rule Studio, Dreamweaver, Fireworks, Java, JavaScript, Flash, are employed during its development. This learning package is tailored for the convenience of students in allowing them to click through to acquire the explanations of key concepts in pipe flow. It is demonstrated that various theories on pipe flow, design, and interactive "What-if" analysis on various design parameters can be performed using this package through an active and dynamic learning environment.

1 Introduction

Nowadays, our society has entered into the information age, in which people intend to acquire the information as quickly as possible. The widely used World Wide Web can be featured by the high availability in Internet, short learning time in using the graphic interface browsers and open standard, and portability between different operating systems and platforms. The information released in the Internet is no longer limited to text and graphics as normally presented in the conventional textbooks. The linked material could be in a variety of formats including sound, picture, video, 3-D modeling, animation or application. When new packages of educational materials are developed, these characteristics are capable to enhance the feasibility of the standard HyperText Markup Language (HTML) generally used in the World Wide Web [1].

If a close watch and detailed review are made on the existing educational systems and the population of students under these systems, quite a wide ranges and variations among students can be detected. In recent years, the demand for higher education at different age groups has been increased, particularly in adult age group. There exists a trend that the society increasingly demands people of better educational quality so as to enhance the productivity. As such, if working adults under time and location constraints desire to earn more money in order to improve living conditions for their family, they have to upgrade themselves through various channels. Web-based learning (WBL) becomes one of these viable alternatives.

With the recent technological advancements in the fields of computer technology, artificial intelligence technology, education and instructional technology, web-based instruction has been becoming somewhat common place in what would be considered traditional higher educational settings [2]. Many schools try to conduct a minimum of some types of web-based instruction. Additionally an entire new industry of web-based instruction has risen to compete with the universities in this endeavor [3]. A knowledge-based system (KBS) is able to encapsulate systematically the heuristic expertise and knowledge and to accomplish a level of performance comparable to that of a human expert. It is considered suitable for solving problems that demand considerable expertise, judgment or rules of thumb, which can be broadly classified into the following categories: interpretation; design; diagnosis; education; and planning. KBS has been widely and successfully applied in different fields [4-8].

One of the vital drawbacks on traditional teaching and learning system is that it offers no facility in tracking student's progress or keeping courseware up to date. It is not enough just to supply materials to the learners. It has to monitor whether they have accessed the pertinent information, or whether they need to be chased at times. It is extremely important that their records are kept up-to-date and that their progresses could be monitored and recorded. So the old style learning and training system often became out of date almost as soon as it was issued, and sometimes even before, thus wasting a great deal of time and money. However, new technology is invented to change this conventional teaching and learning system. Educators can now deliver far more sophisticated and effective pedagogical programs, through the implementation of WBL.

For diverse ranges of individuals who would not normally be able to further their education, WBL furnishes a flexible and cost-effective means and opportunity of access to lifelong educational opportunities. As such, it is generally expected that the groups best served by this learning mode are individuals who work, live in remote areas, have special needs, and have family responsibilities. Furthermore, WBL provides the opportunity for interaction from the learners, thus allowing them to tailor learning experiences to meet their specific needs or abilities. The web-based interactive system allows a student to dip-in and dip-out of the different course sections. As such, participants can directly access to different sections, and if they encounter any queries, they can point straight back into the pertinent sections or into the references and back again. It supports an active and dynamic learning environment and offers the possibility of providing a stimulating learning environment to engage learners in meaningful learning through reflection, application, and interaction. Some organizations use WBL in order to raise the effectiveness of their education and training operations for the ultimate goal in enhancing the productivity. In this way, it allows people work at their own pace from different locations and allows organizations to add their specific knowledge to tailor make the teaching materials.

This paper delineates the development and implementation of a web-based interactive computer-aided learning package on pipe flow, by employing the latest KBS technology and web production software. Custom-built graphical user interfaces are tailored in assisting the learners to acquire the requisite knowledge on this subject.

2 Objectives of the Work

As such, the objectives of this study on web-based computer-aided learning package comprise the followings:

- To illustrate how to apply the web-based interactive computer-aided learning for all learners;
- To offer a user-friendly environment for the users to learn the problem domain using computer-aided learning technique;
- To introduce the topic of pipe flow through WBL;
- To provide less expensive, more convenient, and user-friendly teaching and learning tool for learners;
- To make the users feel inspired and attracted to learn through the Internet instead of textbook;
- To progress from using the Internet to augment courses, to create virtual courses;
- To develop a tool aiming at the integration of textual information and graphical expedients;
- To realize virtual learning for individualized instruction;
- To help arouse the overall awareness of Internet-based teaching options to augment classes.

3 Web-Based Learning Tools

The recent fast-track development of the WBL from a text-only medium to an expanding multimedia communication system has increased and diversified delivery mechanisms of quality education. Commonly used WBL tools include e-mail, listservs, web-based bulletin boards, chat, online courses, electronic performance support system, static web pages and interactive web pages. All of the above Internet-based learning tools can be used together. The numbers of items to be added on the web page depend on the expected requirements of the users. It is worthwhile to emphasize the interactive web pages since they include the ability to search a database, ask questions, customize the look and feel of the site, and perform other types of interaction and online web-based course. Although it can be observed that the number of sites deploying interactive web pages is growing, the number of them are still much less than their counterparts of static web pages, covering the majority of existing WBL sites.

4 Development Environment

With a variety of capabilities provided by different software, it is best to design web pages by coupling the use of several software together, in order to take advantage of their individual functions. Thus, several professional programs, including Visual Rule Studio, Dreamweaver, Fireworks, Java, JavaScript, and Flash, are used in this case.

4.1 Expert System Shell

Expert system shell encapsulating specific representation methods and inference mechanisms is employed in this study, so as to facilitate development of the knowledge base on pipe flow. This system has been implemented with the aid of a microcomputer shell Visual Rule Studio [9], which is a hybrid application development tool under object-oriented design environment. Visual Rule Studio acts as an ActiveX Designer under the Microsoft Visual Basic 6.0 programming environment. Production rules as well as procedural methods are used to represent heuristic and standard engineering knowledge. By isolating rules as component objects, separate from objects and application logic, it produces objects that can interact with virtually any modern development product and thus rule development becomes a natural part of the component architecture development process. Besides, Visual Rule Studio is compatible with Microsoft Internet Information Server and Active Server Pages. As such, in order to allow it to reach any user with a web browser and Intranet or Internet access, the ruleset components can be deployed as part of a web server based application.

With Visual Rule Studio, objects are employed to encapsulate knowledge structure, procedures, and values under the declarative knowledge representation object-oriented programming environment. An object's structure is defined by its class and attribute declarations within a RuleSet. Object behavior is tightly bound to attributes in the form of facets, methods, rules, and demons. Each attribute of a class has a specific attribute type, which may be compound, multi-compound, instance reference, numeric, simple, string, interval, and time. Facets provide control over how the inference engines process and use attributes. Methods establish developer-defined procedures associated with each attribute. The set of backward-chaining rules that conclude the same attribute is called the attribute's rule group. The set of forward-chaining demons that reference the same attribute in their antecedents is called the attribute's demon group. Various types of window display are then defined, which inherit common characteristics and possess their own special properties, with the use of standard Visual Basic classes, including Check Box, Option Button, List Box, Command Button, Text Box, etc.

4.2 Web Page Design Tools

Dreamweaver [10] is used to build the main content, structure, frame, and most of the functions of the web pages. Frames are created by modifying an existing Dreamweaver document and dividing into additional document areas. The contents of the pages are then added by typing or pasting objects. Named anchors, which can set position placemarkers in a document, are used to jump to a specific topic or to the top of a document. Tables, which furnish ways to add vertical and horizontal structure to a page, are used for laying out data and images on an HTML page. Other features include insert layer, insert table, insert image, list the point, swap image, link up each of the web page, insert external program like Java and JavaScript. Java [11] is a programming language that is well suited to designing software that works in conjunction with the Internet. The Netscape Navigator and Microsoft Internet

Explorer browsers can download a Java program from a web page and run it locally on the web user's system. These programs, which are called applets, can be interactive taking user input, responding to it, and presenting ever-changing content. In this interactive package, there are a number of Java programs to illustrate some pipe design calculations. It provides different combinations of variables in the governing equations for users to design their own culverts. The purpose of JavaScript [12] is to add some interactions to HTML, to allow for user interaction and feedback multimedia and animation, and to link HTML to other technologies such as Java and ActiveX. In this learning package, JavaScript is used in the search function to provide multiple web site searching and to add some functions such as the timer in the web page.

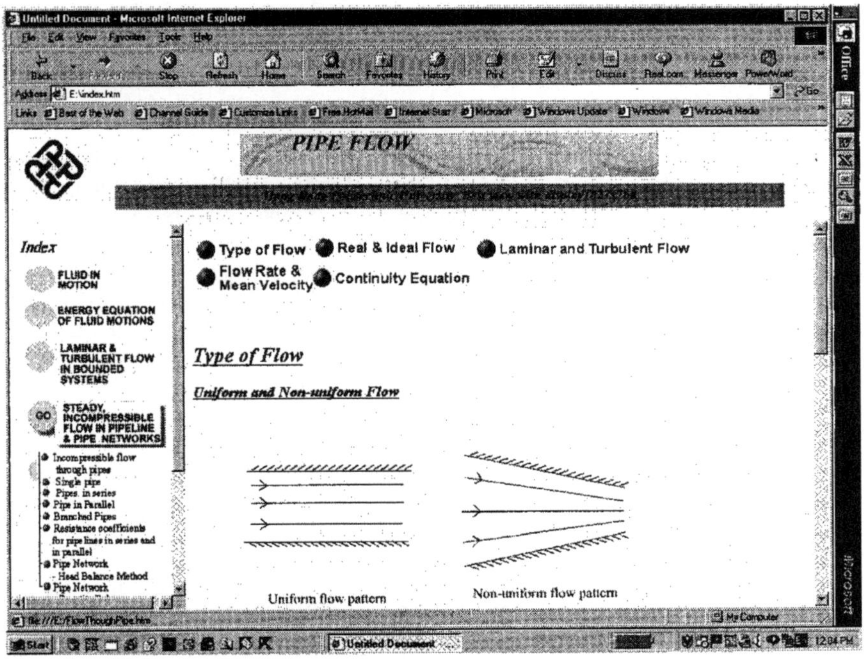

Fig. 1. Screen displaying the opening menu of the computer-aided learning package on pipe flow

Fireworks [13] is mainly employed in making the encapsulated rollover that contains all the possible appearances of the button, representing its various states of use. Each button is designed to have up to four unique appearances or states, namely, up, over, down and over while down. Flash [14] provides the solution for the delivery of vector-based graphics and animation containing multiple scenes. It can create flash animations and interactive activities including vector graphics, interactive movies, buttons with actions, etc. It shows some interactive graphics, which make the web page more active and alive.

5 Learning Package on Pipe Flow

In this learning package, the web pages are basically grouped into two parts. The first part provides the basic concepts of pipe flow [15] to the user, which can be seen to be a one-way information transfer from the webmaster to the user. The second part provides some design exercises and interactive "What-if" analysis about pipe flow for the user to test how they understand the domain topic, which is a two-way information transfer. The user is required to fill in some tables and then the results will be computed automatically. Figure 1 displays the opening menu of the computer-aided learning package on pipe flow. The structures of the web pages are divided into five headings, which include fluid in motion, energy equation of fluid motion, laminar and turbulent flow in bounded systems, steady incompressible flow in pipeline and pipe network, and quasi-steady flow in pipes.

5.1 Fluid in Motion

The user can enter this page by clicking the icon "fluid in motion" on the left-hand side of the main index page. Upon moving the mouse over the icon, the contents of the section, which introduce the basic characteristics of pipe flow, are shown. At the top of the page, there are several icons for switching topics within the section. It is in itself divided into five sub-headings, which are type of flow, real and ideal flow, laminar and turbulent flow, flow rate and mean velocity, and continuity equation. The definitions, together with the principal characteristics, of pipe flow are highlighted.

5.2 Energy Equation of Fluid Motion

This section mainly expounds the energy equation used in pipe flow. This section is divided into two sub-headings, namely, Euler's Equation and Bernoulli's Equation. First of all, the assumptions taken and the derivation of these two governing equations are stated. The concept of net force balance or acceleration on a small elemental stream tube of cylindrical section with uniform cross-sectional area in the direction of the flow is then explained in steps. Pertinent forces acting on the element, including pressure and gravity, are shown together with appropriate graphics. The requisite conditions and assumptions for the derivation of these equations are also described. When a specific command button is clicked, the underlying meaning and significance of these governing equations will be shown. Some illustrative numerical examples with suitable animation graphical effects are then used to demonstrate the application of the equations. Figure 2 shows a screen displaying an illustrative numerical example to demonstrate the application of Bernoulli's Equation.

5.3 Laminar and Turbulent Flow in Bounded Systems

Under this section, the basic concepts of laminar and turbulent flow in bounded systems are articulated. It is further divided into four sub-sections, namely, incompressible steady and uniform laminar flow in circular cross-section pipes, incompressible steady and uniform turbulent flow in circular cross-section pipes, flow at pipe inlet, and separation losses in pipe flow. The assumptions taken and the derivation of the governing equations for both cases are also presented. Figure 3 displays the screen showing instructional knowledge on incompressible steady and uniform laminar flow in circular cross-section pipes. At the top of the web page, several icons are used to switch amongst various topics within this section.

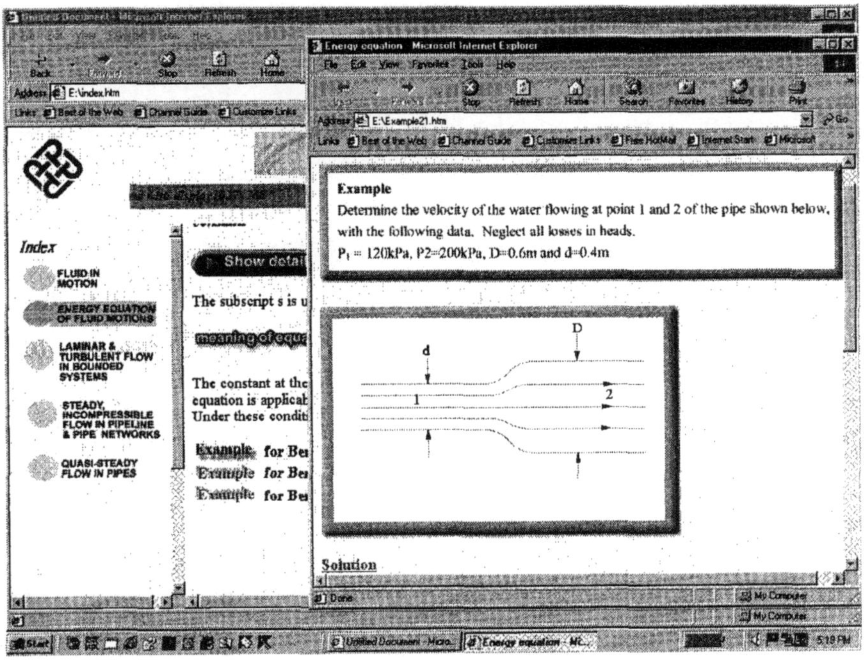

Fig. 2. Screen displaying an illustrative numerical example to demonstrate the application of Bernoulli's Equation

5.4 Steady Incompressible Flow in Pipeline and Pipe Network

This section delineates steady incompressible flow in pipeline and pipe networks. It covers details on incompressible flow through pipes, single pipe, pipes in series, pipe in parallel, branched pipes, resistance coefficients for pipelines in series and in parallel, head balance method for pipe network, and quantity balance method for pipe network. Again, some illustrative numerical examples with suitable animation graphical effects are then used to demonstrate the application of the theories.

5.5 Quasi-steady Flow in Pipes

In this section, the theories on quasi-steady flow in pipes, relating to the time relationship of head loss, discharge rate, and flow velocity, are explained in details. The user can enter this page by clicking the icon "quasi-steady flow in pipes" on the left-hand side of the main web page. The concept is further applied to a few real situations, namely, a tank emptying through an orifice into the atmosphere, the tank or reservoir having a constant inflow, a tank emptying through a pipe into the atmosphere, and flow transfer between two reservoirs having different levels.

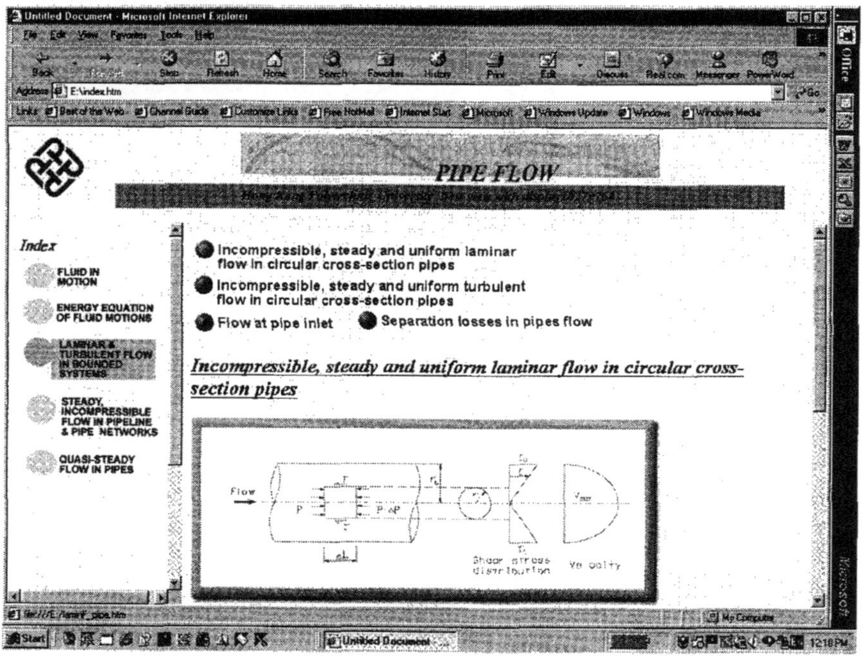

Fig. 3. Screen showing instructional knowledge on incompressible steady and uniform laminar flow in circular cross-section pipes

5.6 Pipe Flow Design

Within this section, knowledge on pipe flow design for pipes with various shapes are incorporated. The user can perform some design exercises as well as "What-if" interactive analyses in this section. Interactive analysis is employed to relieve the intensive computation work for the analytical solution on pipe flow design. In the learning package, it is flexible to perform "What-if" analysis by setting various design parameters through the graphical interface as shown in Figure 4. The user is first required to input the value and then, after having clicked the button, he or she would obtain corresponding results instantly. In total, four different computational options are provided under this section, namely, rectangular culvert, circular pipe, rectangular culvert using end depth method, and circular pipe using end depth method.

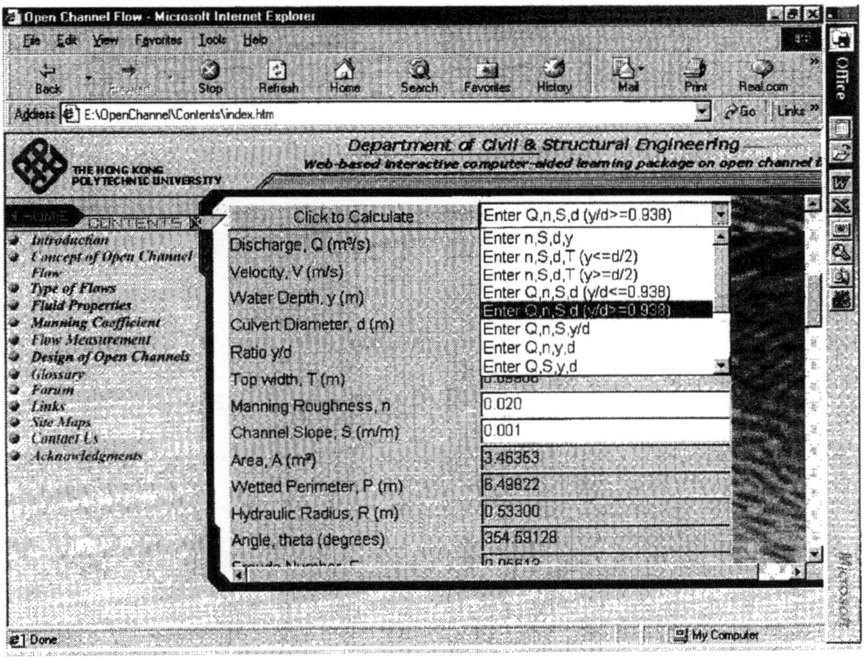

Fig. 4. Screen displaying the interactive "What-if" analysis

6 Conclusions

In this paper, a prototype web-based computer-aided learning package on pipe flow is described. It is illustrated that the hybrid knowledge representation approach applying object-oriented programming technique with various latest software, including Visual Rule Studio, Dreamweaver, Fireworks, Java, JavaScript, Flash, is viable for this domain problem. The flexibility and open infrastructure of Internet have been demonstrated to be able to act as a media for developing teaching and learning application. The student can comprehend easily the domain knowledge on pipe flow theory and design through the interaction with this package. Besides, practical design on pipe flow can be enhanced by the use of the interactive "What-if" analysis. Educational institutions and associated educators should be aware that the world is moving forward and that both employers and students have demands which cannot be met by the extant pedagogical delivery system. The current prevalent environment on financial constraints, as well as both global and private competition, may not be reversed shortly. It may not be possible to find a way out under the existing manner, even if we work more and harder. As such, novice methodologies with a goal of delivering quality education to our students may be required so as to cope with these challenges. The extensive application and implementation of web-based learning is among one of the solutions, which can contribute to overcoming some of these problems. It is strongly believed that, in the near future, the utilization of information technology coupled with other means will drastically change the nature of the teaching and learning process. A universally acknowledged research framework on the new paradigm of teaching and learning in the Internet age should be set up, according to a thorough understanding of the way students learn most effectively, how new tools support and evaluate learning advantages, how to advance the field of teaching and learning, and how educational institutions realize these advantages.

References

1. Kearsley, G.: The World Wide Web: Global Access to Education. Educational Technology Review **5** (1996) 26-30
2. Maddux, C.D.: The World Wide Web: Some Simple Solutions to Common Design Problems. Educational Technology **38(5)** (1998) 24-28
3. Berge, Z.L.: Guiding Principles in Web-Based Instructional Design. Educational Media International **35(2)** (1998) 72-76
4. Chau, K.W.: An Expert System for the Design of Gravity-type Vertical Seawalls. Engineering Applications of Artificial Intelligence **5(4)** (1992) 363-367
5. Chau, K.W., Albermani, F.: Expert System Application on Preliminary Design of Liquid Retaining Structures. Expert Systems with Applications **22(2)** (2002) 169-178
6. Chau, K.W., Chen, W.: An Example of Expert System on Numerical Modelling System in Coastal Processes. Advances in Engineering Software **32(9)** (2001) 695-703
7. Chau, K.W., Ng, V.: A Knowledge-Based Expert System for Design of Thrust Blocks for Water Pipelines in Hong Kong. Journal of Water Supply Research and Technology - Aqua **45(2)** (1996) 96-99
8. Chau, K.W., Yang, W.W.: Development of An Integrated Expert System for Fluvial Hydrodynamics. Advances in Engineering Software **17(3)** (1993) 165-172
9. Rule Machines Corporation: Developer's Guide for Visual Rule Studio. Rule Machines Corporation, Indialantic (1998)
10. Towers, J.T.: Dreamweaver 4 for Windows and Macintosh. Peachpit Press, Berkeley (2001)
11. Farrell, J., Gosselin, D.: Java Programming with Microsoft Visual J++ 6.0: Comprehensive. Course Technology, Cambridge (1999)
12. Barrett, D.J., Livingston, D., Brown, M.: Essential JavaScript for Web Professionals. Prentice Hall, Upper Saddle River (1999)
13. Cohen, S.: Macromedia Fireworks 4 for Windows and Macintosh. Peachpit Press, Berkeley (2001)
14. Kyle, L.: Essential Flash 5 for Web Professionals. Prentice Hall, Upper Saddle River (2001)
15. Douglas, J.F., Gasiorek, J.M., Swaffield, J.A.: Fluid Mechanics. Prentice Hall, Upper Saddle River (2001)

APPLICATION OF WEB-BASED TRAINING (WBT) IN HONG KONG ORGANIZATIONS

SIMON C.H. CHAN
The Hong Kong Polytechnic University
Department of Management
Yui Choi Road,
Hung Hom, Kowloon,
Hong Kong
E-mail: simon.ch.chan@polyu.edu.hk

Web-based training (WBT) is an innovative approach to deliver training through the Web, Internet, Intranet and Extranet. The aim of this paper is to describe the current state of development and adoption of WBT in Hong Kong organizations. It also provides the basis for the development of WBT instruments and theoretical framework. The essentially exploratory aim is dealt with a qualitative study. Thirteen case studies were examined the context in which WBT in Hong Kong organizations. With different internal organizational features and external social forces, top management support is the main immediate factor influencing the decision to adopt WBT. Most organizations perceive that WBT is likely to adopt and implement in Hong Kong, especially suitable for the new generation. However, some respondents believe that WBT will never replace traditional training. WBT acts like an alternative channel to deliver training through the use of high technology and the Internet.

1. Web-based Training (WBT)

Web-based training (WBT) is an innovative approach to distance learning using the technology of the Web, the Internet, the Intranet and the Extranet. Nowadays, employees can be used commonly available training courses called web browsers to access different types of information (i.e. text, pictures, audio, animations) over the Internet (Brown, 1999). No one can deny that WBT have been shown to reduce overall training costs (Whalen & Wright, 2000), reduce training time, and maintain or improve learning.

As the rapid changes in organization learning and widespread of human resource information systems (HRIS) in Hong Kong, human resource practitioners start to concern the use of information technology belonging with the Internet to deliver training to their staff. It seems that web-based training will be one of the most useful tools to fulfill the new process of self-learning and enhance the concept of lifelong learning in future. As there is little prior research on Web-based training (WBT), it is less likely that WBT is widely used in Hong Kong organizations. To better understand the nature of WBT innovation in Hong Kong, the researcher conducted an in-depth exploratory study on the adoption and usage of WBT in Hong Kong organizations.

Given the relative lack of research on WBT adoption, the aim of this paper is to describe the current state of development, and adoption of WBT in Hong Kong. It provides the basis for the development of WBT instruments and theoretical framework. Specific objectives in this paper are: (a) to identify the nature of WBT innovations in

Hong Kong, (b) to identify the factors that affect the adoption of WBT; (c) to evaluate the effectiveness and perceived benefits of WBT in HK organizations.

2. Literature

Web-based training is a formal effort to change job-related knowledge and skill through the use of information and activities presented on the computer via network. After reviewing the literature in training and development and information technology adoption, WBT have several advantages and disadvantages.

2.1. *Advantages*

There are some exciting new developments in the use of WBT that are increasing the effectiveness of training significantly. The Internet offers a rich, collaborative learning environment, available anytime and anywhere (Davis, 2001). The larger and more geographically dispersed the company is, the more likely web-based learning will save money. It will also minimize the time between when employees need training and the time they can receive it. WBT can access to expert instructors regardless of geographic location (Whalen & Wright, 2000). Moreover, WBT allows employees to learn at their own pace, at home or in the office (Davis, 2001). Employees can convert information to knowledge on their own timetable. WBT can offer an individually-tailored learning path through the course program (McDermott, 2001). It may introduce an entirely new model for learning, which is one that focuses primarily on the needs of the learner, instead of on the abilities of the instructor. The use of self-paced WBT experience has grown tremendously because of the growing importance of quality time spent on the job. The use of WBT saves in time if compared with time spend on the job training (Connors, 2001).

Another major benefit of training delivery via the Internet is that different computers and different operating systems can be used simultaneously to share information and communicate worldwide. Employees, whether at home or in the office, can access training at the exact time it is needed. This "just in time" inventory system, facilities continuous access to the most current data and allows individuals more control over their learning process (McDermott, 2001). The information delivered can be standardized and consistent to all users, therefore reducing the possibility for misinterpretations. Consistent delivery of content that would be diluted by filtering through instructors is possible with technology-based training (Kruse & Keil, 2000). WBT tends to cost less than comparable in-person training (Zager, 2001). WBT is seen as offering a cost-effective alternative to more traditional methods (McDermott, 2001). The elimination of costs associated with instructors' salaries, meeting-room rentals, and students travel, lodging, and meals is directly quantifiable.

2.2. *Disadvantages*

No matter what form of instruction is used, some individuals will find that they are at a distinct disadvantage, while in a different environment their disadvantages may disappear. There are some concerns to keep in mind when considering web-based training as an alternate delivery system for training. Accessibility becomes and issue when looking at any technology-based solution. Computer speed, bandwidth and availability need to be compatible with the training package chosen whether delivered through a CD or the Internet (Pritchard-Becker, 2001). Web-based training takes more time and more money to develop than expected. Like any first time challenge, learning about and implementing new technology takes more resources than expected (Hall, 1997). Although costs of equipment have dropped dramatically, small institutions in particular find costs prohibitive, and even the larger, wealthier institutions are concerned over technological changes that lead to obsolescence of expensive hardware (Yaverbaum, 1993).

Technology issues that play a role include whether the existing technology infrastructure can accomplish the training goals, whether additional technology expenditures can be justified, and whether compatibility of all software and hardware can be achieved (Kruse & Keil, 2000). The lack of technological standards at present is a barrier o the growth of WBT (McDermott, 2001). Such standards are essential to the interoperability of the products and services offered by the various vendors. More than one organization has investigated the benefits of WBT only to find that a large number of the employees need substantial upgrades to the current equipment on their desktops (Whalen & Wright, 2000). With the easy access to the web, many organizations want to train their employees on the web. These courses are seldom or never verified for their quality and quantity. Sometimes, it is easy to find that not all training courses were delivered by computer and the Internet.

3. Methodology

3.1. *Research Design*

The essentially exploratory aim was dealt with a qualitative study. A set of organizational case studies was examined the context in which WBT in Hong Kong organizations. The data gathered through interviews and documentary source in this qualitative phase of the research. Data for each case study also collected through a single-semi-structured interview with a very management informant, which was used as the medium to collect the data. A total of thirteen semi-structured interviews were conducted with key senior human resource managers or training managers in Hong Kong organizations. The results from the interviews can confirm the importance of the issues identified from the previous literature and identify additional aspects that may be important in the adoption WBT. In addition to being of interest in their own right, these results are also a great help in establishing the focus and content of the quantitative research instrument.

Yin (1989) states that having a case study protocol is essential if a multiple case design is being used. A case study protocol, which is a data collection instrument, is intended to increase the reliability of case study research. In the interview protocol, a definition of web-based training (WBT) was given, questions were asked on four main aspects, namely "Current Status", "Factors that influence successful introduction of WBT", "Effectiveness of WBT", and "Impact of WBT". For examples, a question in the part of Current Status, "Do you currently use WBT? Please provide details." can meet the first research question in Study 1. Moreover, question on "What is the main principle driver(s) of the implementation of WBT in your organization?" can overview the whole picture on factors affecting the adoption of WBT.

3.2. *Sample*

As mentioned by Sekaran (1992), judgment sampling, a non-probability sampling method, may be used to select appropriate samples on the basis of the nature of the research aims. This is used because it can provide more appropriate information for interpretation, because of the deliberate choice of potentially revealing or interesting cases. There is no attempt here to select typical or statistically representative cases, since statistical generalization is not an objective. Sampling was thus purposive rather than statistical.

The raw data was collected through face-to-face semi-structured interviews between the period of March 2001 to May 2001. These interviewees were invited by sending formal letters or through e-mail. Twenty letters were sent to senior training managers/ officers in organizations, with thirteen of them being successfully interviewed. The interview varied in length from 30 minutes to 45 minutes and all were tape-recording. For analysis, the researcher transcribes the original answers in Cantonese into English. A funnel approach was used in the interviews. First, the definition of WBT was provided and explained to respondents. Second, a predetermined list of questions was provided, i.e. interview protocol. Third, every respondent was asked in the same list of open-ended questions.

As this study was based on multiple case studies, the findings on each case were presented individually. A comparative case study approach (Yin, 1989) and pattern-matching logic were used. The data collected for each company was matched with the research questions. A case study report was written, based on an English translation of the report of the interview, supplemented by information drawn from other sources including the homepage of the organization, recent annual report, etc.

4. Results

Thirteen organizations of different nature were invited to participate in this study. In order to have a clear understanding of the perceived ideas on WBT in Hong Kong, the researcher have tried to interviews those organizations which have (a) well-established, planning of training and development, (b) were willing to consider implementing WBT and (c) were not willing to implement WBT. Just based on the thirteen interviews, it appears that manufacturing industry is more willingly to adopt WBT rather than in service industry.

As all the thirteen organizations were chosen by personal judgement, they all have different types of training practice. Seven organizations have more than one type of training method, where two of them include all three type of training mode, i.e. web-based Training (WBT), computer-based training (CBT), traditional training (TT), two of them include WBT and TT, and another three of them include CBT and TT respectively.

Interestingly, a President and CEO of one organization mentioned that "*Today's business operates in a real-time world where innovation rules, competitors appear from all corners, knowledge provides more leverage than capital, and the old rules no longer apply.*" Furthermore, five out of thirteen of organizations just deliver TT (classroom / face-to-face training) to their employees. For example, organization still used the traditional (face-to-face) training to delivery their training courses. Organization mentioned that "*Striving for the best and focusing on human investment*".

The results of the perceived factors affecting WBT adoption indicated that factors are divided into 3 main aspects. They are organizational factors, support factors and social factors.

4.1. *Organizational Factors*

In application development factors, the findings state that technical infrastructure, cost-effectiveness, and skills and abilities are the factors that affect the WBT adoption. Of course, technical infrastructure is important for organization to build up new information technology. The adoption of WBT for organization will involve several technical infrastructures, e.g. hardware, software, number of computers, the Internet, etc. Interviewees comment "*Technology is a main concern in implementing WBT. Organizations need to ensure that it should have sufficient support in technical infrastructure.*" In addition, cost effectiveness is the key to implement new kind of policy or information technology adoption. Most likely, in business, cost-and-benefit is the key to success. Organizations will concern about the cost effectiveness in everything, even include training and development aspect of human resource functions. Most organizations mentioned that "*The use of WBT can save cost in long term, but not in short one*". Comparatively speaking, skills and capabilities are not as important as the other two factors that mentioned above.

Internally, regarding the task characteristics, two organizations mentioned that different employees have different tasks to do in their job duties. The use of WBT may be useful to meet different training needs of employees. For example, the workload of human resource officer is extremely heavy that cannot deliver so many training courses to their staff. Most HR officer just can fulfill one-third of its organization's training needs. One reason is that they do not have enough skills to handle the variety of training programs and collect large amount of updated information at a time. One respondent stated that "*the responsibility of each employee in his task is becoming wider nowadays. The workload on employees is turning into multi-job tasks. Employees need to have multi-skills to perform different task characteristics.*"

4.2. *Support Factors*

Six organizations mentioned that top management support would be the main factors that affect the adoption of WBT. Without top management support, organizations will not implement WBT in its organization. A respondent stated that "*We have top-down approach to organize with the web-based training program, which means top management level will make the decision for implementing new training practices.*" However, it makes sense that top management support will determine by different situations. Besides top management support, the results indicated that employees support is another factors in support aspects. Employee support will influence the effectiveness of WBT adoption. As most of the employees are not willing to receive technology-based training and learning mode by themselves with the computer, employee support will important to organizations' decisions. To some extent, the participation and acceptance of employees are the important elements in making decision.

4.3. *Social Factors*

Five organizations determined that the adoption of WBT would influence by other organizations. Social Pressure is one of the main incentives to drive organizations to investigate in WBT. WBT adoption just likes a kind of fashion or trendy environment for organizations to follow. The trend of information technology and the continuous importance of self-directed learning, in the recent years, enforce organizations to enhance WBT in their organizations. The market demand of using WBT maybe the underlying factors that force organization to use WBT. Interviewee of organization M stated that "*We want to implement new technology-based training mode to our employees so as to maintain the bargaining power among other organizations. We want to follow the rapid change of market demand and the latest trend of training and development aspects.*" Moreover, two organizations mentioned that the support from government would be another force to adopt WBT.

4.4. *Perceived Effectiveness and Benefits of WBT*

Besides the factors that affect WBT adoption, the results also included the perceived advantages, perceived disadvantages of WBT and nature of training courses as well in order to determine the effectiveness of WBT. Six of the respondents mentioned that WBT could help organizations with a more cost-and-benefit way of training. Organizations identify that WBT is cost-effective in long term. WBT in large size of organizations, where the advantage of having large number of staff to train can make cost-effective in terms of money. One respondent mentioned that "*Although there are no accurate figures and numbers in the return on investment (ROI) in other organizations whose using WBT. Our organization forecasts that the use of WBT can save cost in long term.*"

Furthermore, five of the organizations mentioned that geographical independence, save in time, convenience and flexibility, and increase learner control were another important perceived advantages to organizations. WBT can deliver training to any of the places. It fits with the philosophy of "anyplace, anywhere". WBT is especially good for international organizations those have different branches across different countries. One respondent stated that "*Besides users can access training courses 24 hours a day and they can repeat the programme any number of times until we meet our objectives. Courses can be taken at the office, at home or anywhere users feel comfortable.*" Moreoever, a major problem in training is to be able to provide instruction when it is needed. The capability of WBT to reduce training time is one the most well documented and impressive outcomes. Actually, the time saving with WBT is almost completely due to the individualization of instruction, not the use of computer. The use of WBT can save the traveling time of both trainers and trainees, and at the same time, save the training time in working hours. Sometimes, it is difficult to evaluate the effectiveness of training courses. Different tests and evaluation forms also cannot evaluate employees' participation in a systematic way. However, by the use of WBT, it can easily record down the training time, test results of each participant. It can increase the learner control from organizations point of view.

On the other hand, two organizations mentioned that the development and maintenance cost of WBT is high. The high set up cost and up-front investment required of a WBT solution is larger than for traditional approaches due to development costs. Budget and cash flows will need to be negotiated. Technology issues that play a role include whether the existing technology infrastructure can accomplish the training goals, whether additional technology expenditures can be justified, and whether compatibility of all software and hardware can be achieved. In addition, WBT cannot replace the interactive part of training. They perceived that employees could not have any interactive activities in WBT courses, like delivery communication skills or presentation skills.

Due to the difficulties of WBT, especially the non-interactive problem of WBT, it gives some evidence that the nature of training courses will affect the adoption. As a result, it is interest to investigate the characteristics of different training courses that deliver training through the Internet. From the findings, the most common type of training courses are orientation training, information technology training, product knowledge training, service skills training, management development training, etc. Nearly most of the organizations perceived that procedural course, orientation and information courses can deliver training to employees. One common finding is that all these courses are delivering facts and informative knowledge.

Besides, with the increasing importance of information technology, it is common to deliver the IT skills and PC knowledge by face-to-face training. As a matter of fact, organizations are willing to deliver PC training to their staff by WBT. For example,

Microsoft Word, Excell, Powerpoint can deliver through the use of computers and the Internet to employees. However, eight of the respondents perceived that management training could not be delivered training by the use of the Internet and computers. Management training includes, communication skills, team building skills, sales presentation skills, and leadership skills, etc.

5. Conclusion and Implications

In most organizations, the final decisions of adopting a new system or new information technology is determined by top management. With different internal organizational culture and external environmental forces, top management support is the main immediate factor influencing the decision to implement WBT. In different industry sector, organizations have its own structure design. Surprisingly, structure of an organization is one of the main factors that affects the adoption of WBT. It seems that different nature of organizations have different degree of acceptance in adopting new technology-based training and development methods.

On the other hand, WBT includes a significant amount of multimedia that are expensive to produce. Although the reduced costs of delivery is more than offset production costs when enough trainees need to be trained, this initial investment can intimidate companies considering the use of WBT. The high investment cost blocks the intention to take the risk of implementing WBT without a guaranteed market. Furthermore, there may also be risks associated with not adopting WBT. Market globalization and changing technologies have placed companies under great stress, the need to deliver fast, effective, and updated training materials is more important than ever before. Along with an increasing need for training is the conflicting requirement to operate companies with fewer costs, in order to remain competitive.

Many organizations are presently at the stage of evaluating different type of distance learning, and the focus tends to be on which web-based training best meets the needs of the organization. As more training is delivered via the Web, an increasing number of companies will find that a training management system is required to ensure that employees have easy access to online courses. Web-based courses make it much easier to track whether trainees have taken course and the results of web-based testing.

In concluding the results of training that can be or cannot be delivered through WBT, comparatively, the needs of hard skills seems be delivered by WBT whereas soft skills cannot. Some basic courses, like procedure course, orientation, informative courses may be good in delivering training through the Internet. Specifically, with the increase in demand of information technology, organizations are planned to use WBT as the medium to deliver PC training or IT skills to their employees. However, organizations still think that soft skills, e.g. communication skills, interactive skills, can be delivered through the Internet. Furthermore, many organizations are presently at the stage of evaluating different types of distance learning, and the focus tends to be on which WBT that best meets the needs of organization.

For future plan in training and development, most of the organizations perceive that WBT is likely to adopt and implement in Hong Kong, especially suitable for the new generation. However, they believe that WBT will never replace traditional training. WBT acts as an alternative channel to deliver training through the use of high technology and the Internet. WBT provides different way for trainers to choose, at the same time, and meet different employees' training needs. During the next few years, many organizations will adopt the Web/ the Internet as the core mode of training delivery, and training management systems will be the next area where interest will be concentrated.

To sum up, all these findings (factors affect WBT adoption and effectiveness of WBT) would integrate with the variables which reviewed in the literature of WBT in order to build up a particular instruments for measuring WBT adoption, and a new adoption model related to web-based training.

Acknowledgments

The author would like to thank for the following for their assistance and valuable contribution to this research paper: Hong Kong Institute of Human Resource Management (IHRM); Professor Edward Snape, Associate Head of Department, Department of Management, The Hong Kong Polytechnic University; Dr. Eric Ngai, Assistant Professor, Department of Management, The Hong Kong Polytechnic University. The research was supported in part by The Hong Kong Polytechnic University under grant number G-W058. Last but not least, the author is grateful to all the participating managers and their organizations for the time and effort in providing valuable information for this survey.

References

1. K.G. Brown, *PhD thesis, Michigan State University.* **Individual differences in choice during learning: The influence of learner goals and attitudes in Web-based training,**.(1999).
2. K. Connors, *Managed Healthcare Executive.* **Online Learning can be a cost-effective alternative to traditional training,** 11(7), 45 (2001).
3. F. Damanpour, *Communication Research.* **Innovation type, radicalness, and the adoption process,** 15, 545 (1988).
4. B.Davis, *Professional Engineering.* **Learning just got easier,**14(12),42 (2001).
5. B. Hall, *New York: Wiley.* **Web-based Training Cookbook,** (1997).
6. K. Kruse, and J. Keil, *Technology based trainig.* **The art and science of design, development, and delivery,**_(2000).
7. T. McDermott, *Accountancy Ireland.* **Corporate Training,** 33(4),30 (2001).
8. G. Pritchard-Becker, *Community Banker.* **Learning from a distance,** 10(5),33 (2001).

9. U. Sekaran, *John Wiley & Sons, Inc.* **Research Methods for Business: A Skill-Building Approach,** (1992).
10. T. Whalen and D. Wright, *Artech House, Boston, London.* **The business case for web-based training,** (2000).
11. G. Yaverbaum and J. Liebowitz, *Computers Education.* **Gofigure Inc: A Hypermedia web-based case**, 30,147 (1998).
12. R.K. Yin, *Newbury Park, London: Sage Publications.* **Case study research: Design and methods,** (1989).
13. M. Zager, *Rural Telecommunications.* **Online Training: A practical alternative for small business,** 20(5), 42 (2001).

UNIVERSITY TEACHING IN THE "POST XEROX" AGE SYSTEM E-ULE

L. NABER AND M. KÖHLE

Institute for Software Engineering and Interactive Systems
Vienna University of Technology
Favoritenstr. 11/188, A-1040 Vienna, Austria
larissa@naber.at

Universities trapped between rising student numbers and decreasing budgets are turning to e-learning as the one-stop solution, giving little concern for student or teacher needs. We designed e-ULE[a], a university level teaching and learning environment with a strong focus on usability. In contrast to many ITS/ILE, this system does not aim at replacing the lecturer [20], or the university as a whole, but shall lift some of the burden of information transfer from the lecturer and thus allow the students to spend more "quality time" with their teachers. e-ULE provides the lecturer with an easy to use tool and a strong process, enabling him to create suitably linked, interactive hypertext lecture notes, which support the student in the different phases of learning. In compliance with the meagre university budgets the system is open sourced and relies on several prominent open source projects. Currently e-ULE's core components are being developed at a "proof of concept" stage.

[a] e - Usable Learning Environment

1. Introduction

Despite the swift progress in information transfer and organisation in the last 30 years, university teaching is still much the same as it has been since medieval times: the professor gives a lecture [a], that is, he reads his notes to the class.

This type of information transfer is tedious for both parts: lecturers have to cover nearly the same ground year after year, and students suffer from the often less than perfect pedagogical and rhetoric skills[b]

[a]Middle English, act of reading, from Late Latin lectura, a discourse given before an audience or class especially for instruction

[b]You cannot necessarily expect a top scientist to have first rate rhetoric or pedagogical

Valuable resources (time | space | personnel) are given up to the sheer act of information transfer, information that in many cases could be transferred in a more efficient manner[c], thus freeing up resources for more in-depth discussion and exploration of the topics.

University teaching is basically about getting students to ask the right questions, frame problems, and find solutions themselves, which is rarely reflected in university curricula.

Along the lines of Tsichritzis [22], we believe that university teaching in the "post xerox age" should concentrate less on information transfer, but on aiding the student in the process of knowledge acquisition and furthermore we adhere to Ackoff's 4 step ladder [1] of data - information - knowledge - wisdom.

1.1. *Tools of the trade*

Many commercially available (multimedia design) tools resemble more a *jack of all trades*, claiming to be suited for creation of just anything – from kindergarten age edutainment software to realistic simulations of today's world trade. Mostly they lack support for "expert data types" (formulas, construction plans, chemical symbols, ...) and focus too much on the graphical design and too little on the "flow" of the system.

On the other hand there is a fair number of fully fledged "adaptive hypertext educational systems" or "intelligent tutorial systems" (see Bruslovsky's overview article [2]) which aim at replacing the teacher completely. Besides being arcane, these systems obviously do not accommodate the students' wishes: in a recent study [14] we found, that despite of the harsh criticism of their lecturers, students are not bent upon replacing them with an ITS/ILE[d], but rather wish for a highly interactive "question and answer" type of "non-lecture" (and better learning materials). More student-lecturer communication was also established a major "pro e-learning" factor in a study by Schell [18].

Many forward thinking lecturers battle a conglomerate of unrelated tools like university provided lecture web-sites, third party hosted discussion forums and their choice of word processors to support their lecture.

In fact, it is possible to build usable educational hypertext systems using any of the above mentioned tools, but you might as well be using assembly

---

skills as well

[c]to be well contrasted to so-called e-learning in the form of down-loadable Powerpoint™ presentations plus moderated newsgroups.

[d]ITS = Intelligent Tutoring System, ILE = Intelligent Learning Environment

language. A specialised university level hypertext system is called for, that provides support for all the tasks specific to creating engaging and effective hypertext study materials: that is the motivation for the *e*-ULE system.

1.2. *e-ULE– a jack of one trade*

A university level e-learning system should reflect the academic nature of the contents to be taught as well as the limited budget most universities are confronted with. It also must take into the account that most university teachers are neither trained information scientist nor educationalists. Thus the system must provide a very easy to use authoring system and a process to guide the lecturer towards the creation of a usable educational hypertext system.

The aim of the *e*-ULE system is threefold:

- ☞ creation of an educational hypertext design process (EHDP) and an educational hypertext markup language (*e*-ULE_doc).
- ☞ generation of a server backend to handle adaptive and collaborative features as well the generation of personalised/specialised versions of the material.
- ☞ generation of an authoring tool geared towards the creation of university level hypertext.

1.3. *Common e-learning traps*

One of the leading arguments against e-learning lies in the *e* itself: new – electronic – media require new means, and little is still known about structuring hypertext. Even though hypertext has been researched since the 1950s it became popular only at about 1995, with the rise of the web. As book publishing has gone a long way since Gutenberg, we will require some time to adapt to hypertext publishing. Many of today's hypertext lecture notes cannot deny their print origins - the structure is completely linear, organised in separate subsequent chapters. Only the transport medium has changed, the power of the new medium has not been unleashed.

Also, e-learning involves computers, which adds an additional dimension to the whole problem: to learn with a computer, you'll first have to learn about computers (compare [5]):

In [8] Mitchell, Dipetta and Kerr compare the evolution of e-learning to the exploration of Americas wild west, complete with *Lone Rangers*, *Greenhorns* and *Band Wagons*. E-Learning is driven by *Lone Rangers*, interested individuals with the necessary technical and educational knowledge. The occasional *Greenhorn*, an interested person without the necessary knowledge either evolves to a *Lone Ranger* or has to wait for the *Band Wagon*, e.g. the department organising a large scale e-learning venture. They conclude that e-learning is still one big adventure game.

Although everybody likes a little adventure now and then, many of the adventurous experiments are at the students' expense. Even web-based courses designed by experienced *Lone Rangers* can fail, a *Greenhorn's* first foray into web-based courses can easily proof disastrous for the students [9].

2. User requirement

Usable e-learning must lend itself to support different computer literacy levels of lecturers and students. Aside from literacy aspects user needs and requirements are to be clarified.

2.1. *Support of different learning phases*

In individual interviews, that were part of our survey of students' requirements [12,14], we found that the students' use of learning material changes according to different "learning phases".

Phase 1 – reconnoitring: Before deciding on taking a lecture or exam the students want a detailed overview of the topics covered. Some students refer to is as the "90 minutes notes" or "executive summary". Many lectures fail in providing support for this stage.

Phase 2 – learning the basics: After having decided to take the exam most students read through the material available (and try to solve the exercises). In this stage they try to focus on the main points. Many lecture notes do not differentiate between *essential*, *important*, and *additional* information. Support is generally there, but it could be improved from the student's point of view.

Phase 3 – exam preparation: Most students make custom notes of the topics they need to study further. Most classic materials provide no support for this stage, all excerption is done by hand. Although these excerpts can be of great pedagogical value, they cannot efficiently be integrated with classical materials.

Phase 4 – reference: Lecture notes should not be worthless after the exam. Human memory being as it is, it is often necessary to return to previous "haunts", to look up what has been forgotten. While some books come with a somewhat decent index, most lecture notes do without, so information retrieval can be quite tedious.

Phase 5 – selective retrieval: This phase is set apart from the other four phases: without detailed knowledge on the provided information the student wishes to retrieve selective parts thereof which might be required for a different subject matter. Chances for solely extracting *relevant* information are slim. Prerequisites to later chapters tend to be scattered over various chapters, forcing the student to completely canvas the material.

A full-blown learning environment obviously should take the different learning phases into account.

2.2. *Most wanted features (students)*

Nearly all students were in favour of discussion groups. Obviously one of the reasons to attend lectures is to stay in touch with colleagues. The virtual meeting room is even more popular with commuting students.

Another popular feature was an "intelligent" search function, which is capable of helping in cases like "I know, I read it last week ...".

The possibility to annotate the material was also well received. The students favoured a possibility to make private annotations as well as public ones.

A must have feature was the possibility to rearrange the material to one's own liking and the generation of "sub notes" which might serve as an additional, direct path to a special topic. This highlights another common computer usage problem: as pointed out by Shackelford [20] users are so brainwashed by the myth of the "smart computer" that they will blame themselves if they encounter stupidity on the software's part. Instead of questioning the design of the software they assume that nothing can be done about it.

Everybody wanted an intelligent print feature: material is frequently read while in transit, in the park, etc.

A feature to use the online version on a mobile device was mostly discarded. Nobody considered these devices ripe for such a task. About half of the students conceded that that would be an interesting option once the devices reached a certain maturity.

2.3. *Lecturer requirements*

Ease of use was the main requirement[13]. Cutting down on the number of tools involved was another major aspect. So was collaborative editing. The easy (non-technical) integration of features as discussion forums and online chat was much welcomed and many lecturers reacted positively to the idea of involving the students in the creation of the materials.

Many lecturers confessed to a somewhat chaotic creation process, which often involves writing many chapters concurrently, while trying to figure out the most intuitive order. All this is done while juggling a plethora of scientific papers which might "come in handy". Support for such a working style is slim in commercial software. Writing university level educational materials obviously is quite a world apart.

Courses do not only require study materials: courses tend to come with an administrative overhead like student enrolment, times and places of the lectures/labs, ... Some universities offer support for the distribution of this kind of information, but again, this is done via additional tools and not integrated in the work-flow.

3. *e*-ULE Design

e-ULE consists of three major building blocks *server*, *authoring tool* and*student's client*. These building blocks are used to create, distribute and view *e*-ULE documents. The various materials (*e*-ULE document, papers, meta-information) pertaining to a course are collected in an *e*-ULE project. Figure 1 depicts the various parts of the *e*-ULE system.

3.1. *Automatic generation of hypertext*

Hyperlinks – naturally – set hypertext apart from ordinary textual material [10,11]. Unfortunately the manual generation of hyperlinks is quite tedious, as can easily be seen by the number of "brochureware' or "electronic page turning" [7] web-sites on the web. Educational hypertext is no exception.

The main feature of *e*-ULE is the automatic generation of hypertext features. A process similar to a spell checker is used to build custom dictionaries of lecture keywords. These keywords are used to automatically generate hyperlinks and custom views of the material.

3.2. *e-ULE Documents*

e-ULE relies on XML as document format. XML is ideally suited to describe the type of semi-structured content usually found in lecture notes.

Additionally XML offers a host of other XML based languages like MathML (Mathematical Markup Language) or CML (Chemical Markup Language) which will be most useful in the university field.

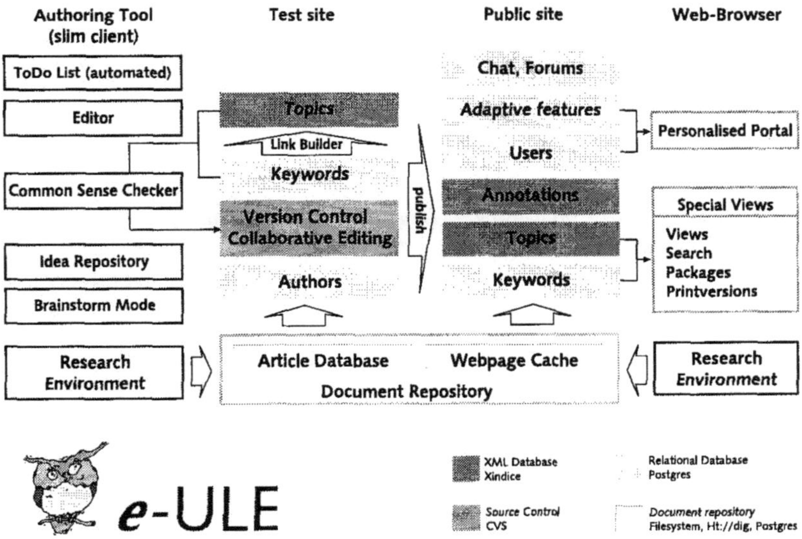

Figure 1. The diagram shows the various components of the *e*-ULE system plus their implementing technology. Most of *e*-ULE's features are located on the server, with a slim authoring client and a standard web browser on the student side.

3.2.1. *XML educational applications*

Major industrial players have consorted and produced the SCORM [19] and the IMS [6] standards for educational environments. Although these standards are very complete and cover everything from content description to learner data exchange and meta data, they are somewhat of an overkill for a university-centred learning environment. Implementing a system that conforms to these standards is likely to result in yet another "jack of all trades" authoring environment that requires months of training to master.

The Open University of the Netherlands has recently released a new version of their EML (Educational Markup Language) [17]. Although this specification looks promising, the system is naturally geared towards the needs of a virtual campus, thus containing many concepts that are of no use for *e*-ULE. Basically it will be possible to convert *e*-ULE_doc[e] to and from EML.

More information about XML standardisation can be obtained from Oasis' XML.org [15].

[e] *e*-ULE's XML based document format

3.3. *Structure*

e-ULE documents fall into one of four categories: *Content, Information, Discussions, Annotations*

3.3.1. *Content*

e-ULE centres around *topics.* Topics are information "atoms" which can not be subdivided[f] meaningfully. A strict process ensures that all meta information necessary to automatically build structures is available. Every topic comes with:

- ☞ a title, an optional subtitle, keywords, an abstract
- ☞ prequel and sequel information
- ☞ level information
- ☞ optional extends / requires informations
- ☞ optional objects, examples, exercises
- ☞ optional server modules (see below)
- ☞ optional bibliography and web-links

Topics are contained in blocks and are linked by prequel and sequel identifiers, thus resembling book-like structures. In addition topics come in three flavours: *essential, important* and *additional.* This *level information* allows the student a faster access to the core elements of a lecture. Relations between the levels of the topics are marked by *extends* and *requires* identifiers. Figure 2 depicts the interplay between related topics.

Abstracts are used to generate a padded table of contents (the often wished for "90-minutes notes" or "executive summary"), which are suitable for a first overview of the lecture (see 2.1 - phase 1.)

Keywords denote the actual topic and semantic variations thereof. This information is used by the link-builder to automatically create a glossary, an index and appropriate hyperlinks. The keywords play a crucial role in the generation of "views" (see 3.4.1).

Objects are digital non-textual information that can be transfered via the web like images, sound or video. Any digital content can be included in a topic via a hyper-link.

---

[f] You can think about them as subsections, or subchapters

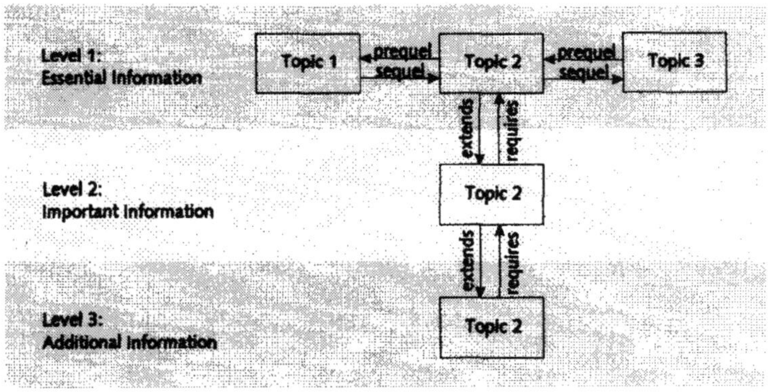

Figure 2. The diagram shows the interplay between related topics.

Server modules add interactivity to the lecture notes. Currently available modules are discussion groups (forums) and online assignments (with peer review option). Each topic can be annotated by the students. These annotations can be public or private.

3.3.2. *Information*

The information section comprises information about the lecture and the *e*-ULE site. This may include: lecture times / dates and places, an introduction to the *e*-ULE client, contact information, technical support, and other relevant information.

3.3.3. *Discussions*

Communication is a vital aspect of learning. Since the aim of the *e*-ULE system is to further student - lecturer communication by reducing the pure information transfer aspect of the lectures there is room for communication in the lecture hall. Still there will be the need to communicate electronically: In the forums students can talk to each other, to the lecturer or to tutors. Different communication needs are served by different types of communication channels: asynchronous, newsgroup like systems (forums) and synchronous chat systems.

3.3.4. *Annotations*

Annotations are another means of communications. In a notice board manner they can serve as platform for collecting additional information about each topic, like errata, implementation examples, notes about practical applications or additional web-links.

3.4. *Server*

For the sake of usability most of *e*-ULE's features are implemented on the server. The number of *e*-ULE projects is only limited by the servers resources. A single server could serve a whole university. The authoring of new *e*-ULE projects is done via a *slim client.*

The *e*-ULE Server includes a *talk-back* function which will report back to the main *e*-ULE site, thus building a network of *e*-ULE sites. Thus *e*-ULE documents from other sites can be integrated seamlessly, but will bear a copyright notice. Of course the editor can hide his own *e*-ULE project from unauthorised access.

The server's tasks include:

- ☞ serving the content
- ☞ providing interactivity (forums, chat, annotations)
- ☞ providing adaptive features
- ☞ enabling collaborative editing
- ☞ ensuring version control
- ☞ student and course management

3.4.1. *Views*

The server acts as portal to the student: content, information, discussions and annotations can be accessed in the usual fashion. Furthermore the server can generate any number of customised views for the student.

These customised views include:

- ☞ print version of selected parts for reading while commuting, ...
- ☞ packaged versions for download and offline reading
- ☞ restructured notes for exam preparation (see 2.1 - phase 3)
- ☞ goal oriented mini notes that highlight a special subject (see 2.1 - phase 5)

The views can be composed of selective parts of the content, information, annotation and discussion sections to the liking of the student. Glossary entries, and corresponding topics are automatically selected by the automated linking mechanism. The student can control the creation of these auxiliary informations by de-/selecting the associated keywords individually.

3.4.2. *Link-builder*

The link-builder takes on the tedious task of generating the necessary hyperlinks. After all, a HTML document without hyperlinks is no improvement as compared to a conventional printout. The link-builder relies on the keywords provided by the lecturer and builds hyperlinks to the main topic connected to the keyword, the glossary entry and the other occurrences of the word.

3.4.3. *Collaborative editing and version control*

The server provides collaborative editing and version control [21], [3], [4], [16] on a "test site". The *editor* can name various *authors* and grant them access to certain parts of his *e*-ULE project. He can assign work to the authors who transparently check it out of the test site along with the latest keyword list. After editing (or inactivity timeout) the respective topic is checked back in, together with the (changed) keyword list.

Topics can be marked as "in progress", "ready for review", "reviewed" and "finished". Unfinished topics appear in the to-do list. The topics of the test site can be published either all at once or individually to the public site.

3.5. *Authoring Tool*

Any learning environment aiming at usable, interactive materials for students' use must provide an equally usable tool for authoring these materials. As pointed out by Shackleford [20]

> Typically, such software does little or nothing to support teachers[...]. The teacher still has to do all the various preparation, teaching, grading, and documentation tasks, and in addition must also devote time and energy to "dealing" with the educational software.

3.5.1. *Research*

Efficient hypertext generation must be integrated in the overall work-flow of lecture design. Writing lecture notes usually starts with research on the topic in question. In consequence, support for the research phase is a crucial part of the authoring tool.

Even tough the web is now a major source of information, there are hardly any tools available to harness the power of the web. Many scientific journals can be read online, and many more are to follow, but handling of this wealth of information proofs rather tricky. Every publisher has his own system - incompatible with everybody else's system – and once the articles are safely downloaded, the real hassle begins. The articles cannot efficiently be organised, categorised and processed. In the end many users capitulate – articles are printed and filed in binders.

Of course there is a number of document management tools on the market (from full-blown systems like Convera, to SoHo[g] products like Paperport) but aside from being expensive they are not specifically designed for use in educational environments and do not lend themselves to further processing of the information.

e-ULE's research support will provide extensible support for literature search and management. Articles can be searched, downloaded, indexed, annotated, categorised and quoted without ever leaving the authoring tool. The same applies to any type of web-based information. Web-sites can be bookmarked and stored offline for further reference. Even if the site vanishes from the web, the information is still accessible.

3.5.2. *Work-flow*

Depending on the individual liking, the creation of academic study material can be a rather chaotic process. Although the picture of the "scatterbrained professor" is a little bit too farfetched, it should be taken with a grain of salt. Complex systems – as lecture notes – involve complex, even chaotic processes – processes that are often out of the reach of common authoring tools like word processors.

Modern word processors frequently provide an outline mode, to facilitate the generation of structured, treelike documents, thus forcing the author to think in chapters, sections, subsections, and so on. *e*-ULE goes one step further and allows for a "semi-chaotic" authoring style by providing a *brain storm mode* and an *idea repository*. At any given time the author can jot down a new idea or start a brainstorm session. The ideas will be kept in the idea repository. The system will compare and group these ideas and repeatedly ask the author to formulate upon.

The all important (and universally disliked) *to-do lists* will be taken care of by *e*-ULE: if a topic misses compulsory parts (like the abstract or a level mark), a need for completion will be listed. Topics can be marked as draft, ready for review, reviewed and completed. Tasks can be assigned

[g]Small Office Home Office

to members of the authoring team.

e-ULE will also help in planning a new course. The lecturer can formulate goals and assign topics to them - complete with a time frame for each topic/goal - and thus build a course table from it.

3.5.3. *Collaborative editing*

As many lectures are held by a group of lecturers, collaborative editing is another crucial feature. In line with the Constructivistic learning theory, the lecture notes could even be written in cooperation with the students. See 3.4.3 for details.

3.5.4. *Common sense checker*

The common sense checker lays the foundation for the automated link-builder. In a process similar to a spell-checker, the authoring tool will mark all unknown words. The actions on the unknown word include: correct spelling mistake (choose from list), mark as new keyword, mark as a deviation from a known keyword (choose from list).

New keywords come in two flavours: prerequisites, which are used to generate a special list of "should know" items and real keywords. The real keywords are immediately associated with a new topic and a glossary entry. Every topic can be manually associated with several keywords. These entries can be selected from each occurrence inside the text.

The common sense checker of course relies on user input to point out useful keywords. This cannot be avoided, as the very same word could be a keyword or just ordinary word, depending on the audience. An integral in a freshmen's course on mathematics of economists has a meaning different from an integral in postgraduate course of particle physics. In addition to the automatically detected words, the user can convert a word to a keyword at any time.

3.6. *Client*

The client in fact is an up-to-date web-browser. For the sake of usability we decided against a specialised client to minimise the need for technical support.

Today's standard browsers like IE5+, Netscape 6, or Mozilla 1 are sufficiently equipped for this task. In addition modern browsers can integrate various specialised file formats via plug-ins, and some[h] are even able to natively display XML application such as MathML.

The creation of specialised versions or views (see 3.4.1) of the content is left to server, the result can be browsed in the usual manner.

The major drawback in relying on the server to handle all student side interaction lies in the fact, that a permanent connection to is needed. This disadvantage is mitigated by the possibility to download chunks of the material for offline viewing in the browser, allowing the use of dial-up connections to the Internet.

4. Summary and future plans

e-ULE's main idea is to produce usable and highly functional educational materials. We aim at lifting the burden of information transfer from the lecture and allow the students to spend more "quality time" with their lecturers.

Based on a students' and lecturers' requirements analysis we designed a system for the collaborative creation of educational university level hypertext materials.

e-ULE helps the lecturer in all phases of course development by providing an integrated environment for: research, authoring, adminstration, and communication plus a strong guiding process.

On the student side *e*-ULE features support for different learning phases, and learning styles including the possibility to tailor the materials to the inidividual liking (specific views, annotations, adaptive features).

The system will be open-sourced and released under the GPL, building on open standards and the wealth of already available open source software.

Currently *e*-ULE is under active development and a number of lecturers are looking forward to give it a spin and have already volunteered for usability testing the prototype.

References

1. R. L. Ackoff. *Creating the Corporate Future : Plan or Be Planned.* John Wiley & Sons, 1981.
2. P. Brusilovsky. Methods and techniques of adaptive hypermedia. *User Modeling and User-Adapted Interaction*, 6(2-3):87–129, 1996.
3. W. Cellary, D. Durand, and et al. Things change: deal with it! versioning, cooperative editing and hypertext. In *Proceedings of the the seventh ACM conference on Hypertext*, 1996.

[h] Mozilla has just completed MathML support

4. J. Conklin and M. L. Begeman. gibis: a hypertext tool for team design deliberation. In *Proceeding of the ACM conference on Hypertext*, 1987.
5. W. D. Pedagogy before technology: Re-thinking the relationship between ict and teaching. *Education and Information Technologies*, 6(4), 2001.
6. IMS. IMS specifications. WWW: http://www.imsproject.org/, 2002.
7. V. Jones and H. Jo. Interactive multimedia based on learning theories to enhance tertiary education. In *Conference proceedings ICCMA'98*, 1998.
8. C. Mitchell, T. Dipetta, and K. J. he frontier of web-based instruction. *Education and Information Technologies*, 6(2), 2001.
9. W. J. Montelpare and A. Williams. Web-based learning: Challenges in using the internet in the undergraduate curriculum. *Education and Information Technologies*, 5(2):85–101, 2000.
10. S. Moulthro. Beyond the electronic book: a critique of hypertext rhetoric. In *Proceedings of the third annual ACM conference on Hypertext*, 1991.
11. B. Mynatt, L. Leventhal, and . et al.". Hypertext or book: Which is better for answering questions? In *Conference proceedings on Human factors in computing systems*, 1992.
12. L. Naber. Hypertext support for learning phases, tech. report ifs01-36. Technical report, Viennna University of Technology, 2001.
13. L. Naber. Authoring tool requirements analysis. tech. report ifs02-33. Technical report, Viennna University of Technology, 2002.
14. L. Naber. Student motivation survey. tech. report ifs02-31. Technical report, Viennna University of Technology, 2002.
15. OASIS. xml.org. WWW: http://www.xml.org/xml/registry.jsp, 2002.
16. Osterbye. Structural and cognitive problems in providing version control for hypertext. In *Proceedings of the ACM conference on Hypertext*, 1992.
17. OUNL. EML specifications. WWW: http://eml.ou.nl/, 2002.
18. G. Schell. Student perceptions of web-based course quality and benefit. *Education and Information Technologies*, 2001.
19. SCORM.
Advanced distributed learning initiative. WWW: http://www.adlnet.org/, 2002.
20. R. Shackelford. Educational computing: Myths versus methods. why computers haven't helped and what we can do about it. In *ACM SIGCAS Computers and Society, Proceedings of the Conference on Computers and the Quality of Life*, 1990.
21. N. A. Streitz. Designing hypermedia: a collaborative activity. *Communications of the ACM*, 38(8), 1995.
22. D. Tsichritzis. Reengineering the university. *CACM*, 42(6), 1999.

ON THE DESIGN OF MATHEMATICAL INSTRUCTION MATERIAL FOR DISTANT LEARNING PLATFORM

PAO-TA YU, CHUNG-MING OWN, HUNG-PING YU

*Department of Computer Science and Information Engineering**

National Chung Cheng University

160, San-Hsing, Ming-Hsiung

Chiayi, Taiwan 62107, R.O.C

The aim of this paper is to introduce a convenient and efficient way to transform presentation slides written in Tex/Latex document editors to an equivalent file of the Microsoft PowerPoint application. In this paper, we announce a new system, Tex2Ppt. This system can be used to strengthen the weakest part of the Microsoft products, inconvenient, homely and unfriendly of mathematical equation editing. We translate the most popular Tex/Latex source file into the PowerPoint file. Hence, we not only can use the formal Tex/Latex typesetting, but also can use the handy of the application of PowerPoint.

1 Introduction

Computer applications such as spreadsheets, material representation, molecular modeling, and data acquisition are essential tools for teaching. These educational tools, used wisely, could provide the key to unlock a treasure chest of academic knowledge for students. Hence, teachers tend to put more and more effort to find useful educational tools. The representation tool is the one. Besides, students often have a difficult time to visualize concepts and struggle to grasp information that is presented either in verbality or in writing. This situation certainly exists in traditional classrooms, but it can improve in today's multimedia environment. Thus, multimedia computer-based representation tool provides a means to infuse more experiential components into a classroom.

Hence, for the sake to obtain the good quality of multimedia computer-based instruction, most users take Microsoft PowerPoint as the editor for their learning materials. Furthermore, the requirement that translating learning materials from other editors to Microsoft PowerPoint has been getting stronger. As we know, most of the Microsoft applications don't follow the open source license. Unless Microsoft releases or built-in this translator, it's difficult to translate those other learning materials into PowerPoint compatible files.

In addition, there are many deficiencies in the multimedia computer-based environment especially in mathematics. For example, if we want to show some mathematic notations in a web page, we have some ways but it's not an easy way to do. Thus, most of the symbols and terminologies in mathematics can't be notated in plain text without some specific applications support; like Microsoft equation editor. On the other hands, in the academic community; most users prefer to use Tex/Latex to present their papers or professional typesetting works, because this tool has fully functioned and variety of supports by importing packages. Moreover, Tex/Latex not only can produce highly professional output, but also support several kinds of document formats; such as PostScript files, DVI files, and PDF files.

Hence, for the purpose to overcome the deficiencies of PowerPoint and strengthen the utility rate of Tex/Latex system, we want to construct an integrated environment of Tex/Latex system, This system, Tex2Ppt translation system, can conveniently translate different documents written in Tex/Latex into the format of Microsoft PowerPoint.

2 Basic Concepts

Even though Microsoft PowerPoint has getting more and more popular, there still are some deficiencies. First, if you have ever used Microsoft PowerPoint, you would know how inconvenient to insert a mathematical equation into your representations. Users have to launch the Microsoft Equation Editor to edit their desired equations, then; these equations will turn into a bitmap graphic and be located where the users design. However, the problems will occur when many equations are inserted into the writings. Because the equations are not the contents of representations, the more equations we uses, the more difficulties we try to arrange the typesetting. In common with teachers to prepare their teaching representations, their representations always contain many mathematical equations. Assume that each bitmap graphic equations occupy 5Kbyes hard drive capacity, how many resources can you imagine to handle these presentations?

Second, the Tex/Latex systems are still major typesetting tools for scientific researches. The typesetting style is more formal then typesetting in Microsoft products. Hence, if users use the Tex/Latex system to arrange the typesetting, but they want to represent by the tool like PowerPoint, there is no easy way to achieve their goal. Hence it's impossible for him to be complete in both respects.

Then, a breaking point for Tex/Latex users is shown. In 1. , they propose a solution to solve the problem mentioned above. They address a tool which follows the Tex/Latex syntax, can produce slides like PowerPoint. It means that this tool can translate the Tex/Latex source into a DVI file, then the TrueTex DVI Previewer are used to render the result of the document. Finally, the program "Latex 2 ppt" will be used to translate the slides made by the TrueTex DVI Previewer to Microsoft PowerPoint.

However, the performance of their solution is negated due to either the support of Chinese language for the TrueTex DVI Previewer is quite pool, or the "Latex 2 ppt" is a commercial and expensive software contained in Scientific WorkPlace application 2.

3 Tex2Ppt translation system

In the Tex/Latex system, the Tex/Latex source can be transformed into not only the DVI file format, but also Postscript (.PS) file format and Portable Document Format (.PDF) file format. Note that, one of those file formats, Postscript, it not only supports the Chinese language, but also the viewer of GSView is a freeware 3. Hence, if we take advantage of GSView, we don't need to use the expansive software TrueTex Previewer anymore.

In our proposed approach, we implement the Tex2Ppt translation system to control the whole translating process. Before launch our system, we first edit the Tex/Latex source in the editor that supports traditional Chinese language (such as cwTex 4.), then compile it into the postscript file format. Then, we execute our system Tex2Ppt. The system structure is described in Figure 1.

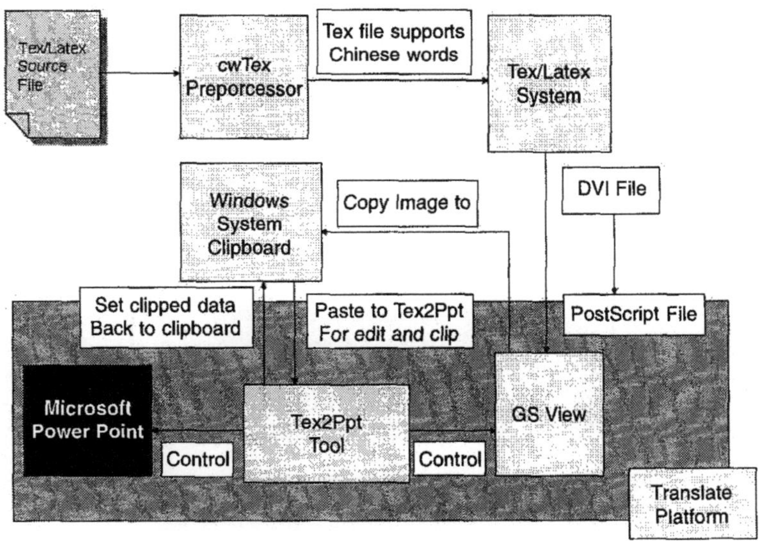

Figure 1: The architecture of the translation System

In the beginning of executing our system, we need to select the translated postscript file. Then, a sketch of the first page of the postscript file will show up in the default resolution at the upper-left part of the system. The user can change the display resolution, text depth, text alpha and graphics alpha values of the postscript file by controlling the GSView application through our proposed system. When we change the resolution of the postscript file, the size of the designated power point file will depend on the resolution we changed. In our case, the resolution value of 92 is suitable for the monitor resolution of 1024×768. In addition, if we change the value of the depth of the resolution, text alpha, and graphics alpha, the rendered quality of the postscript file will change. For example, by decreasing the depth of the resolution from 24 to 8, the colors can be rendered within the postscript file are reduced from 16777216 to 256. Then, the presenting quality will be a quite different. The quality representation is demonstrated in Figure 2 with depth of 24 at the left and with depth of 8 at the right.

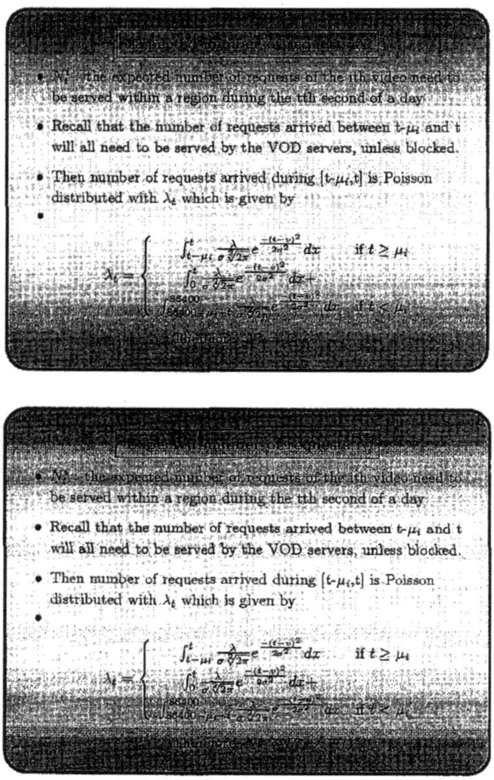

Figure 2: Demonstrating of different rendered qualities.

Moreover, by changing the value of the text alpha parameter, the quality of rendering the words will change too. The difference is demonstrated in Figure 3 with text alpha parameter equalizing to 4 at the left part, and the text alpha parameter is set to 1 at the right part of the Figure. It's obviously clear that the words are much smoother with higher text alpha parameter value.

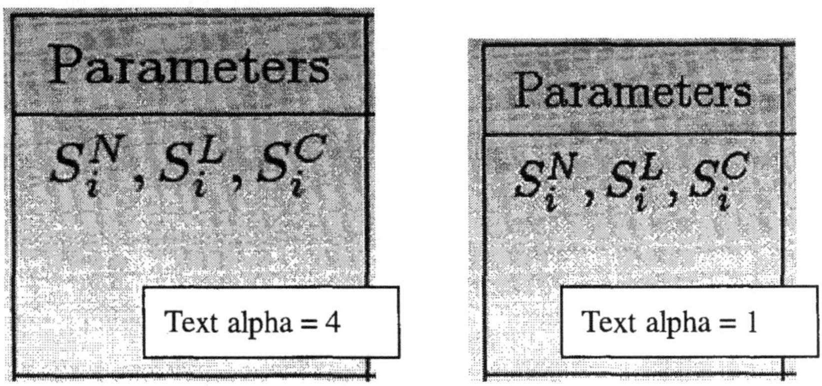

Figure 3: rendering qualities with different text alpha value

After setting up the quality parameters, the user needs to decide how many pages will be translated. Then the pages will be clipped and pasted to the Microsoft Power Point. Moreover, our system provides the cutting function to make the user adjusting his representation region. This function increases the flexibility on editing.

Figure 4 shows three components of our system:

Comprehensive Area: this area shows up the sketch of the each page of the target postscript file, and this content will be pasted to the Microsoft PowerPoint application. This area enables the user to examine the content matched their expectation or not. When the user takes a starting point on the comprehensive area and presses the mouse and then dragging the mouse to form a region, there will be an actual-sized sketch of the page. The purpose of the action is to let the user examine whether the starting and the ending points of the selected region are exactly what they expected.

Verification Area: the purpose of this area is to help the user to verify the detail of each page. This area will show the actual size of clipped part selected by the user.

Control Area: This area is composed of control buttons and text fields. The control buttons can adjust the perform resolution and the scale. The greater of the scale is, the worse quality of the representation is.

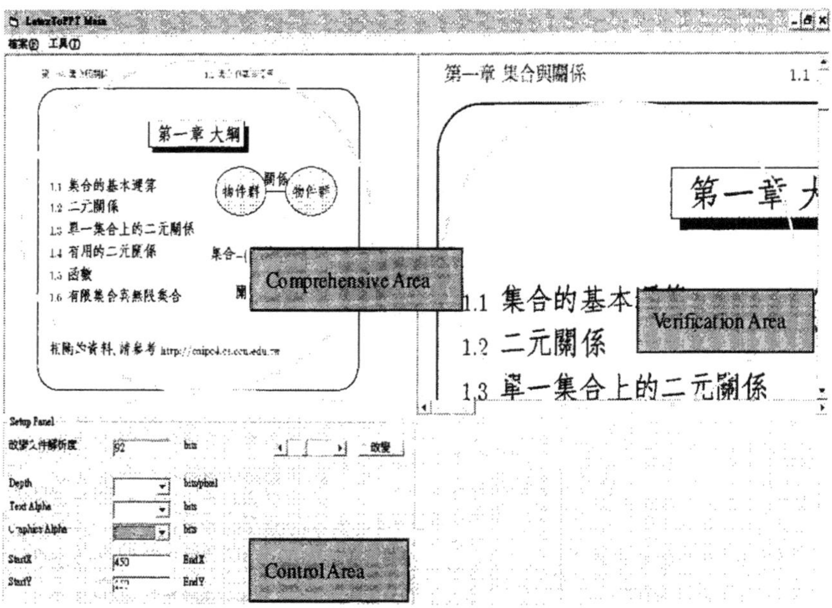

Figure 4: The components of Tex2Ppt translation system

4 Experiments and Comparisons

In our experiments, we compare the different approaches of Mathematic equation editor. Figure 5 shows the vavilov theory edited by the Microsoft equation editor. Figure 6 shows the vavilov theory edited by Scientific WorkPlace and views by TrueTex DVI Previewer. Figure 7 shows the vavilov theory edited by cwTex and viewed by GSView.

Table 1: Comparison of three approaches

Viewer	No. Page(s)	Size	Chinese support	Editing Tool	Flexibility when edit	Render quality
MS Equation	2	60.5KB	Y	MS Equations Editor 3.0	NO	Bad
Scientific Work Place	1	35.5KB	N	Scientific Work Place	NO	Good
GSView	1	37.5KB	Y	WinEdit+ cwTex	YES	Good

In Table 1, under the comparison about size, Chinese support, Flexibility and quality, we can figure out the best choose is edited by cwTex and viewed by GSView. It means that our system can translate the best representation what we want.

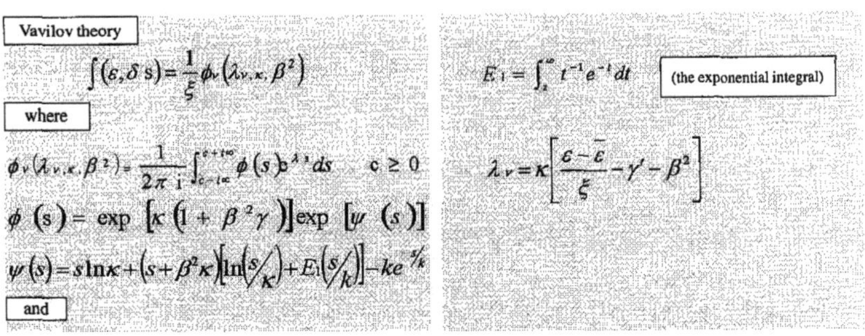

Figure 5: Vavilov theory with Microsoft equation editor（60.5KB）

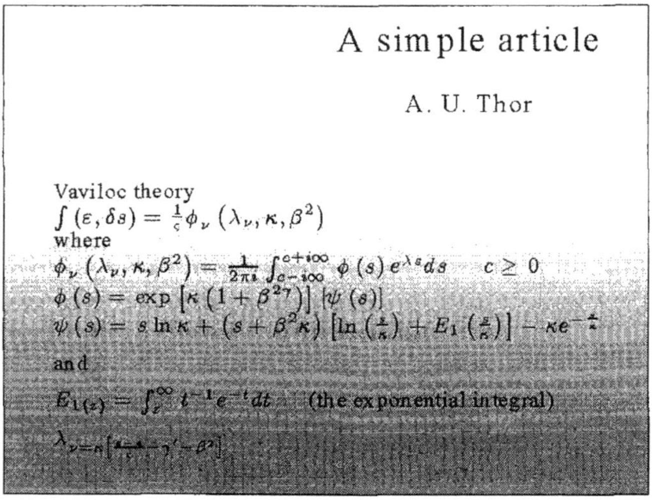

Figure 6: Vavilov theory with Scientific WorkPlace 2.5, TrueTex DVI Previewer（35.5KB）

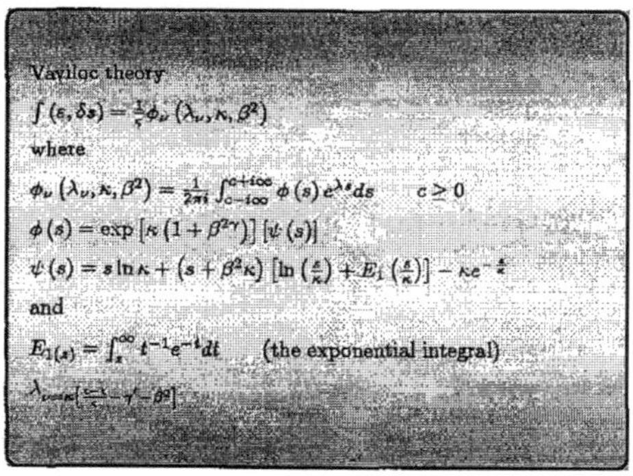

Figure 7: Vavilov theory with cwTex, GSView（37.5KB）

5 Conclusion

In this paper, we proposed a translation strategy between Tex/Latex files and Microsoft Power Point files. On one hand, our major contribution is that the Tex/Latex users can easily translate their works into Microsoft product, they don't waste time to re-write the content again, and the representation quality is reserved. On the other hands, we provide a solution to strengthen the weakest part of the Microsoft product, the unfriendly of mathematical equation editing. We also settle the problem of supporting of multi-language, especially the Traditional Chinese.

References

1. Latex to Power Point, http://www.drake.edu/cbpa/ARC/LaTeX_to_PPT.html
2. Mackichan software, http://www.mackichan.com
3. GSView Homepage, http://www.cs.wisc.edu/~ghost/
4. 吳聰敏、吳聰慧, CwTEX排版系統(第二版), 2000.
5. CWTEX Homepage http://ceiba.cc.ntu.edu.tw/tmwu/index.html#cwtex
6. Michel G., Sebastian R. and Frank M., The LaTeX graphics companion, Addison Wesley, (1997) pp. 338-345.
7. Latex Project Homepage, http://www.latex-project.org/

LEARNING THROUGH WEB-BASED ASSESSMENT

CHI KUEN WONG, WAI WONG, AND CHOR HUNG YEUNG

Computer Science Department,Hong Kong Baptist University, Waterloo Road, Kowloon Tong,HONG KONG.

E-mail: {kckwong, wwong, chyeung}@comp.hkbu.edu.hk

Although the Internet has become widely used in various aspects of the education process, the attention of its use in assessment has not been well received. This paper describes the development of a web-based assessment system, Quadrille, the proposed teaching and learning model with it and the preliminary feedback from teachers.

1 Introduction

The Internet has become widely used in the education process as a means of communicating, conducting discussions, exchanging ideas and for the dissemination of information [1]. However, the attention of its use in assessment has not been well received. Assessment is an important aspect in the educational process. It strongly influences what students attend to, how hard they work, how they allocate their study time, and what they can afford to get interested in [2,3]. This paper describes the development of a web-based multimedia assessment system, Quadrille, and presents the learning model with it and the feedback from teachers.

2 Development of Quadrille

Studies showed that student performance improved with frequent class testing [4]. One possibility for this improvement is that feedback on tests allows students to identify their own weak areas and work on them. Another study gives evidence that the frequent continuous assessment can lead to some positive effect on student work rates [5]. However, frequent testing increases the teachers' workload and the time delay in the return of the tests, thus, hampers these advantages. The development of a computerized assessment system will provide a possible solution to this problem.

Quadrille is a web-based assessment system which provides a subject independent platform. This allows the subject contents to be revised and updated very easily without the need to modify the programs. A list of the perceived requirements of the system is presented below:

- Ease of access
- Provision of a variety of question types
- Provision of setting marking scheme
- Provision of setting time limitation
- Flexibility of question selection
- Recording student performance
- Inclusion of feedback

2.1 Ease of access

The target users of the system are primary and secondary school teachers and students. They are not expected to have strong computer background. Fortunately, with most Windows-based software, once you have learned a package, the same 'look and feel' applies to others. Therefore, anyone who knows to use a Web browser can use this system without too much specific instruction.

The hardware and software requirements for accessing this system are very low. A personal computer with a Web browser and capable to access Internet is sufficient for using this system.

2.2 Provision of a variety of question types

Multiple-choice question is the most common question type in computer-assisted assessment. Text and numeric input are the second most common question types [6]. This may be mainly due to the ease of development. Unfortunately, text-based questions may cause boredom in the exercises. Hence, multimedia is used to arouse students' interest and capture their attention in the Quadrille system. It currently can support seven types of multimedia questions such as multimedia multiple choices, drag and drop, clicking, matching and so on.

2.3 Provision of setting marking scheme

Score is one of the feedbacks to students. This system allows teachers to set the marking scheme for individual question. They can also set the weighting of each exercise/test contributed towards the final grade.

2.4 Provision of setting time limitation

Due dates are normally set for exercises. Hence, the system allows the teachers to set the due date and time of an exercise. In addition, the teacher can also set the start date and time of the exercise so that no students can access the exercises before the specified time although the exercise has been deposited on the server. This time limitation feature also applies to tests; thus, the tests can be administered under a situation similar to an examination.

2.5 *Flexibility of question selection*

All the questions are stored in a question bank which is organized by courses. Each course can contain a number of units under which the questions are stored. An exercise or a test can contain questions from any unit of the same course. There are three ways to select questions. The simplest way is to select the questions of the teacher's choice. The second way is to request the system to select the questions according to certain conditions (e.g. question types, difficulty levels) set by the teacher. The final way is to allow the system to select the questions according to the conditions specified by the teacher when each student starts to attempt the exercise/test. All students will receive the same set of questions with the first two selection methods while they will receive different question set with the last method.

2.6 *Recording student performance*

Student performance data is recorded in a database. These data include individual student score and time spent for each question, the facility of each question, the number of attempts before a correct answer is achieved and so on. They can be compiled to provide various timely reports for teachers.

2.7 *Inclusion of feedback*

The system provides feedback to both students and teachers. The system can give immediate feedback on the correctness of the student answers. Hints are available when the student chooses a wrong answer or get stuck with a question. Even when the student gives a correct answer, further explanation or information related to the question/answer can be given in order to enhance student learning.

As the student performance data is stored on a database, teachers can request for various reports for individual student, for the whole class and for each course.

3 System Architecture

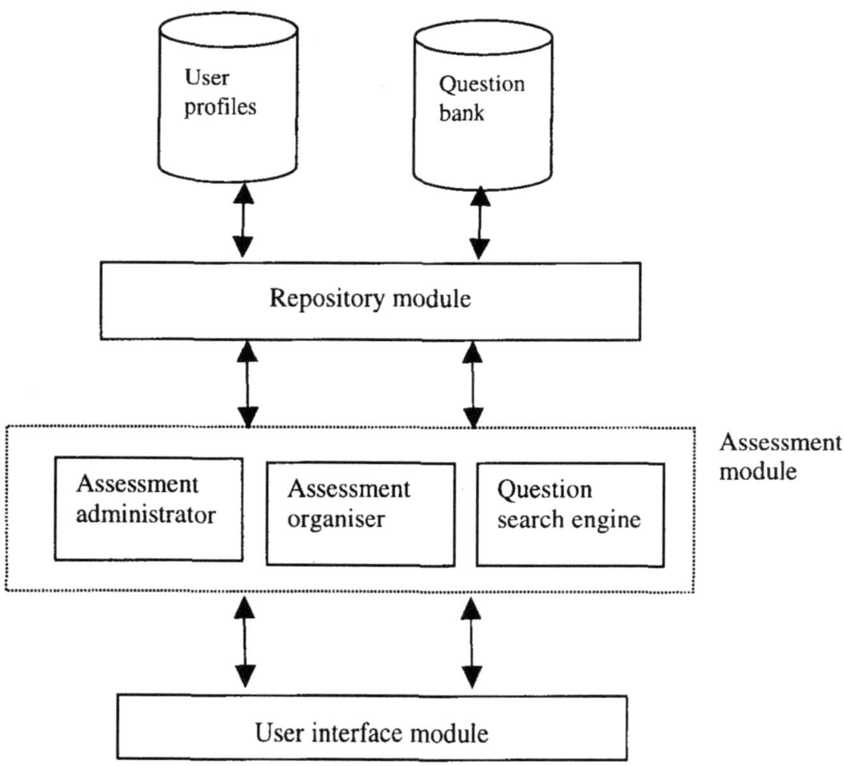

Figure 1: System Architecture

The system is built on a modular architecture (Figure 1). The user interface module consists of Web interface sub-models for students, teachers and system administrators. Each submodule provides different functionality to fulfill the needs of different classes of users. The repository module provides facilities to access data records from the databases. The assessment module consists of three sub-modules, namely assessment organiser, assessment administrator and search engine. The assessment organiser organises the questions from different courses/units into various types of exercises/tests. The assessment administrator administers the exercises and tests, and records the students' performance data. The search engine selects questions according to the criteria set by the teachers.

4 Teaching and Learning Model

The term 'assessment' is often associated with the testing of whether learning has occurred. But this is only one of the assessment roles. Scriven [7] used the terms 'formative' and 'summative' assessment to distinguish the two roles of assessment. Formative assessment refers to the use of evaluation in the development or improvement of some educational process. Summative assessment is the use of evaluation in decision-making about the end result of an educational process. They refer to functions, not a particular kind of assessment [7,8]. Hattie and Jaeger suggested that assessment needs to be an integral part of a model of teaching and learning if it is to change from its present status as an adjunct to measure if learning has occurred, to a new status of being part of the teaching and learning process [9].

The power of assessment is feedback. It informs the students' understanding of the taught materials. Quadrille system provides feedback to both students and teachers. The proposed model of teaching and learning with it is shown in figure 2.

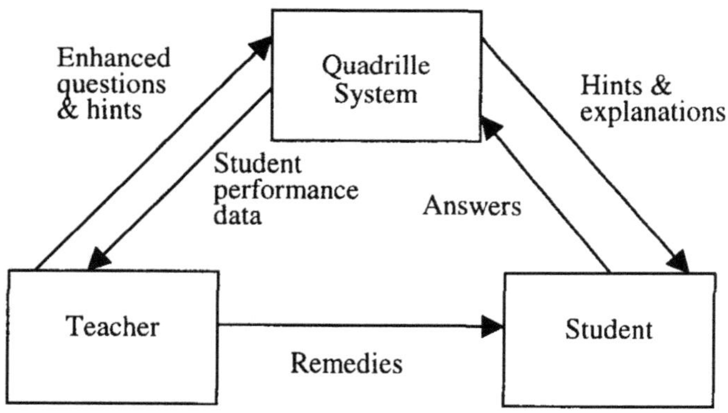

Figure 2: Teaching and Learning Model

Various forms of feedback are the major feature which makes Quadrille as a formative assessment tool. Students receive immediate feedback when they have given an answer to a question. If the answer is incorrect, hints and/or explanations of why the given answer is incorrect are given. In order to reinforce learning, further information or explanation on the question/answer is given even though correct answer is provided. Attainment level is another form of feedback. The system allows teachers to assign a difficulty level to each question; hence, the exercises/tests can be arranged in a progressive level of difficulty. This may help students know the level of attainment they have reached. All the above-mentioned feedback allows students to identify the areas that they need to improve.

As well as feedback to students, Quadrille system also provides feedback for teachers. Because the student performance data is stored in the database, various performance reports can be generated. They can be related to the performance of individual student or the whole class. Hence, teachers can adjust their pace of teaching and plan the necessary remedies for their class. The system can also produce reports on the effectiveness of individual questions with question facilities, average number of attempts before a correct answer is given, average time spent, etc. This information may help teachers identify the problem areas in terms of question quality and student performance. Hence, the teachers can enhance the questions and the associated hints and explanations, and adjust the difficulty level of some questions. This improvement in question quality will also enhance student learning.

5 Preliminary Teacher Feedback

The Quadrille version 2.0 Beta 2 was released on November 18, 2001. In order to promote this system, a number of workshops were held for primary and secondary teachers and IT coordinators. A simple questionnaire was administered at the end of each workshop. A total of 274 questionnaires were distributed and 203 questionnaires (84%) were returned.

Over 90% of the respondents indicated that they would tryout the Quadrille system and 87% would recommend this system to their school management. However, only half of the respondents expressed that their schools were capable to install and manage the system. This result is consistent with our informal discussion with the teachers participating the workshops. Many of them prefer us to host the server for them. It means that they will put their question banks and student records on our server. It is understandable because managing a system is more demanding in terms of computing knowledge than using a system. Therefore, some workshops on system administration are required.

The system is distributed under Gnu Public License, an open source license. This allows schools and teachers to use the system freely. We recorded 41 downloads of the software package of Quadrille from our web site during the period of December 9, 2001 and January 23, 2002 (44 days). Thirty-seven (90%) of them have left their school names and telephone numbers to us.

6 Discussion

Writing multimedia questions is seen to be the greatest obstacle to successful implementation of the web-based assessment system. Scanning/drawing graphics, audio file production and writing explanations/hints are very time consuming. In addition, not every teacher knows how to produce the multimedia materials. That is why we suggested that teachers could apply funding from the Quality Education Fund or other sources for employing a technician to assist in the multimedia materials production. Hence, the teachers can concentrate on writing questions. Once the question bank has been built up, the questions can be reused in the future.

Since Quadrille is an open-source software, it is available to everyone free. Textbook publishers are encouraged to use it to produce Web-based exercises and test banks accompanying with their textbook as instructors' supporting materials.

The supports from the school management and its willingness to change are also the critical factors for the successful implementation of the web-based assessment system. The teachers need the management to allow them to install the system on the schools' servers. Although the interface of Quadrille is user friendly, system installation and maintenance require some computer knowledge. The provision of technical support from the computer technician also requires the permission from the management.

As we cannot have sufficient resources to provide long-term substantial supports to schools, we are planning to form a Quadrille users' club for the teachers to share their experience in using the system, the question banks and the new system enhancement and modifications. Collaboration is the best way for them to help each other.

7 Conclusions

Quadrille is a web-based assessment system. It can provide feedback about student performance and effectiveness of individual questions in the question bank. Hence, it can be used for either formative or summative purposes. The automated grading capability of the system frees up human resources that can be used for providing additional personal attention to students.

From the feedback, this system is well received by teachers. However, the success of implementing web-based assessment is largely depended on the supports from school management and the availability of good quality question banks.

8 Acknowledgment

The development of this system was made possible by the provision of a grant from the Quality Education Fund (QEF), whose support we gratefully acknowledge. We would also like to thank all principals and teachers who supported this project.

References

1. Mudge, S.M. Delivering Multimedia Teaching Modules via the Internet, *Innovations in Education and Teaching International*, Vol. 36, No. 1, (1999).
2. Sadler, D.R. Evaluation and the Improvement of Academic Learning, *Journal of Higher Education*, Vol. 54, No. 1, (1983).
3. Stallings, W.M. and Leslie E.K. Student Attitudes Toward grades and Grading, *Improving College and University Teaching*, Vol. 18, (1970).
4. Black,P and Wiliam, D. Assessment and Classroom Learning, *Assessment in Education: Principles, Policy & Practice,* Vol. 5, No. 1, (1998).
5. Mulligan, B. Pilot Study on the Impact of Frequent Computerized assessment on Student Work Rates, *On-Line Proceedings of the Third Annual Computer Assisted Assessment Conference*, (1999).
6. Bull, J. Update on the National TLTP3 Project 'The Implementation and Evaluation of Computer-assisted Assessment', *On-Line Proceedings of the Third Annual Computer Assisted Assessment Conference*, (1999).
7. Scriven, M. The methodology of Evaluation, in: Tyler, R.W., Gagne, R.M. and Scriven, M. (Eds) *Perspectives of Curriculum Evaluation*, (1967).
8. Brookhart, S.M. Successful Students' formative and Summative uses of Assessment Information, Assessment in Education, Vol. 8, No.2, (2001).
9. Hattie, J. and Jaeger, R. Assessment and Classroom learning: A Deductive Approach, *Assessment in Education: Principles, Policy & Practice,* Vol. 5, No. 1, (1998).

ARCHITECTURE AND ALGORITHMS OF CPS – AN AGENT-BASED TUTORING SYSTEM FOR COACHED PROBLEM SOLVING ON THE WEB

ELVIS WAI CHUNG LEUNG AND QING LI

City University of Hong Kong {iteleung, itqli}@cityu.edu.hk

Abstract: *Currently, guiding students to reach the learning goals through problem-solving approach is quite primitive in most cyber-courseware systems on the Internet. In particular, these systems do not provide integrated learning-domain solutions for responding student enquiries based on individual student's background and interests. In order to offer student-specific problem-solving tutorship, dynamic generation of case-based solutions is a positive step towards this objective, which can accommodate individual student's needs accurately at anytime anywhere. In this paper, we present architecture and algorithms for developing an agent-based tutoring system called Coached Problem Solver (CPS) which, among other features, supports dynamic generation of student-oriented solutions on the Web. The facilities and capabilities of user profiles, rules, schema, XML and SMIL are incorporated and utilized by CPS so as to provide a better support to the interactive learning environment in which student-specific, content-based learning styles can be adequately entertained. A prototype system of CPS manifesting these algorithms has been built in Java, using IE on the PC platform.*

Keywords: Web-based education, agent-based approach, user profiles, XML, and SMIL

1. Introduction

In the past few years, many education providers have launched a number of online courses on the Web [8,9,10]. In order to enhance interactive learning, many different kinds of multimedia-based courses have been developed for attracting students to learn on the Internet. Many students enrolled in such online courses initially, however, the drop out rate seems to be quite high. One of the reasons is that these on-line courses do not have an effective tutoring system to help students who are in the learning process and encounter trouble to understand the subjects (learning domains) and/or in problem solving. For example, students with different background and knowledge of a given subject are most likely given the same tutoring support (such as FAQ). The heart of the problem is the lack of "content/user awareness". These systems are not designed with powerful intelligent knowledge base facilities, such as personal profiles, which can help understand students' behavior and interest in order to provide student-specific, content-driven results to individual students. The learning and teaching performance is thus inevitably affected under this phenomenon.

To provide effective problem-solving tutorship based on user profiles, dynamic generation of case-based solutions is one of the possible solutions, which can tailor to students' needs accurately at anytime anywhere. For example, when a student requests a solution for some self-studying problem, the system would understand the question from the student first before generating a suggested solution. In this paper, we put forward an approach of developing an agent-based tutoring system called Coached Problem Solver (CPS), and describe in detail the architecture and algorithms of CPS to address many of the challenging issues involved in developing such a flexible and cooperative system.

1.1 Practical Issues Involved: an Overview

In CPS, we propose to use *rule-based paradigm* coupled with *user profiles*. In particular, the rules will be utilized to interpret a student question in the initial stage. After that, filtering the relevant concepts for answering the question becomes critical. Normally, some concepts are included in a learning domain and the relationship among the learning domains is the concept/point. In order to provide integrated learning domain solutions, we advocate using user profiles to find out the relevant concepts from different learning domains [13]. Actually, each student will have some form of learning domains collected from previous experiences, and the agents (programs) of CPS will fetch relevant concepts from his profile history, and provide the suggested answer based on the question. Thus, the agents can provide the student-specific solution for matching with the individual needs.

Moreover, an effective media for storage of concept/point is also important. The ideal media should be easy to manipulate and of low bandwidth usage. XML is a meta-markup language. It uses a DTD for any application to describe its data to be used. One of the advantages of XML is low bandwidth usage. It can provide a repository as the central storage for all concepts. Also, the concept of *data islands* [17] can be introduced for a connection-less approach for knowledge delivery.

In order to reduce the cost, we adopt the concept of *solution schema*, a well-defined template for concept generation. In particular, it ensures the generation process to be in an accurate manner, which will be stored into the user profile as part of the history. When the student recalls a similar question, the system can consult his profile history to provide the relevant concepts directly, so as to reduce the required resource and response time.

In addition, it is necessary to identify an efficient way for checking all learning domains in each generation of an individual solution. We introduce an index server that stores all the concept paths and the relevant parameters. When a suggested solution generation is initiated, the system will first search the index server (by SQL statement) to identify all the relevant paths of the learning domains and fetch the solution schema for the actual solution generation. Thus, it can reduce the response time and increase the efficiency.

Interactive learning [1] is a primary goal for online courses on the Internet. No matter what tutoring facilities are provided to individual students, the support by an interactive learning environment is needed to motivate the students to continue studying on the Internet personally. SMIL [19], a language for describing interactive, synchronized multimedia applications on the Web, is therefore chosen and used for the multimedia presentation in our CPS in order to enhance the interactive learning.

1.2 Paper Objective and Organization

In this paper, we present the details of our CPS in terms of its architecture and algorithms for coached problem solving through dynamic generation of student-oriented solutions on the Web. The user profile, rules, schema, XML, and SMIL are incorporated in and utilized by the algorithms in order to provide better support to the student-specific, content-based learning styles within an interactive learning environment.

Through the designing architecture and algorithms for coached problem solving, we aim to address the following main topic in this paper: How to effectively serve individual student's needs in providing concepts for a particular question? In fact, the main contribution of this paper is not so much on the performance efficiency side, but to bring out a feasible approach in an innovative way. For this purpose, our prototype system is developed to demonstrate the feasibility of the proposed approach.

The rest of this paper is organized as follows. The related work for reviewing the current systems for coached problem solving is reviewed in section 2. The specific features of the CPS architecture and algorithms are detailed in sections 3, which includes agent-based architectural framework for coached problem solving, 4-staged conceptual model and algorithms. The prototype system is discussed in section 4. The final section concludes this paper and makes suggestions for further research.

2. Related Work

In this section, we briefly review some representative intelligent tutoring systems (for coached problem solving) on the e-learning domain [14,16].

Andes [11] is a collaborative project started since 1995 between the University of Pittsburgh and the US Naval Academy. It has a modular architecture, and is implemented in Allegro Common Lisp and MS Visual C++. Before execution, a problem author creates both graphical description of the problem and the corresponding coded problem definition. The problem solver uses this definition to automatically generate a model of the problem solution graph. Then an Action Interpreter and a Help System refer to the student model to make decisions about what kind of feedback and help to give the student. The central component of the student model is a Bayesian network that is constructed and updated by the Assessor, which provides probabilistic estimates of the student's mental state.

LANCA [15] adopts an intelligent agent's approach to distance learning in a distributed environment. It uses a constructive approach instead of user profiles to assist students in difficulty. Also, it assumes that all the questions and solutions related to the problems and given by a learner should be applicable to other learners, building a common and useful databank. To realize this approach, it uses intelligent agents able to detect the difficulties of the learner and to delegate specific help to be provided.

DT Tutor [12] uses decision-theoretic methods for coached problem solving to select tutorial actions that are optimal given the tutor's beliefs and objectives. It employs a model of learning to predict the possible outcomes of each action, weighs the utility of each outcome by the tutor's belief that it will occur, and select the action with the highest expected utility. Also it decides the action topic, such as a specific problem step or related concept. A dynamic decision network is used to implement most of the intelligent, non-user-interface part of DT Tutor. GeNIe is an experimental project from the University of Pittsburgh, and it uses SMILE and C++ for building the prototype system. However, it does not yet have suitable user interface, and so has not been evaluated with human students.

A comparison between CPS and the above-mentioned systems is shown in Table 1. Compared with the other systems, CPS takes a step forward to providing suggested solutions from integrated learning domains. For example, a suggested solution will take into account the previous concepts and expected concepts for a question raised by the student. Consequently, the suggested solution will be more specific and pertinent to the students' learning process.

Purposely, CPS takes the advantage of web technology to place the operation on the Internet. Java (JSP and Servlet) [18] will be used in the middle-tier, while XML and SMIL are used for delivering and presenting the solutions. As a result, CPS can provide a truly interactive, multimedia-enabled intelligent tutoring system on the Internet.

Adopted Approach	**LANCA**	**Andes**	**DT Tutor**	**CPS**
Architecture	Agent-based	Modular	Decision-theoretic	Web-based, Agent-based
To Model of Student Knowledge/Problem/Question Method	Constrictive Approach	Bayesian network	Dynamic belief networks	User profiles, Rule Base, Schema
Represent Suggested Solution Method (Concepts)	Adaptive	Dynamic	Dynamic	Dynamic
Coverage of Suggested Solution (Concepts)	Within a learning domain	Within a learning domain	Within a learning domain	Integrated learning domains
Adopted Tools for the System	Java	Lisp & C++	GeNIe, SMILE, C++	Java, XML, SMIL

Table 1: A comparison between CPS and other systems

3. Architectural Framework

To build a flexible, knowledgeable and self-improving system to support e-Learning, our approach is to develop (using Java) an agent-based framework for intelligent tutoring [2,5,6,7]. In this section we describe the detailed architecture and a set of algorithms for CPS.

3.1 CPS Architecture and Components

The overall architecture for CPS is as illustrated in Figure 1. As shown in Figure 1, the agent-based architecture for CPS is a collaborative environment that includes *Tutor Agent, Interface Agent, User Profile,* and *Knowledge Domain*. Based on their own knowledge, each agent should take an efficient and effectiveness way to complete their own task and provide information to each other. The detailed elaboration of each component is given below.

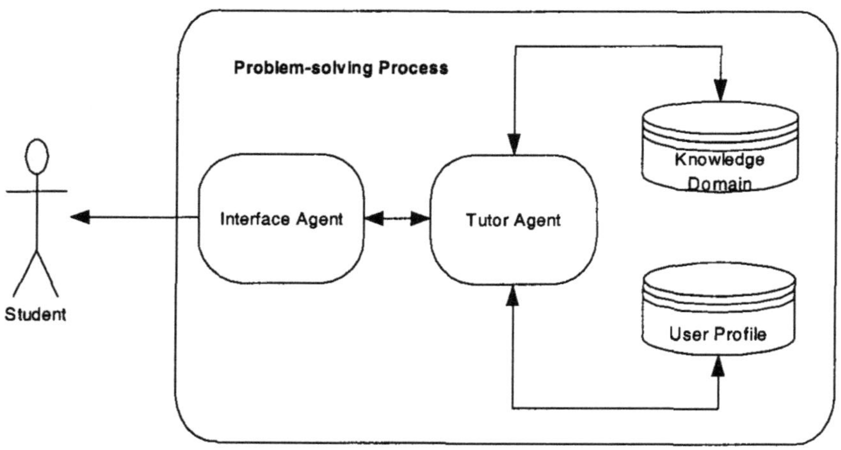

Figure 1. Agent-based architecture for CPS

Interface Agent: Its main function is to link students and the Tutor Agent for coached problem solving. It has four states as shown in Figure 2. Normally, the Interface Agent is on the Listening State. When a student makes a request to the Interface Agent for some problem solving, the state will be changed to the Processing State for handing the student's input event. After the input event, it will pass the question to the Tutor Agent, and the Processing State will be changed to

Waiting State (to wait for the Tutor Agent to return the solution). Once the Interface Agent receives the return from the Tutor Agent, it will start to present the solution. Then the Processing State will be revisited and the Interface Agent starts to take over the system resources to present the solution (which may involve displaying the XML file by XSL through applet on the client-side, and playing the multimedia through SMIL). After the student reads through the solution, CPS will arrive at the Termination State so as to release the hold-up resources and return to the Listening State again.

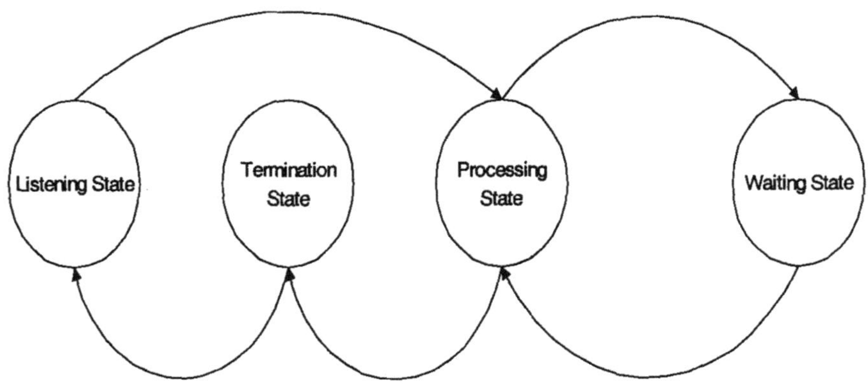

Figure 2. 4-state processing of the Interface Agent

Tutor Agent: This is the heart of the CPS mechanism. The Tutor Agent receives a request from the Interface Agent, then connects to the Knowledge Domain and User Profile databases (cf. Figure 1) for refining the question and providing a solution. The refined question and suggested solution will be saved in the user profile as a history for future use. To better manage these processes, a layered conceptual model is introduced for the Tutor Agent (to be detailed in the next section). After the necessary processing steps, a student-specific solution will be generated and sent back to the student.

User Profile: It is the primary storage for all student-specific information such as study history (Figure 3), personal information, study status, and history of the question and solution of each request. It provides the relevant information to the Tutor Agent for refining the question and then determining the related concepts for the question. Normally, the user profile will provide the latest student's information on demand. Detailed operations will be discussed in the following section.

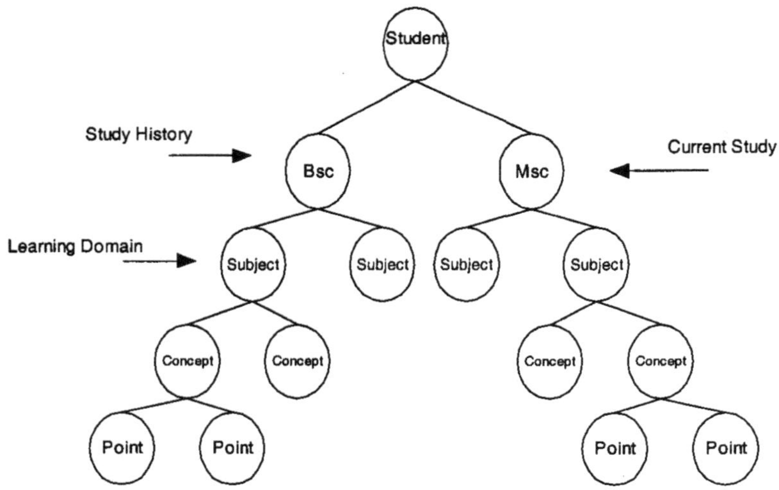

Figure 3. Study history

Knowledge Domain: It is the primary repository for all course notes (learning domains). The relevant information will be extracted from the Knowledge Domain in providing solutions for the questions. In order to enhance the retrieval performance, all course notes are stored in XML and all location paths of each course note stored in an index server. The retrieval operation will be based on the index server to locate the expected information for a given question. The details of retrieval and reconstruction of the concepts will be explained in terms of the staged conceptual model to be described next.

Some Assumptions**:** A student is required to enroll some courses in order to obtain an academe award. Each course has a number of subjects (*learning domains*) to ensure the student acquiring new knowledge from the course. Also, each learning domain has some topics (*concepts*) and *points* manifesting the whole learning domain.

3.2 Staged Conceptual Model

In order to provide a conceptual framework for governing each component's work, a *4-Staged Conceptual Model* is introduced as illustrated in Figure 4. Based on this conceptual framework, we can clearly identify the individual works for each component and the relationship among these layers.

Definition 1. *The **Staged Conceptual Model** consists of 4 different layers, which are Problem Classification, Verification, Filtering, and Construction. Each layer has a graph model instantiating a set of rules for determining its decisions. For the flow of each operation, the result should be transferred from an upper layer to the next layer below for further processing until it reaches the solution.*

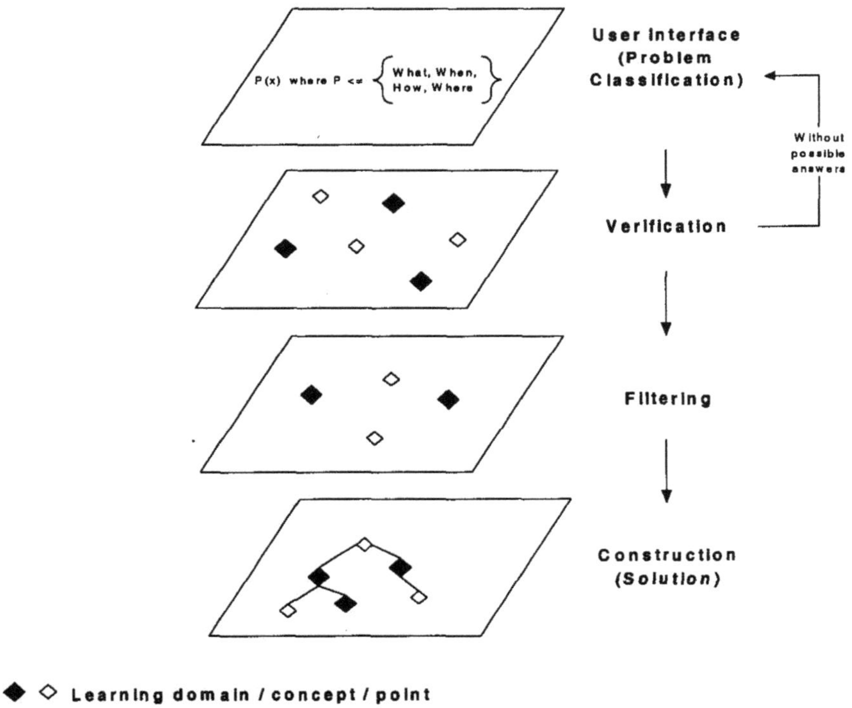

Figure 4. Staged conceptual model

The main functions of each stage are as follows:

Problem Classification Stage: In this stage, a question x that is provided by the student will be classified into one of the four categories, p, such as what, how, when and where.

Verification Stage is based on $p(x)$ to verify whether or not any relevant learning domain/concept/point for the particular question exists in the Knowledge Domain. If it is found, the verification process is completed; otherwise, return the question to the student for reconfirmation.

Filtering Stage: This stage is to, based on the result from the Verification Stage, filter the most relevant learning domain/concept/point for the question.

Construction Stage: In this stage, the relevant learning domain/concept/point hierarchy has been constructed by the relationships between each node pair for the solution.

Typically, a web-based graphic user interface is provided at the Problem Classification Stage (PCS) for a student to input a specific question. Then the question will be transferred to the next level, i.e., the Verification Stage. At this stage, the question will be made more specific to the relevant learning domains and the Knowledge Domain will be checked to see if it has the relevant information for this question. The Filtering Stage will next find out the student-specific's concept of the learning domains for the student. Likewise, this information will be passed to the Construction Stage for developing the actual solution in XML format. Finally, this XML document will be transferred to the PCS for presentation. The detailed operations in each stage will be explained in the subsequent subsections.

3.2.1 Problem Classification Stage

In order to identify the *core theme* of a student's question, we employ a rule-based paradigm to manage this process in the PCS [3,4]. The employed rules are as stated in Rules 1-4, where x in the question (x) [e.g. x = "Java Programming"] can be either a subject or a concept (refer to Figure 3).

Rule 1. If what (x) then definition(x);
Rule 2. If how(x) then example(x);
Rule 3. If when(x) then situation(x); and
Rule 4. If where(x) then relationship(x, y) where y is another knowledge domain.

Generally speaking, students who are in trouble for learning a subject may likely to have insufficient knowledge to well define a question. Also, a student may be confused (overloaded) if too much information for the question is provided by the tutoring system. According to the above rules, the PCS will classify the question into the *what*, *how*, *when*, and *where* categories and keep the solution concisely, thereby guiding the student to form a (preliminary) question in a positive way. However, a student may select more than one rule in getting more information for a question.

3.2.2 Verification Stage

The main responsibility of the Verification Stage (VS) is to refine the question from the PCS. To enhance the refinement performance, the user profile's history will be checked in this VS first (cf. Algorithm 1).

```
r := HistoryChecking(x,k)
If History(r) = true
            Pass the question to Filtering Stage
Else
            Starting the refinement process
            /* see Algorithm 2 */
Endif

HistoryChecking( x, k )
x : Learning domain/concept/point from Problem
    Classification Stage
k : History of all questions from the student
r : Expected result

r:= false
For each k
            If k = x then r:= true
Return r
```

Algorithm 1. Finding out a similar question from the history of User Profile

Words to be ignored in a Question
a, an, the, and, for, is, are, or, be, were, have, has, same, what, when, how, where, etc.

Table 2. Ignoring Word Table

Sometimes, the history may not have any similar question, in which case a refinement process will be initiated. In this refinement process, the main issue is on matching the words' combination with particular learning domain(s). Normally, student inputs a question with more than one word. For understanding the words' meaning pertinent to a learning concept, a Learning Directory (Figure 5) and an Ignoring Word Table (Table 2) are introduced and utilized in CPS, as explained below.

Ignoring Word Table: It contains the words that should be ignored for determining the words' meaning such as a, an, the, etc. Normally, ignoring these words will not affect the meaning of the question. Thus, the complexity for the understanding words' meaning can be reduced without sacrificing the accuracy.

Learning Directory: It is for building a categorized tree based on the learning subjects in a major study. For the example in Figure 5, the main categories are Programming, Networking, and Software Engineering. Under the main categories, the sub-subjects are described in next level and so on. According to this categorized tree, the words in the question will be compared with the nodes for identifying the relevant information/concept for the question. Algorithm 2 illustrates the process of understanding a question (in terms of the words' meaning) pertinent to a learning concept.

The main algorithm for understanding the question

```
a)  Read through the question into a Java object
b)  Take out some words by the Ignoring Word Table (For this example, "What is" will be ignored)
c)  Identify the relevant Main Category based on the remaining words of the question (see Figure 5)

    If word(s) has been found in the Main Category(s)
        GoNext:= DirectoryChecking()
    Else
        GoNext:= CourseChecking()
    Endif
d)  /* In worst case, relevant learning concept also may not be found in Learning Directory. Thus,
    we need to inform the student that no relevant answers for this question */
```

```
    If GoNext :=False
        Re-inputting the question are requested due to lack of relevant learning concept
    Endif
```

<u>DirectoryChecking</u>

```
Continue := False
If more than one Main Category has been located
  For each Main Category has been located
  Ignoring the word matching with the current Main Category
     For each nodes of the Main Category
        If the word(s) of the question = node's keywords
                Continue := True
        Endif
Else
  Ignoring the word matching with the Main Category
  For each nodes of the Main Category
        If the word(s) of the question = node's keywords
                Continue := True
        Endif
Endif
Return Continue
```

<u>CourseChecking</u>

/ In order to select one directory starting the searching, User Profile will be employed. Normally, student finding a solution for a particular question is about current study, so we assume that the best answers are relating to the current study. Thus, the User Profile will provide a list of current subjects for the following algorithm. */*

```
Continue := False
While the list of current subjects is not null
        Continue : = DirectoryChecking()
Endwhile
```

/ However, relevant learning concept may not found in current subjects. Thus we need to continue searching the other Main Category */*

```
If continue := False
While the Learning Directory is not null (Only the subjects has not been checked)
        Continue : = DirectoryChecking()
Endwhile
Endif
Return Continue
```

Algorithm 2. Understanding the words' meaning pertinent to a learning concept

Based on Algorithms 1 and 2, the student's question can be determined in this VS as valid or not. In addition, an important checking step is taken in the VS to ensure that the question must have a relevant solution in the learning domains before transferring it to the Filtering Stage, thereby increasing the problem solving efficiency.

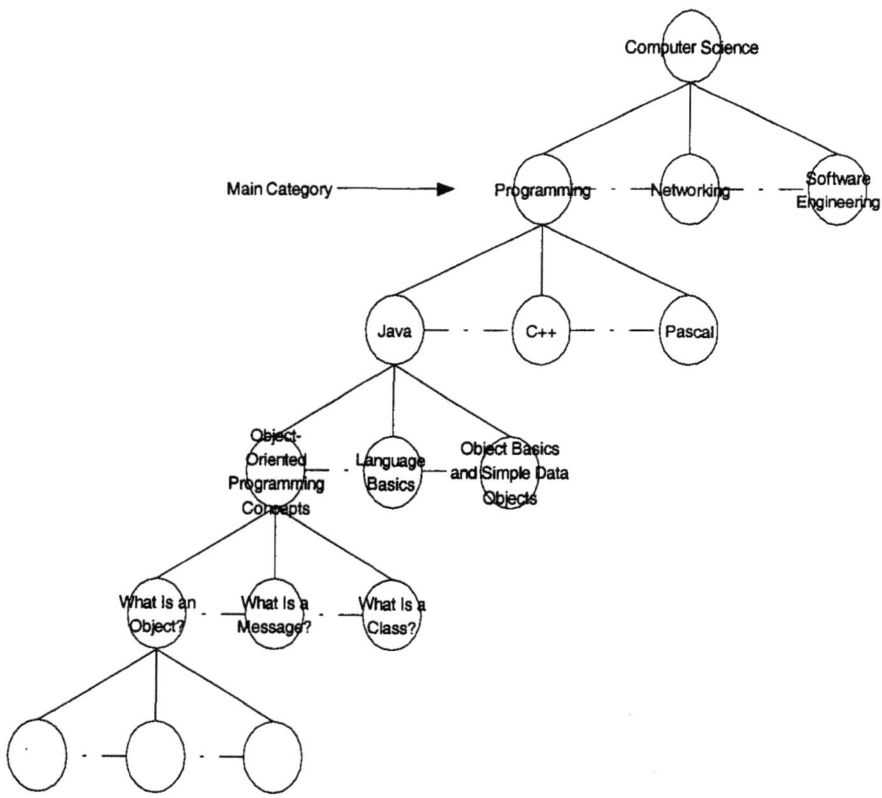

Figure 5 . Learning Directory

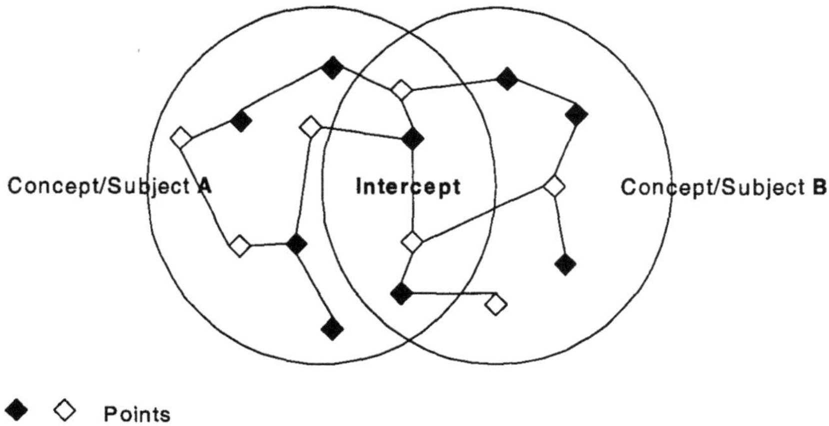

Figure 6. Knowledge Domain in the intercept between Learning Domains A and B

3.2.3 Filtering Stage

The main responsibility of the Filtering Stage (FS) is to process the confirmed question from the Refining Stage to find out relevant and suitable learning domains for the specific question. Two cases exist: If a specific question exists in the user profile's history, this request will then be passed directly to the Construction Stage. Otherwise, it will start the filtering process as described below.

Case 1: Acquisition of new knowledge based on pervious relevant knowledge. First of all, our CPS tries to identify what are the student's needs. Quite often, a student's expected solution is supported by the pervious knowledge (learning domains). The relationship among pervious learning domains and suggested learning domain for the question needs to be identified in this FS so as to fulfill the student expectation. Figure 6 intuitively illustrates a possible inter-domain relationship, where the intercept of learning domains is regarded as most suitable for the student.

Definition 2. *A suggested solution is an intercept* $\gamma = (\alpha, \beta)$, *where* α *is a Concept/Subject in relation to the student's problem,* β *is another Concept/Subject in relation to* α *.* α *and* β *are stored in the Knowledge Domain.* $\gamma \in \alpha$ *and* $\gamma \in \beta$, *where* γ *is a set of points.*

Based on Definition 2, we can formulate the relationship between the learning domains and the question. As shown in Figure 7, a given question can have several related and/or unrelated solutions (of different learning domains) around it. Subsequently, we introduce an algorithm for finding out the relevant learning domains.

Case 2: Acquisition of new knowledge without pervious relevant knowledge. A student may not have previous knowledge relating to the question. In that case, CPS is only providing the knowledge about the question.

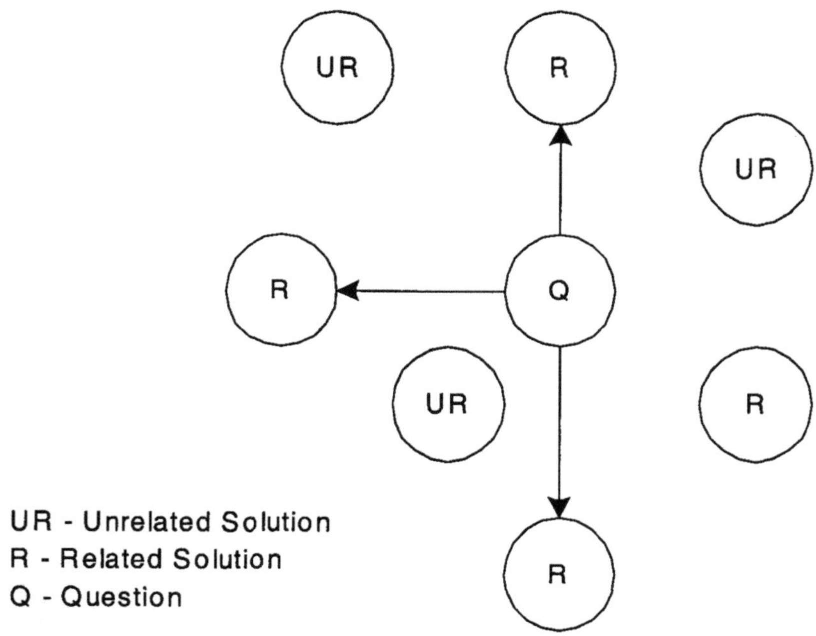

Figure 7. Determining related solution for a given question

Based on Algorithm 3, all suitable learning domains for the current question and a maximum of 5 previous learning domains will be stored in *f*. These parameters will be passed to the next stage for generation of XML document before sending the result to the student.

```
rc, rp := FindAllLearningDomain(i, x)
x : Question
k : Concept/Point
f : Result of all Concept/Point

if rc and rp = null
  /* Case 2 */
  f:= x.k

else

  /* Case 1 */
  /* Find concept/point in relation to current study */
  /* p(x) see rules 1-4 */
  For each r
     If rc.k ∩ x.k  and rc.k = p(x) then f:= f + rc.k + x.k

  /*Because previous learning domains may be so
   much, so only take the maximum nearest 5 domains
   for return to the student */
  For maximum nearest 5 rp
     If rp.k ∩ x.k and rp.k= p(x) then f:= f + rp.k + x.k

FindAllLearningDomain(i, x)
i: Study history (learning domains) from User Profile
x : Question
rc : Expected result for current studying
rp : Expected result for previous studying

For each i
            If i = current learning domains
                        If i∩ x then rc:= rc + i
            Else
                        If i∩ x then rp:= rp + i
Return rc,rp
```

Algorithm 3. Finding out all concepts from relevant learning domains for the question

4 Prototyping Development

To demonstrate the validity and effectiveness of our approach, we have been developing an experimental prototype system of CPS. This prototype is based on IE browser which supports XML document and uses the built-in Java Applet (for handling the XML DOM parser function).

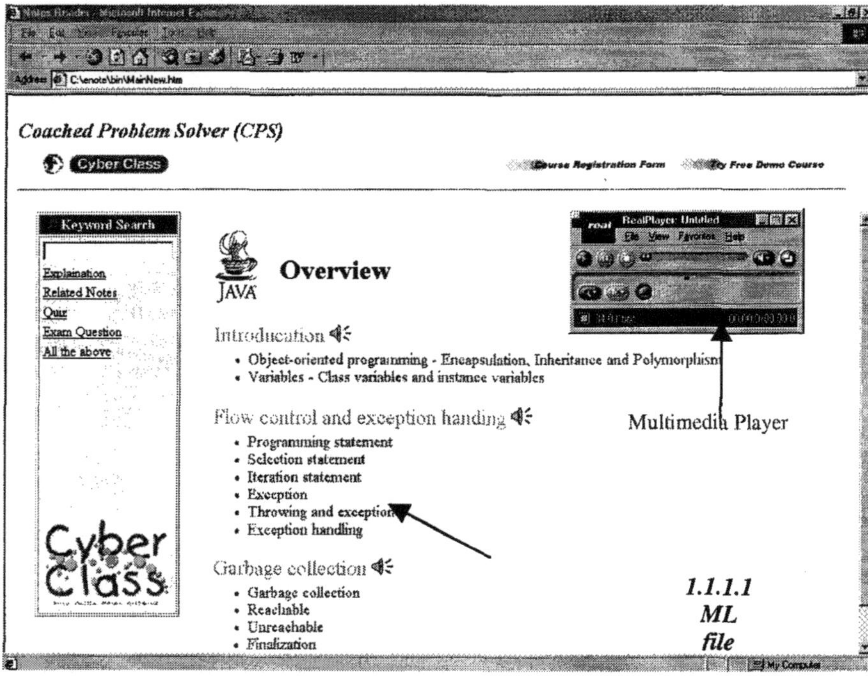

Figure 8. Generation of result from CPS

Figure 8 shows an overall interface for presenting a generated solution*. The center part is the suggestion notes, the XML document presented by XSL. Also, the user may play the multimedia video by clicking on a specified symbol.

5. Conclusion and Future Work

In this paper, we have presented an agent-based architecture and a set of algorithms that form the core of the Coached Problem-Solver (CPS) mechanism in our e-Learning system on the Web. Among the many desirable features offered by CPS, the following advantages are worth particular mentioning:

---

* The solution is actually a response generated by CPS on the user query of "What is Java programming language?".

- **Intelligent Coached Problem Solving on Demand**. Based on our proposed architecture and algorithms, student can get the solution on demand for their own question at anytime anywhere. In addition, a solution can combine the previous learning domains and new knowledge for a given question, thus, the learning performance can be increased.

- **Active Learning.** The suggested solution is generated based on individual student's question and expectation, which supports the ideas of personalization and interactive learning effectively. The new and previous learning domains and their links are transparent to the student. It is easy for a student to understand the structure of the suggested solution and the relationship between a subject and a sub-subject.

- **Connection-less Approach.** We note that our CPS is a suitable mechanism for advocating a connection-less approach for the e-Learning environment. In particular, it can reduce the demand on the server support by avoiding a large number of connections within a particular period. Also, by combining with Java, XML, and SMIL capabilities, CPS can provide a flexible, knowledgeable and self-improving system to support student learning.

Thus, it becomes possible to guide students to solve their problems in learning their subjects on a timely basis. This hopefully can have a positive influence on the drop out rate, since the learning interest of students on the Internet can be more likely maintained. For our further research, one of the immediate issues is to develop an interface to support the initial creation and preparation of the course notes (learning domains). Adopting a proactive approach for the agent to learn from the interaction process between reading the course notes and the assessment result is also an interesting issue to explore. Such an approach can allow us to find out "hot topics" and issues of concern from the e-Learning users. Moreover, we will incorporate more multimedia technology to the e-Learning environment in order to enhance the traditional teaching method. Finally, we plan to investigate the possible utilization of our system and support more advanced techniques (such as data mining) based on the CPS sophisticated/advanced facilities.

References

[1] Jonassen, D.H., Supporting Communities of Learners with Technology: A Vision for Integrating Technology with Learning in Schools. *Educational Technology*, 35(2). 60-63, 1995

[2] Leung E., and Li Q., Agent-Based Approach to e-Learning: An Architectural Framework, in Kim, W., Ling, T.W., Lee, Y.J. and Park, S.S., *The Human Society and the Internet*, LNCS 2105, pp.341-353, 2001.

[3] Forgy, C. L., *Rete: A Fast Algorithm for the Many Pattern/ Many Object Pattern Match Problem,* Artificial Intelligence 19, 17-37, 1982.

[4] Riley, G., *CLIPS, A Tool for Building Expert Systems.* http://www.ghg.net/clips/CLIPS.html.

[5] Lesser, V. R., *Cooperative Multiagent Systems: A Personal View of the State of the Art,* IEEE Transactions on Knowledge and Data Engineering, vol. 11, no.11 Jan –Feb 1999

[6] Ciancarina, P., Tolksdorf, R., Vitali, F., Rossi, D. and Knoche, A., Coordinating Multiagent Applications on the WWW:A Reference Architecture, *IEEE Transactions on Software Engineering*, vol. 24 , no. 5, May 1998

[7] Lashkari, Y., Metral, M. and Maes, P., Collaborative Interface Agents, *Proceedings of the Twelfth National Conference on Artificial Intelligence*, 1994

[8] Pimentel M. G.C. and Abowd G.D., Ishiguro Y., Linking by Interacting: a Paradigm for Authoring Hypertext, *Proceedings of ACM Hypertext*, May 2000

[9] Stern M., Steinberg J., Lee H. I., Padhye J. and Kurose J.F., MANIC: Multimedia Asynchronous Networked Individualized Courseware, *Proceedings of Educational Multimedia and Hypermedia*, 1997

[10] Mukhopadhyay S., Smith B., Passive Capture and Structuring of Lectures, *Proceedings of ACM Multimedia*, October 1999.

[11] Gertner A. S. and VanLehn K., Andes: A Coached Problem Solving Environment for Physics in Gauthier G., Frasson C. and VanLehn K., *Intelligent Tutoring Systems*, pp. 133-142, 2000

[12] Murray R. C.and VanLehn J., DT Tutor: A Decision-Theoretic, Dynamic Approach for Optimal Selection of Tutorial Acitons, in Gauthier G., Frasson C. and VanLehn K., *Intelligent Tutoring Systems*, pp. 153-162, 2000

[13] Bradley K., Rafter R. and Smyth B., Case-Based User Profiling for Content Personalisation, in Brusilovsky P., Stock O. and Strapparava C., *Adaptive Hypermedia and Adaptive Web-Based Systems*, pp.63-72, 2000

[14] Trella M., Conejo R. and Guzman E., A Web-Based Socratic Tutor for Trees Recognition, in Brusilovsky P., Stock O. and Strapparava C., *Adaptive Hypermedia and Adaptive Web-Based Systems*, pp.239-249, 2000

[15] Frasson C., Martin L., Gouarderes G. and Aimeur E., LANCA: A Distance Learning Architecture Based on Networked Cognitive Agents, in Goettl B., Halff H., Redfield C., Valerie R. and Shute V., *Intelligent Tutoring Systems*, 594-603, 1998

[16] Sanrach C. and Grandbastien M., ECSAIWeb: A Web-Based Authoring System to Create Adaptive Learning Systems, in Brusilovsky P., Stock O. and Strapparava C., *Adaptive Hypermedia and Adaptive Web-Based Systems*, pp.214-226, 2000

[17] http://www.microsoft.com/

[18] http://www.javasoft.com

[19] http://www.w3.org

INTEGRATING MULTIMEDIA AND SOFTWARE AGENTS FOR EFFECTIVE WEB-BASED LEARNING

TANKO ISHAYA, STAMATIS GUSSIOUS AND CHARLOTTE M. JENKINS

Centre for Internet Computing, The University of Hull, Scarborough Campus, Filey Road., Scarborough,, YO11 3AZUK,

{T.Ishaya, S.Gussious, C.M.Jenkins}@dcs.hull.ac.uk

The web is increasingly used as a platform for e-learning applications. The sophistication of these applications varies from simple libraries of static lecture presentations to fully integrated, dynamic multimedia applications enabling interaction between students and between student and lecturer. Replacing the physical presence of the lecturer who answers queries, motivates students and generally supports the whole learning process is clearly the most challenging aspect of any development effort. In a web-based learning environment the presence of the virtual lecturer may be required 24 hours a day and at any physical location around the globe. This paper provides both an evaluation of existing web-based learning applications and an introduction to a framework for integrating multimedia and software agents in web-based learning. An implementation of the proposed framework is presented which addresses two key issues: firstly, the effective integration and synchronisation of multimedia within applications; and secondly, provision for 24-hour interactive student support through the use of intelligent software agents.

1 Introduction

The Internet has been the most influential technology in the transformation of modern commerce and society. Although it has proved its potential for creating online learning environments to support education (Yazon, 2002; Harris, 1999; Fetterman, 1998), the full potential of the Internet for transforming education is only just being tapped. Yet, even in its current stage of development, the web as a learning aid is bringing us closer than we ever thought possible to making learning of all kinds, at all levels, any time, any place, any pace a practical reality for every individual. The educational community has been lured into using web technology for promoting student learning and today there are hundreds of thousands of online learning materials, tutorials, and courses supported by different learning tools with varying levels of complexity.

Discussions about the educational potential of the Web have been particularly salient within and among education and Internet research (Cummings et al.2002; Harris, 1999). The need to link pedagogy to the prevailing technological infrastructure was highlighted by Roschelle and Pea (1999) and Mergebdollar (1996). They however, emphasised the need for additional frameworks for Web-based learning. In answer to this requirement, several researchers have offered frameworks for learner-centred Web instruction (Bonk and Cummings, 1998), the integration of the Web in one's instruction (Bonk et al., 2000), the role of the online instructor (Bonk et al., 2001) and the types and forms of interaction made possible by the emergence of the Web (Cummings, et al, 2002).

Despite the on-going evolution of these educational frameworks, the web is used primarily as a virtual library, where webmasters and teachers distribute their publications, tutorials, and lecture materials in electronic format. However, web technology has permitted the use of multimedia in the presentation of teaching materials (Jesshope, et al., 2000) and the creation of interactive, and thus more interesting, online courses and tutorials. Moreover, there is on-going development of new online teaching tools as web-based learning tools such as (Jesshope et el., 2000).

Another emerging technology that could be beneficial for web-based learning is web agents. The development of agents is still in its early stages but is promising for future applications. Web agents can be thought of as software (robots) that reside on a web site or within an application to help guide the learner. Such agents could be used in online education to support the student throughout their learning process. Employing this technology in online education could provide great benefits by enabling an interactive web-based learning paradigm to support or replace conventional learning techniques. This will yet provide another answer to some of the questions raised and explored in Cummings et al.(2002).

The main purpose of this paper is to describe an ongoing research investigation with the aim of providing an improved understanding of the role of multimedia and web agents in online learning. We aim to show how their integration could provide efficient web-based learning tools. In the next section, we provide a brief overview of some existing web-based learning tools. In section 3, we provide a framework for integrating multimedia and agents for web-based learning. Section 4, presents and describes a simple application of the framework defined in section 3 with a discussion of initial results. Section 5 concludes the paper with further research questions.

2 Review of some learning environments

The key advantage of the Internet is the ease with which it enables information exchange between people across the globe. The HTML-enabled integration of text with other media formats provides the ideal platform on which to build online applications. The first example of this was seen in the simple transformation of books, publications, tutorials, and course content to electronic format (Cummings et al., 2002). Initially, web-based learning was seen as a means of providing access to static instructional-educational materials such as Microsoft PowerPoint presentations Boettcher (1997). Thus, Web-based learning in its most basic form can be defined as learning in an online environment. However, using these basic online learning tools, the isolated learner is unable to interact with the teacher making it much more difficult for them to focus, read and understand the material. This is one-way communication with little or no support for an interactive learning process.

There are now a number of web-based (asynchronous as well as synchronous) online learning tools designed to provide varying levels of complexity and flexibility. The tools have been designed to facilitate content delivery via standard web browsers over the Internet. While we provide a thorough review of only a few tools, the features for reviewing such tools should be:

- Support via a web browser
- Support for asynchronous discussion groups and /or threaded discussions

- Support for course planning and management
- Support for instructional design, information presentation and testing
- Support for online testing
- Support for student self assessment, progress tracking and building motivation
- Support for synchronous learning

There is significant variation in depth and quality of these features with its associated costs and complexity.

2.1 An evaluation of BSCW

Basic Support for Cooperative Working (BSCW) is one of the first free available web-based learning tools developed by the research group of German National Research Center for Information Technology (GMD). It is a shared web-based workspace system that supports collaboration in heterogeneous environments (a different-time different-place situation) (Klöckner, 2000; Bentley et al., 1997). The shared workspace is the central access point for common data and learning resources to all students and a log to keep track of individuals' participation. The shared workspace can contain files, text, documents, photos, graphics, calendars and discussions. All these contents can be available to individuals that have the corresponding access rights to read or manipulate them. It also provides some facilities for synchronous communication among students and teachers. BSCW provides some important features for online collaboration such as authentication, production of joint materials, document versioning, notifications, flexible graphical user interface for customization, and multi-language support. These features have been summarised by Appelt (1997) in terms of events and activities as shown in Figure 1.

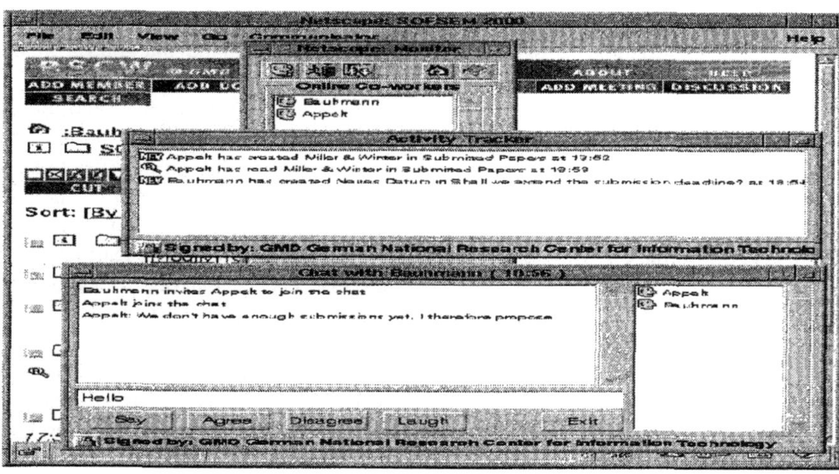

Figure 1. BSCW Event Monitor

According to GMD, since 1994, more than 100,000 users have registered and have been using the BSCW system. Reasons for its popularity and acceptance are because of its wide range of synchronous and asynchronous communication facilities, and the fact that the system including is automated configuration is offered free to anyone. This has enabled lecturers from various universities to register online and reserve a workspace for their courses.

The functionality of the BSCW system seems very impressive. It provides most of the synchronous or asynchronous communication means available today. Lecturers and students have multiple choices of communication using email, discussion forums, chat sessions, and audio or video conferencing. The teacher is able to engage the students in online discussions using the chat or the forum services. They can ask questions and request students to post their answers online. Furthermore, the various event functions of the BSCW platform enable on time notification of students for special events, for instance group meetings, and there are adequate means for monitoring students' progress by the lecturer.

Furthermore, the shared workspaces enable students to download or upload documents and files and work simultaneously on the same project. The lecturers are able to upload the teaching material online so that students could download it at any time. Students can also upload their essays or assignments in order to be examined by their teacher.

On the other hand, there are two major disadvantages of this system that must be taken into consideration. Firstly, BSCW is mainly a communication and collaboration platform not a presentation tool. The BSCW system does not provide any means to support the preparation and the demonstration of the lecture presentation. Thus, the author needs to use another tool, such as Microsoft PowerPoint, to develop the presentation material. Apart from this, the lecturer is limited on publishing the teaching material online either as documents to download or as slides embedded in web pages. Thus, while the BSCW system offers various channels of communication among users, learning requires a means for supporting students' problems at appropriate times. The lecturer cannot be online at all times to support this learning process with limited alternative source for finding help.

2.2 An evaluation of AudioGraph

AudioGraph is the result of a collaborative project between Surrey University in the United Kingdom and Massey University in New Zealand (Jesshope et al., 2000). Their research first discovered that there was a lack of simple professional tools and applications that would help an online teacher in their tasks. Two main reasons motivated the development of AudioGraph- firstly, the small number of the existing tools required usually expert knowledge of programming, suitable for multimedia professionals rather than academics, secondly, most of the tools were very costly (Jesshope et al., 2000; Jesshope, 1999). These problems motivated the AudioGraph team to develop an application that would be free of charge to use and that would require no specialist programming knowledge.

The presentation model of AudioGraph closely follows the traditional lecture in a classroom model. The presenter can use already prepared slides and use the player to present them. In addition to this, the online presenter is able to add comments, animations and audio clips to reinforce the presentation material. Because of the similar presentation styles in both AudioGraph and conventional teaching, AudioGraph presents a shallow learning curve to the potential author. The goal of this tool was to place the production of media, for online education purposes, in the hands of the educators rather than the technologists (Jesshope, 1999). AudioGraph allows authors to use pre-prepared slides, usually made with Microsoft Power-Point, and record these with the AudioGraph recorder tool. The author indicates the number, names and order of the slides and AudioGraph integrates them into a presentation allowing subsequent playback. Another great feature of this tool is that it offers a number of drawing and pointing tools to be used while playing back a presentation. For example, the highlighter allows the author to draw the attention of his audience at specific elements. AudioGraph will authomatically generate web pages for each presentation. The following figure shows the tools provided by the AudioGraph..

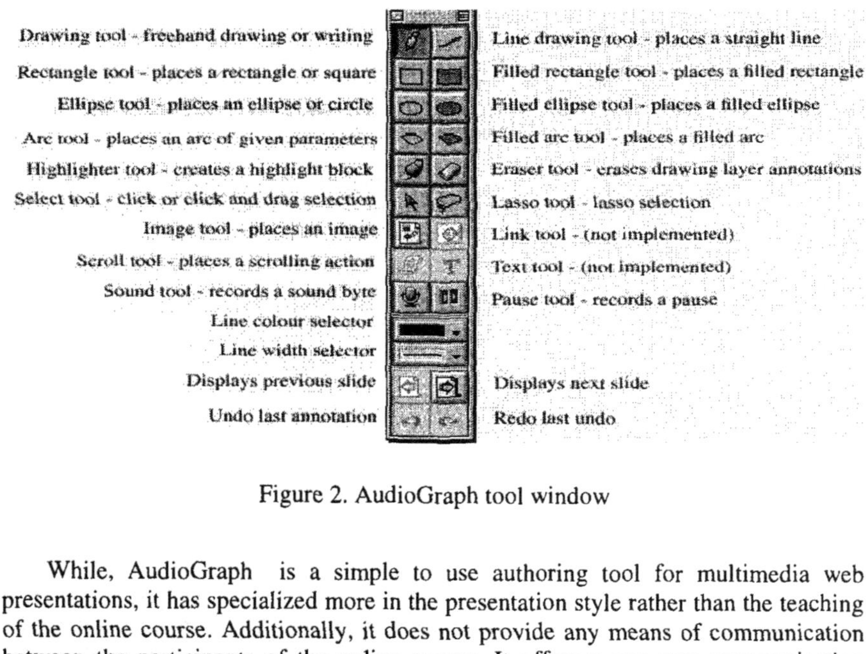

Figure 2. AudioGraph tool window

While, AudioGraph is a simple to use authoring tool for multimedia web presentations, it has specialized more in the presentation style rather than the teaching of the online course. Additionally, it does not provide any means of communication between the participants of the online course. It offers a one-way communication between the teacher and the students. So, students are left responsible to follow the course at their own pace, which requires students' motivation and self-discipline. There is no interaction among the students, and the lecturer has no means of monitoring student's performance and progress.

From this analysis, we can see that most existing web-based learning tools only support a subset of the traditional learning pedagogy. Face-to-face communication is currently impossible in web-based learning. Thus, the hundreds of pedagogical innovations need to be unified into a single acceptable web-based learning pedagogy. The unidirectional flow of information from instructors to students and a lack of interaction amongst students can be addressed by integrating multimedia and web agents. The next section describes a framework that integrates multimedia and agents to provide the stated functionality.

3 A framework for integrating multimedia and agents for web-based learning

The role of multimedia and computer mediated communication has been examined for web-based learning in Section 2 through a review of two existing online learning solutions. The two systems both employ different technologies and utilize a number of facilities provided by multimedia and computer mediated communication. However, even with all these technologies, neither of the system provide the potential for 24-hour online support for learning. The BSCW was able to provide asynchronous or synchronous support but only for a certain time. Thus, in most cases the student relies on asynchronous support. In this section, we provide the concept of agents and describe a framework for integrating multimedia, computer mediated communication and agents for effective web-based learning.

As in conventional teaching, past experience shows that every student needs support or advice when faced with complex learning problems and preferably at that specific moment. This certainly raises the question of how to achieve any time and any place support. Obviously, the teacher cannot be available 24-hours. The challenge for 24-hour support has forced academics, technologists and researchers to investigate the possibility of employing other technologies for supporting this important feature of web-based learning. We believe that the integration of web agents will provide this functionality. Thus our framework for developing web-based learning tools is the integration of agent technologies, computer mediated communication technologies, and multimedia technologies interfaced with web technology. Figure 3,presents the diagrammatic representation followed by a description of each component.

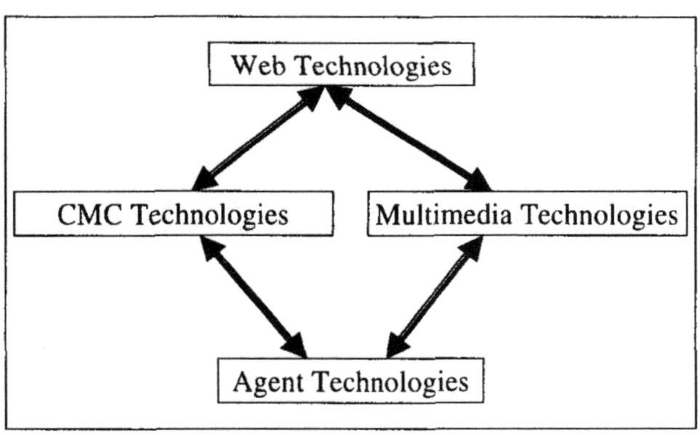

Figure 3. A framework for effective web-based learning tools

3.1 Agent technologies

The integration of agents at the bottom layer of the framework is in order to provide the required 24-hour support in web-based learning. The technology of intelligent agents is being advocated as a next-generation model for engineering complex, distributed and open systems (Jennings, 2000; Wooldridge, 1997). Agents are increasingly used in a large variety of application areas. For example, the role of software agents in Groupware and CSCW has been discussed by Ellis and Wainer (1999) and Intelligent Tutoring Systmes by Potska (1988). Wenger (1987) states that although agents build upon previous research on intelligent tutoring systems, they bring a fresh perspective to the problem of facilitating online learning. Agents are defined by Roesler and Hawkings (1994), as independent computer programs operating within software environments such as operating systems, databases or computer networks. Kay (1990) defines an agent as something that shares and helps to accomplish user's goals. Looking at these two definitions, key characteristics of agents can be summarized as follows:

- Agents are independent computer software
- Agents can be flexible by providing the ability to reside and interact within various software environments
- Agents are able to communicate with humans
- Agents can perform complicated tasks in respect of humans

See (Sounders, 2000; Jennings, 2000; Wooldridge, 1997; Ellis and Wainer 1999; and Woolf, 1992) for a more comprehensive discussion of agents. Th interaction flexibility of agents in various environments such as the web could be used to utilise the information repository to provide 24-hour support.

The approach will be to design and employ a range of intelligent agents that vary in their architecture and functionality. Thus, each agent will utilize Artificial Intelligence techniques to provide the required functionality of agents in web-based learning.

The following list shows some of the many required features.

1. 24-hour online support for the student.
2. Support interactive e-learning environments
3. Answer simple queries during course presentation.
4. Answering sophisticated queries and start discussions around these queries
5. Retrieve additional information from external sources to aid the student
6. Provide references of books, electronic papers and control the online library transactions
7. Link various key issues/concepts of the course from different pages, combine them and output knowledge (data-mining)
8. Guide students throughout the course, understand student's needs and apply accordingly. So, agents can have multiple personalities
9. Start friendly discussions on general subjects to encourage and motivate students
10. Co-work with students' in-group projects to understand to understand and evaluate their needs and monitor their progress

11. Evaluate the online course using the students' criteria

3.2 Multimedia technologies

Most existing web-based learning tools do not provide support for multi-mode communications. Those that attempt to provide a medium where audio, video and data are transmitted are designed to be meeting-centric. For example, BSCW has limited support for synchronous data communication. There is therefore, the need for, audio, visual and textual communication combined with synchronous and asynchronous communication. The most effective method is synchronous PC-based videoconference between the teacher and the students. However, such a method requires expensive hardware and the development of private networks or extranets to facilitate the direct communication among the remote users.

The teacher will need to prepare presentation slides and add sound support. Thus, students will be able to read the text and listen to their teachers' voice simultaneously. Sound and video are probably the two most important components that define multimedia. There are many advantages from the utilization of sound in online teaching. The sound of the teacher would increase the motivation of the students, draw their attention to important points and provide a high level of virtual socialization.

3.3 Computer mediated communication technologies

Computer Mediated Communication offers a great range of technologies either synchronously or asynchronously. The system should include computer conferencing such as email, discussion forums and text based chat facilities. The email, chat and discussion forums would provide an asynchronous communication. Advanced synchronous communications such as audio or video conferencing are very important for an e-learning system although, such communications require the purchase of special software, hardware and network programming to synchronise the communications.

These forums can encourage online active participation and collaboration between and amongst students. The teacher obtains the e-moderator role for this activity. The teacher should take the role of a moderator to promote active learning and teamwork of the students with various techniques. For instance, he could oblige all his students to contribute their ideas to online discussions in the forum.

3.4 Web technologies

Commonly various e-learning components are integrated on a website in order to provide an online platform. Browser capabilities and the creation of appropriate plug-ins enable the integration of a wide range of programming languages, multimedia and communication technologies to web pages. There are now many web-authoring tools with varying levels of complexity.

4 A tool for teaching Java using multimedia and agents

The previous section defines a framework for developing effective web-based learning tools. In this section, we provide a simple application of the framework with a discussion of the initial results. A summary of the requirements of our application is as follows:

1. The system should provide online JAVA tutorials for students
2. The system should be simple to use and navigate
3. The system should be interactive as possible including interaction capabilities among students and between students and the teacher
4. The system should provide possible means of 24-hour support for the student
5. The system should be as autonomous as possible
6. The student should feel comfortable and fulfilled with the delivery methods without needing further interaction or teaching
7. The system should have minimum hardware or software requirement with no cost.
8. The application should reduce the teacher's efforts
9. The system should focus on the e-learning concept and its delivery methods rather than the presentation content

From these specifications, the system will focus on the delivery methods of the content, the communications methods, the interactivity and usability level of the e-learning solution. The student should be able to study the course online with minimum hardware or software requirements. The delivery methods should be adequate enough for the student to understand the tutorials. Moreover, the system should provide various means of interaction to satisfy students with different learning and communication tactics. The e-learning application should provide a 24-hour support for the student and mainly about the course material. Figure 4, is the architectural design of the application.

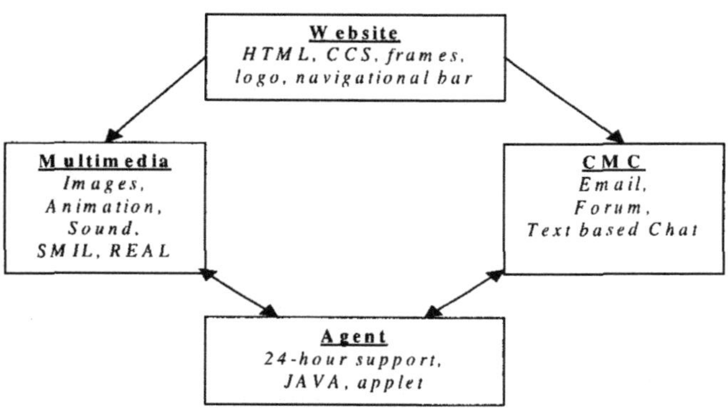

Figure 4. Architectural design of the system

4.1 System Implementation

The website is the main interface of the e-learning system, thus it needed to be simple, usable and compatible with different types of browsers. Easy navigation with clear links throughout the website is always important. Its interface consists of two main frames – static and dynamic frame. Figure 5, shows structure of the website interface.

The website was implemented with the use of HyperText Markup Language (HTML) version 4.0 to provide browser compatibility. Furthermore, Cascading Style Sheets (CSS) were used to improve the visualisation and structure of the website content. CSS was used to provide a consistent structure throughout the site.

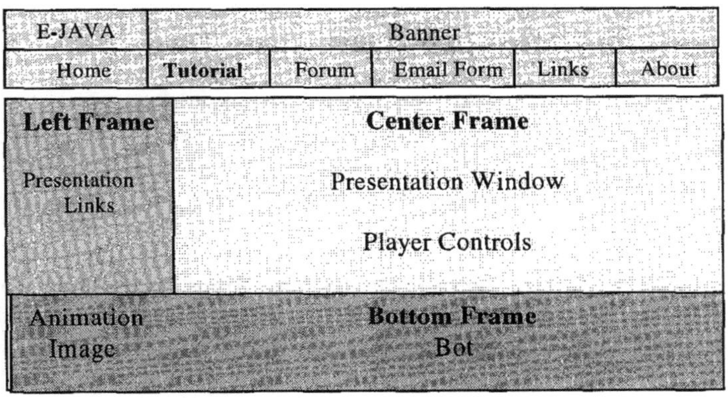

Figure 5. Frame structure of the website interface

According to the design plan, CMC features included email, discussion forum and text-based chat. Video conferencing requires expensive hardware and network programming and thus it was outside of the scope of the prototype. A Common Gateway Interface (CGI) script was written to accomplish these features. CGI is server-based and ensures the delivery of the form input and the appropriate presentation format at the other end (teacher). Furthermore, a confirmation message is shown whenever the student's input is sent successfully to the server. The purpose of the email form was to provide a quick communication facility for he student. The student is not required to have any email program installed since the CGI script is server based.

Multimedia technologies such as images, animation, sound and video clips have been used for this application. The presentation is demonstrated with a linear series of slides (like PowerPoint) with audio. Both the presentation slides and the sound take advantage of streaming technologies to enable playback, easy navigation, total flow control of presentation and reduce downloading time. The implementation is based on Synchronized Multimedia Integration Language (SMIL) for visual presentation. SMIL provides a good solution for synchronising each slide with the corresponding audio file. However, in order to view documents, a special tool is needed to make SMIL files readable online, a REAL player from REAL Networks Technologies was used for this purpose. SMIL tags can handle different types of files such as videos, images or sound. Unfortunately, SMIL is still under development and only provides a limited number of tags to do basic functions such as specifying starting or ending time of viewing a file and synchronising different multimedia files. SMIL does not provide tags for special effects like fading or highlighting that could be very useful during a tutorial presentation.

A .smil file was created for each JAVA tutorial that holds information about the timing of the sound files. The SMIL files are called from the HTML page of the particular tutorial. Real Player includes plug-ins that enable web developers to embed its control system on the HTML page using the control attribute. The appendix section includes partial code for this purpose. The following figure demonstrates a presentation of a JAVA tutorial. The student can watch it from the embedded display of the Real Player and handle the presentation with the player's control bar. The detailed design of our agents is similar to the Information Gopher. The agent can answer any possible queries from students about the presentation material, which complements teacher's support 24-hour per day. The agent was implemented in Java.

A JAVA Swing applet was used for the implementation of the intelligent agent's interface. This interface consists of three main GUI components: a text field, buttons and a text area. The text field that is in the top position is used for the student's input. So, students are able to type a question in this field. At the middle of the applet there are three buttons. The first button is used to submit the input of the user to the agent. The second one is used to play the audio clip of the corresponding answer. This function was added to serve as an additional accessibility facility for disabled students. The last button is used to stop the sound. At the bottom of the GUI lies a text area that provides the answer to the student. Figure 6 shows the graphical user interface of the agent. The main functionality of the agent uses a keyword matching technique.

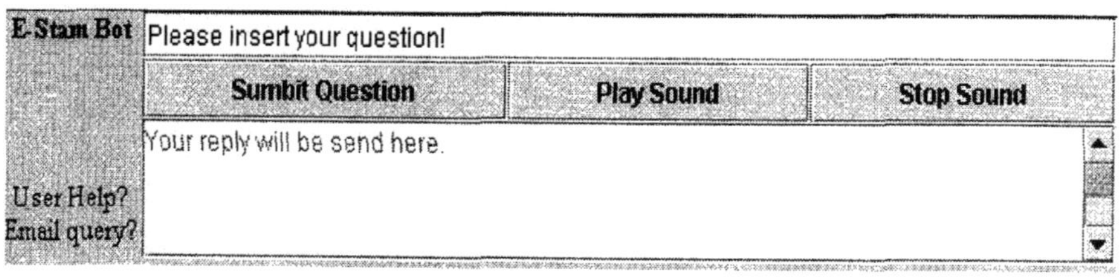

Figure 6. The Agent GUI

4.2 *Evaluation of the system*

The prototype was evaluated using 15 MSc students from the University of Hull, Center for Internet Computing. These students had already completed a Java module in a traditional classroom environment. During the course the module material was online, presented as PowerPoint slides. The only means of online interaction was by email. Every student had a different background and most of them did not have past experience of programming.

An evaluation was conducted to assess the overall effectiveness of the prototype. Tutorials used were just a small portion of the MSc. Java programming module and students were requested to use the prototype and express their views by filling in a questionnaire. The questionnaire needed to focus on the following objectives:

1. Effective use of multimedia
2. Effectiveness of the agent as a support tool and
3. Effectiveness of the online communication facilities.

Analysis of students responses revealed the following analysis. 50% of the students indicated that the multimedia component was adequately efficient and 60% of the responses shows effectiveness of the sound components. When multimedia was compared with the PowerPoint delivery method, 43% of students found multimedia as the best solution and 57% regarded the integration as the best approach to effective e-learning. Furthermore, results revealed that majority of the students appreciated the role of the agent during the presentation process. More specifically, 53% of students found it useful in improving their learning experience. 45% of students agreed that CMC provided the essential facility required for interactive communication.

5 Conclusion and further research

With an awareness of current discussions about the educational potential of the Web in education, this research in progress presents a proposed framework for developing web-based learning tools. The framework has been tested with very promising results. We have demonstrated that even primitive agents can provide valuable assistance as human teachers, serving as cognitive tools. Erickson (1997) states that we have to move beyond the adaptive functionality were agents acts as "butlers" to the metaphor where agents have full human characteristics. Our test prototype focused on the delivery methods of the material rather than its pedagogical perspective. It is therefore, important that a unified learning pedagogy for adoption in web-based learning is defined.

Agents need to have an appropriate persona like actors in a play. They should be cooperative, honest and be able to motivate or draw the attention of the student. Intelligent agents should be able to start a conversation, guide and provide appropriate feedback to the students. Most academics agree that agents should show some human emotions to students, using video picture.

References

1. Appelt, W. (1997). Basic Support for Cooperative Work on the World Wide Web. *International Journal of Human Computer Studies: Special issue on Novel Applications of the WWW*. Academic Press, Cambridge. Spring 1997.
2. Bentley, R., Appelt, W., Busbach, U., Hinrichs, E., Kerr, D., Sikkel, S., Trevor, J. and Woetzel, G. (1997) "Basic support for Cooperative work on the World Wide Web." *International Journal of Human-Computer Studies: Special issues on innovative applications of the World Wide Web.*

3. Boettcher, J. V. and Conrad, R. 1997. Distance Learning: A Faculty FAQ. Florida State University. Available online : http://microsoft.com/education/planning/online/distance_faq.asp [Accessed 16 July 2001].
4. Bonk,C.J., Kirkley, J.R., Hara, N. and Dennen, N.(2001). Finding the instructor in post-secondary online learning: pedagogical, social, managerial, and technological locations. In: Stephenson, J., Editor, , 2001. *Teaching and learning online: pedagogies for new technologies*, Kogan Page, London, pp. 76-97.
5. Cummings, Jack A., Bonk, Curtis J., and Jacobs, F. Robert. (2002). Twenty-first century college syllabi; Options for online communication and interactivity, *The Internet and Higher Education, Volume 5, Issue 1, May 2002, Pages 1-19*
6. Ellis, C. and Wainer, J. (1999) "Groupware and Computer Supported Work", In: Weiss, G (ed)., *MultiAgent Systems: A Modern Approach to Distributed Artificial Intelligence*, New York, The MIT Press: 425-457.
7. Fetterman, D.M., 1998. Webs of meaning: computer and Internet resources for educational research and instruction. *Educational Researcher* **27** 3, pp. 22-30.
8. Harris, M.H (1999). Is the revolution now over, or has it just begun? A year of the Internet in Higher Education. *The Internet & Higher Education* **1** 4 (1999), pp. 243-251.
9. Jennings, N. R. (2000) "On Agent-based software engineering", *Artificial Intelligent*, **117**(2): 277-296.
10. Jesshope, C., Heinrich, E. & Kinshuk (2000). Technology Integrated Learning Environments for Education at a Distance. DEANZ 2000 Conference, 26-29 April 2000, Dunedin, New Zealand. Online publication.
11.
12. Jesshope, C (1999). Web-based teaching-Tools and Experiences. *Austrian Compter Science Communication*, 21 (1), PP 27-38
13. Mergendoller, J.R., (1996). Moving from technological possibility to richer student learning: revitalized infrastructure and reconstructed pedagogy. *Educational Researcher* **25** 8, pp. 43-46.
14. Sounder, J. H (2000). A primer on artificial ntelligence technologies. Available on line: http://users.erols.com/jsounders/papers/aitechniques.htm. [Accessed August, 2001]
15. Wooldridge, M. (1997) "Agent-Based Software Engineering", in IEE Proceedings in Software Engineering, IEE
16. Yazon, Jessamyn Marie O., Mayer-Smith, Jolie A., and Rosemary J. Redfield, Rosemary J. (2002) Does the medium change the message? The impact of a web-based genetics course on university students' perspectives on learning and teaching, *Computers & Education, Volume 38, Issues 1-3, January-April 2002, Pages 267-285*

PART TWO Models

VEGA-KGQA: A KNOWLEDGE-GRID-BASED QUESTION-ANSWERING APPROACH[1]

HAI ZHUGE, YANYAN LI, JIA BI AND JIE LIU

Knowledge Grid Research Group, Key Lab of Intelligent Information Processing
Institute of Computing Technology, Chinese Academy of Sciences, 100080, Beijing, P.R.China
E-mail: zhuge@ict.ac.cn

A Knowledge Grid is our newly proposed mechanism for uniformly sharing and managing knowledge resources across the Internet, based on which, a new question-answering approach VEGA-KGQA is proposed. It can intelligently answer users' questions by incorporating five distinguished features: the semantic-web-based representation, the multi-level knowledge support, the human-machine-cooperative knowledge collection mechanism, the knowledge-based template and the knowledge reasoning and navigation mechanism. The VEGA-KGQA mechanism is a part of the engine of the Knowledge Grid VEGA-KG.

1 Introduction

Information Retrieval focuses on the problems associated with retrieval of documents from a collection in response to user questions. The main metrics used to test the accuracy of the retrieval are precision and recall. The precision measures the relevance of the items retrieved and the recall measures the relevance of the information retrieved relative to the items in databases. However, with the increasing availability of information in the WWW, users are confused in finding useful information from large amount of retrieval results. Thus, there is a great demand for new evolutionary technology to improve the performance of IR.

Traditional IR systems assist users to locate documents but leave it to the user to extract the knowledge from the top ranked documents. As users are overwhelmed by rapidly growing web information, there has been an increasingly need to develop Question Answering (QA) technology. QA is an IR paradigm for discovering concise answers to an open-domain natural language question from a large target corpus. Over the past two years, work in QA has been encouraged by the inclusion of a question-answering task in the experimental work of the TREC conference series. The goal of the QA task is to "retrieve small snippets of text that contain the actual answer to a question rather than the document lists traditionally returned by test retrieval systems." Participants use various techniques to extract answer texts. These techniques include traditional passage retrieval [1,3], document retrieval plus passage ranking [7], and document retrieval plus linguistic processing (such as entity extraction, entity classification, and entity ranking) [8]. So far, many systems have been developed to attempt to fulfill the QA goal [e.g. 2,9].

AskJeeves (http://www.askjeeves.com) and Ulika (http://www.ulika.com.cn) is respectively an English and Chinese question-answering search engine, which adopt the idea of avoiding the natural language understanding by two-times template retrieval. The

[1] The research work was supported by the National Science Foundation of China (NSFC)

system START developed by Boris Katz at MIT's Artificial Intelligence Laboratory translates the question into a T-expression template that can be used to search the annotated knowledge base for T-expressions that contain information relevant to providing an answer to the question.

A Knowledge Grid is a mechanism that shares and manages the distributed heterogeneous resources spread across the Internet in a uniform way [11, 13, 14]. The main purpose of this paper is to propose a new question-answering approach that enables an intelligent QA by making use of the Knowledge Grid mechanism.

2 Cooperating among Information Space, Knowledge Space and Service Space

The information space uniformly specifies various data types including *text*, *database*, *picture*, *audio*, *video* and *multi-media*. The knowledge space uniformly specifies knowledge at the *conceptual level*, the *axiom level*, the *rule level*, and the *method level*. The service space uniformly specifies versatile services. The three spaces can be regarded as the special cases of a general resource space, where resources refer to information, knowledge and services. The resource Grid provides users the uniform resource-using interface to share and manage the resources across the Internet.

The three resource spaces can work independently or cooperatively to accomplish complex tasks. The information space is the lowest level, the knowledge space is the middle level, and the service space is the highest level. The low-level space can provide support to the high-level space. The information space retrieves information from the web and then provides information support to both the knowledge space and the service space. Information is the origin of knowledge generation, which in turn supports information understanding and classification. The knowledge space provides knowledge support to the service space. The service space can get information from the information space or get knowledge from the knowledge space for performing information processing or knowledge processing. A piece of knowledge in the knowledge space can be linked to a set of supporting documents in the information space that gives reasons and evidences for the knowledge. The linkage between two resources can be built by users while inputting knowledge or by automatic knowledge-based reasoning and indexing.

3 Knowledge-Grid-based Question-Answering Model

3.1 General Process Specification

The general process of the VEGA-KGQA is illustrated in Figure 1. Users put questions and get the required QA service in the service space, and then the search process is executed. The Analyzer module processes the question by referring to the knowledge of the concept level and the axiom level in the knowledge space, which is denoted by the arrows with the round head. The Q-Refiner module matches the processed question with any appropriate template in the template repository, and refines the abstract questions to concrete questions and then return to users. The Answer Processor module fulfills the task of normalizing the attained answer and returning answers to users in an easily understood form. The Template Repository Manager is responsible for managing the template repository with the help of GUI, which will be further discussed in section 4. Each template links to the corresponding knowledge and then depends on the other levels of knowledge. The links are denoted as the dashed arrows.

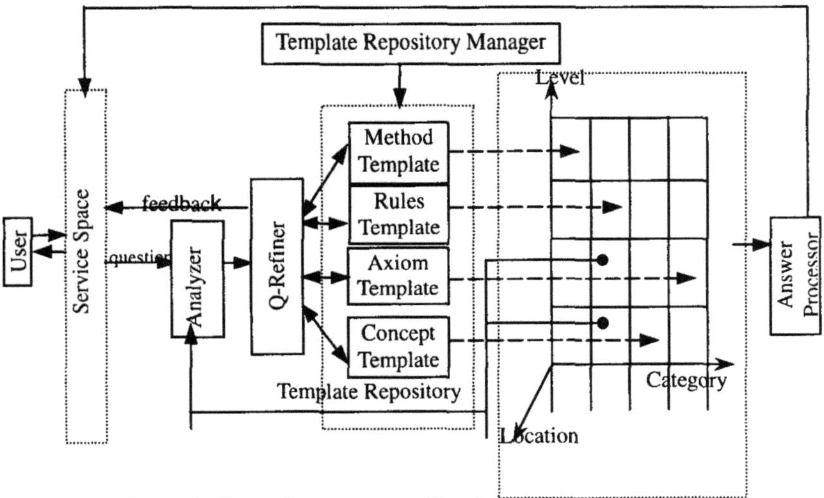

Figure 1. General process specification of the VEGA-KGQA.

3.2 The Semantic Web Representation of Knowledge Resources

By consulting WordNet [10], knowledge resources are represented with XML, which have common tags as FLAG, PRIVILEGE and RELATED-MATERIALS. The FLAG indicates whether this piece of knowledge is logically deleted or not, the PRIVILEGE indicates the knowledge provider, and RELATED-MATERIALS indicates the related knowledge or the sources of knowledge. Concept can be either an atomic concept or a composite concept. Atomic concepts constitute the basic building blocks of sentences (e.g., "driver", "mammal", "subway", etc.), conveying the most fundamental cognitive knowledge, while composite concepts are built up from atomic concepts through the concept conjunctive operator "AND". An axiom takes the form of a natural language statement or a mathematical equation that describes the relationships between the concepts. For example, the "SUPERC (CONCEPT, CONCEPT)" specifies the first concept is more abstract than the second concept. Generally, the relationships between concepts can be various besides the appointed in the DTD file, such as "be composed of ", "happen in" etc. Rules are in the format of "IF * THEN * ", where the "IF" portion denotes premises and the "THEN" portion refers to the conclusions or consequences. Rules also indicate the relationships between axioms such as "TRANSITIVE (AXIOM)", SYMMETRICAL (AXIOM) etc. Method takes the form as the <problem, solution> pair where the solution can be a one-step action, multi-steps actions jointed by "AND", or a complex process. Furthermore, we use "OR" conjunction to denote several optional solutions to the same problem.

3.3 Question Analysis

The system accomplishes part-of-speech tagging and parsing of question [6], then forms the semantic context of the keywords by consulting the knowledge space, and then specify the questions corresponding to the four levels of knowledge.

- Concept-level questions

The concept-level questions are the simplest ones, which mainly concerns the explanation or definition of a concept as well as some attributes of a concept. "*define*", "*describe*" and "*introduce*" concern the explanation or definition of concepts, while "*when*", "*where*" concern the time and place attributes of concepts. As for "*who*" and "*what*" question words, in some cases, they imply searching answers at the concept level. The recognition of the concept-level questions is based on matching the users' questions with a small set of question templates. Some of the templates are:

T1: *What {is | are} <noun_description>?*
T2: What's the definition of <noun_ description >?
T3: Who | Whom {is | was | are | were} <person (organization)_description>?

It's worth to note that there are two exceptions. When the question is too abstract to get an answer, several refined questions will be returned for users to choose. For example, "Please introduce Beijing" can be refined into "the resorts in Beijing", "the shopping center in Beijing", "the custom in Beijing", etc. The other exception is the type of question with the interrogative "*how*", which is determined by the meaning of an adjective or an adverb following the interrogative. As for the example of "How far is the earth from the sun?", the adverb *far* is represented as being an attribute of "*distance*" in the concept level of knowledge, and then we can get the answer by searching this attribute of "*earth*" at the concept level.

- Axiom-level questions

This type of question is relevant to some common sense and the relationship between concepts, and the answer is "yes" or "no" with validating documents. Moreover, in some cases, the questions began with "*what*", "*who*", "*name*" and "*which*" interrogatives are relevant to the axiom. Such questions are the most ambiguous when it comes to determining the question type. Some of the templates are:

T4: *Is <noun_description> a <noun_description>?*
T5: *{Do | Does | Did} <noun_description> <verb_description> <noun_description>?*
T6: *Which <noun_description> is <adj_description>?*
T7: *Name <noun_description> <clause_description>?*

This type of questions can be formulated as an embedded expression *Relation (concept, concept)* after being pre-processed. Some other parameters (adjectives, possessive nouns, prepositional phrases, etc.) are used to create additional expressions in which prepositions and several special words may serve as relations. For example, T4 can be simplified into a form of *Is-a(A, B)* where A and B respectively indicates a concept; T5 can be formulated as *verb(A, B)*; T6 can be formulated as *adj_comparative (A, B)*; and as for T7, the verb in clause decides the specific relationship between the concepts. Of course, the relationship can be various types such as *Super(A, B)*, *Part-of(A, B)*, *has(A, B)* and so on.

- Rules-level questions

Rules mainly indicate the logical relationship between axioms, and causality relationship is typical, so this type of questions includes the questions began with "*why*" interrogative and other semantics similar questions that ask the reason for some axioms. The following are some of the templates.

T8: Why {can | do | does} <clause_description>?

T9: Why <verb_description> <noun_description>?

T10: What's reason for <clause_description>?

In some cases, rules can facilitate the answering of questions by mapping several semantics similar questions to one question

- Method-level questions

This kind of question takes into account finding a solution to a given problem, which is mainly related to the *how*-term and other semantics similar questions such as "The approach of …". We can formulate the questions as $O_1.m_i \rightarrow O_2$ (i=1 to n), where O_1 and O_2 respectively denotes the resource objects and the target objects, m_i denotes a method of O_1 such as the operation of searching, comparison, computation and etc. Some of the representative templates are as follows:

T11: How to <verb_description> <phrase_description>?

T12: How {do | did | can | could} <clause_description>?

Obviously, this type of questions is the most complicated and the solutions to them will probably involve the reasoning according to the other three levels of knowledge.

4 Knowledge-based Templates

A template represents the common features of a class of questions with the same type. We incorporate knowledge reasoning into template so as to realize flexible and automatic answer searching. The root template takes the following form:

```
Question Template {
Question-type: <string>
Question-Pattern: <question-description>
Solution: <solution-process-description>
Related-knowledge: [
   Rules: Rules<knowledge-category, knowledge-level, knowledge-location>;
   Method: Method<knowledge-category, knowledge-level, knowledge-location>]}.
```

In the above root template, the "question-type" denotes the type of question falls into the concept-level, the axiom-level, the rule-level and the method-level. The "question-pattern" is the description of one class of questions. The number of parameters in the pattern can be one or more, and we use @*I* to denote the parameter, "*I* "means the capital letter from A to Z. The "solution" describes the steps or process that is taken to deal with the given question, where the simple knowledge reasoning among the four knowledge levels is embodied. The "related-knowledge" specifies the reference rules and methods used in the solution, and the "Rules" and "Method" respectively links to the corresponding general rules and methods in the three-dimensional knowledge space. As Figure 2 illustrates, in the knowledge space, the "*knowledge-category*" can be set as "*Template*" and other semantic categories, and the "*Template*" can be further expanded as a coordinate hierarchy such as "*common*", T_1, T_2 and etc. The "*common*" denotes the rules that can be used by all templates, while T_i denotes the rules that can only be used by the *i*th set of templates. For example, the <Template.Common, Rules, http://kg.ict.ac.cn/~zhuge> and the <Template.T_1, Rules, http://kg.ict.ac.cn/~zhuge> respectively specifies that the rules located in http://kg.ict.ac.cn/~zhuge can be used by all templates and only be used by the first set of templates. By this means, the general rules are grouped according to their application scope, which improve the performance of QA while reducing the redundancy of knowledge.

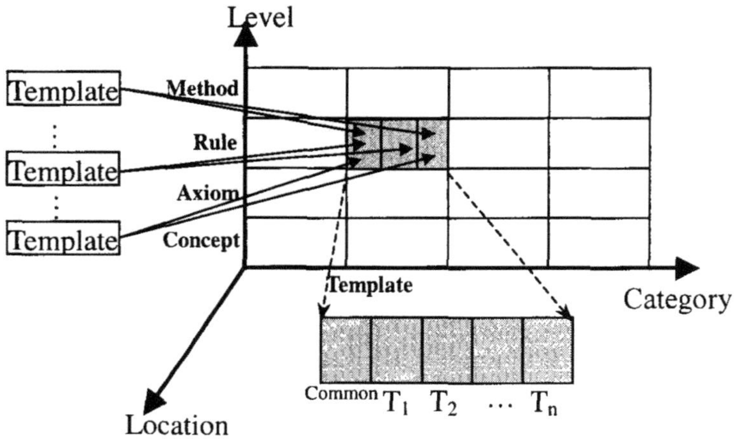

Figure 2. Templates link general rules in knowledge space.

A *Frame* consists of five parts including comment, a group of templates, a set of assignments, refinement functions and matching keywords, which can be formulated as 5-tuples: *Frame(Comment, Templates, Assignments, R-Functions, M-Keywords).*

The comment describes the main content of the frame; the templates belonging to one frame should have the similar question pattern or semantics; assignment appoint the possible value of parameters in the templates; refinement function is a mapping from one template to a set of refined templates for a given assignment; in order to improve the performance of matching templates, each frame is equipped with many keywords that represent the special meaning for the questions in the frame. If some of the keywords appear in the user's question, then the corresponding template will be probably selected. If the keyword in the question is synonymous to the matching keywords, the template will also be probably selected. The matching keywords can be obtained semi-automatically.

Convenient template management requires flexible template retrieval. The VEGA-KGQA uses a binary frame inheritance relationship between frames, which provides rich semantic information for the template retrieval mechanism, so it improves the flat template repository structure. Descendants of an ancestor are classified by different values with which descendants inherit from the ancestor as discussed in [12]. As Figure 3 illustrates, the whole template repository includes four sub-repositories composed of many frames, and each frame consists of many frames linked by real lines jointed with arc or broken line. The former denotes the "*abstraction*" relationship that means the templates in parent-frame is more abstract than those in children-frames, while the latter denotes the "*composition*" relationship that means the templates in parent-frame is composed of templates in children-frames.

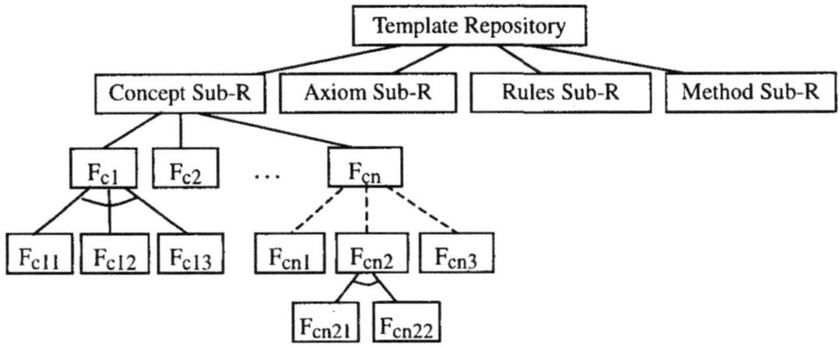

Figure 3. The structure of Template Repository.

The templates repository is maintained semi-automatically. On one hand, the personal manager can manually maintain the template repository with several operations such as *ADD, DELETE, UPDATE*, etc., on the other hand, the Template Repository Manger can automatically analyze the set of questions from different users, extracting the common features to construct new templates, delete the seldom used templates or update the templates. Particularly, in the face of unexpected question formats, the "Q-Refiner" cannot match the question with any of the templates, and then we adopt the traditional keyword-based method to directly search answer in the corresponding knowledge domain. In the meantime, we post the special questions on a Knowledge Collection Board (KCB) for public sharing.

5 Answer Formation Mechanism

With respect to a given question in natural languages, the mechanism carries out the following steps to obtain an answer in the knowledge space:

1. Analyze the question and check whether the question is too abstract or not, If it is too abstract, then return the refined questions for users to choose.
2. Match the question with the appropriate template in the specific knowledge level to obtain the solution.
3. Follow the solution of the template to get the answer in the knowledge space.
4. Normalize the answer and then return to users.

In the following, we take two types of questions to briefly illustrate the process of providing intelligent answers to various types of questions, especially the idea of the knowledge reasoning.

Question type 1: IS * A *?
Example: *Is buffalo a mammal*?

According to the above steps, the answer formation mechanism firstly pre-processes the question to get the keyword focus "*buffalo*" denoted as *@A* and the reference keyword "*mammal*" denoted as *@B*. Then, determines that the question type corresponds to the axiom level, so the question is formulated as *IS-A (@A, @B)*. Next, it searches in the template repository to get the matching template as follows:

```
<Axiom>
  <Pattern>IS * A * </Pattern>
```

```
  <Solution>
        1. Determine the corresponding knowledge domain (denoted as D) based
       on keywords
       2. Function IS-A (@A, @B)
       3. IF @A = @B THEN
                RETURN "yes"
            ELSE
                S = {X | SUPER (@A, X), X∈D}                    //axiom level
            END IF
        4. IF S = □ HEN
           RETURN "no"
      ELSE
         FOR each X in S
               IF X=@B THEN
              RETURN "yes"
                  END IF
            Call function IS-A (X, @B)               //use related rules in
rule level
                  END FOR
            END IF
        5. RETURN "no"
  </Solution>
  <Related-knowledge>
     <Rules>
               Rules<knowledge-category=Template.Common,knowledge-level=
               Rules,knowledge-location=http://kg.ict.ac.cn/~zhuge>
       //use the common rule such as transitive rule, e.g., A→B,B→C ⇒ A
→C
       </Rules>
       <Method/>
  </Related-knowledge>
</Axiom>
```

As above template shows that the solution to this type of question includes the following steps: Firstly obtains the set of axioms in which one of the concepts is *@A*, and then decides whether the other concept is *@B* or not. If the concept is *@B* then return "yes", or refers to the related rules and thus recursively calls the function with *IS-A (X, @B)* till the cycle ends. Meanwhile, in the information space, substantial information analysis involving the navigation and cross-correlation of information items needs to be done so as to return supporting documents to the final answer.

The above example involves knowledge of the axiom level and the rules level. In addition, we take another instance to explain the relatively complex process of answering questions by synthetically using the concept, axiom and method levels of knowledge.

Question type 2: WHAT IS * FOR NUMERICAL COMPARISON?
Example: *What's the farthest planet from the sun?*

Just as the first example, the answer formation mechanism firstly pre-processes the question to get the keyword focus "*planet*" denoted as *@A*, and the reference keywords are the noun "*sun*" denoted as *@B* and adjective "*far*" in form of superlative degree that indicates the question is about the comparison. By consulting knowledge of the concept level, "*far*" is an attribute of distance, and then the question is formulated as *max-distance* (*@A, @B*), so this type of questions begins with "*what*" interrogative and relate to the "*numerical comparison relation*". Then, it matches template and one of its assignments to get the following template, and then by employing the solution of the template and normalizing the answers, intelligent answers are returned to users finally.

```
<Axiom>
  <Pattern>WHAT IS * FOR NUMERICAL COMPARISON</Pattern>
  <Solution>
     1. Determine the corresponding knowledge domain (denoted as D) based on
        keywords
      2. IF there exists max-distance (X, @B) THEN                    //axiom
level
                   RETURN X with maximum distance from @B
           ELSE
                   S = {X | SUPER ( X, @A ) , X∈D}                     //axiom
level
              END IF
    3. FOR Each X in S
          Get the value of distance attribute and put into a array    //concept
level
      END FOR
       4. Assign the max to flag
    5. CALL sort method with the parameters of array and flag
                                    //call related method in method level
    6. RETURN X with maximum distance from @B
  </Solution>
  <Related-knowledge>
      <Rules/>
        <Method>
             Method<knowledge-category=Template.T1,knowledge-level=Method,
             knowledge-location=http://kg.ict.ac.cn/~zhuge>
              //call the sort method in T1 for getting the corresponding value
              of the array according to the flag
        </Method>
  </Related-knowledge>
</Axiom>
```

6 Implementation

The general architecture of the VEGA-KGQA system is illustrated in Figure 4. The dashed arrow denotes the question and the solid arrow denotes the answer. In this system,

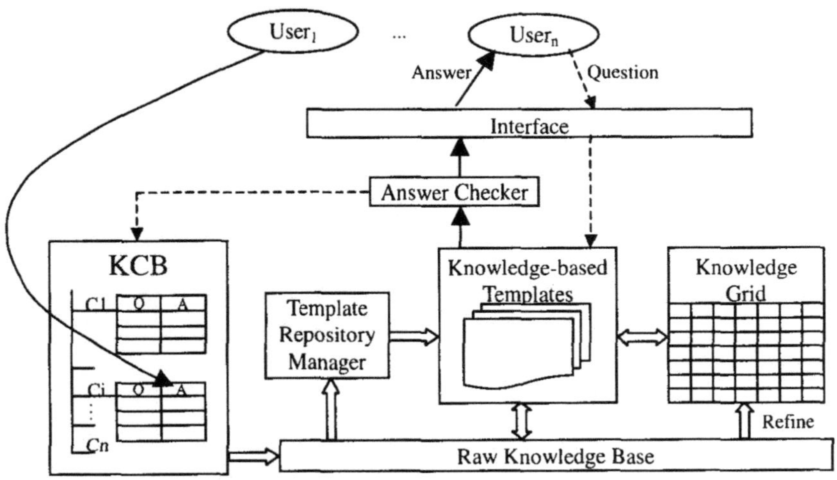

Figure 4. General architecture of the VEGA-KGQA system.

the Knowledge Collection Board is used for different users to share their experience knowledge. In case a question has no matching template, the system will automatically poster it on the board, and other users can also poster their answers to the questions on the board. The questions are classified into different categories so as to facilitate the knowledge extraction process. The function of the Answer Checker is to decide whether the answer to the question is found, if the answer is already attained then return it to the users, otherwise poster the question on the board.

Each user puts the questions and gets the answers through the interface. For a given question, the system will firstly retrieve the matching template. Once the template is located, the system will mark the question with "Yes" and then follow the solution to get the answer in the Knowledge Grid. On the contrary, if there is no matching template for the given question, the system will find the answer in the Knowledge Grid based on the keywords, and then mark the question with "No". Then, the Answer Checker returns the normalized answer to users if the mark is "Yes" or poster the question on the board if the mark is "No". Moreover, the system will put the question with corresponding answers into the Raw Knowledge Base periodically, then refine the knowledge and put into the Knowledge Grid. Meanwhile, new templates are generated semi-automatically. On one hand, the system analyzes many problems and extracts the general patterns. On the other hand, the Template Repository Manager analyzes the answers manually to form the solution to a class of questions with the same question pattern. Thus, when other users put the similar questions later, the system will return correct answer to the question automatically.

So far, we have implemented the knowledge collection board and the supported Knowledge Grid platform Vega-KG (http://kg.ict.ac.cn), and the design of templates in one specific domain is also completed. The implementation of the other parts is ongoing.

7 Discussions and Comparisons

Most of the works that have been done in IR and QA fields essentially find the exact answer to the user's question in a large collection of documents, such as [2,4,5] and etc. In this study, we extend the traditional text-based information retrieval to knowledge-based QA. The main different points between the traditional QA and the VEGA-KGQA are listed in table 1.

Table 1. Comparison between *traditional QA* and *VEGA-KGQA*.

Features	*Traditional QA*	*VEGA-KGQA*
Question analysis approach	Determine the question type	Determine the question type and the knowledge level concerned.
Answer extraction approach	Relevant document retrieval	Template matching and knowledge navigation
Answer selection approach	Complex process of candidate answer ranking	Simple process of normalizing answers
Answer	Sentences of pre-specified	Concise words or sentences

restriction	length	with validating documents if needed
Knowledge reasoning assistant	No	Yes
Support resources	Information (web documents)	Services, knowledge, information

The improvement of the efficiency and precision of QA due to the effective resources and templates organization, the rational question type classification, the knowledge-based templates, and the close linking resource spaces.

8 Conclusions

This paper proposes a new question-answering approach VEGA-KGQA based on our previously proposed Knowledge Grid model. The approach enables users to get not only the answers but also the relevant supporting resources by incorporating the semantic-web-based representation, the multi-level knowledge support, the human-machine-cooperative knowledge collection mechanism, the knowledge-based template and the knowledge reasoning and navigation mechanism. The interface of the VEGA-KGQA will be incorporated into the operation interface of the Knowledge Grid to form an integrated Knowledge Grid browser, and the main VEGA-KGQA mechanism is a part of the Knowledge Grid engine that support the browser.

Ongoing works include three aspects. (1) Real-time knowledge extraction, updating and refinement. (2) Coupling different types of resource for uniformly using and reasoning. (3) Domain-specific applications.

References

1. J.Allan, J.Callan, F.F. Feng and D.Malin: INQUERY and TREC-8. In proceedings of the Eighth Text Retrieval Conference (TREC-8), Gaithersberg, MD, USA (1999).
2. R.J.Cooper, S.M. Rüger: A Simple Question Answering System. In Proceedings of the Ninth Text Retrieval Conference (TREC-9), Gaithersburg, Maryland (2000) 249-255.
3. M.Fuller, M.Kaszkiel et al: The RMIT/CSIRO Ad Hoc, Q&A, Web, Interactive, and Speech Experiments at TREC 8. In proceedings of the Eighth Text Retrieval Conference (TREC-8), Gaithersberg, MD, USA (1999).
4. A.Ittycheriah, M.Franz, W.J. Zhu: IBM's Statistical Question Answering System. In Proceedings of the Ninth Text Retrieval Conference (TREC-9), Gaithersburg, Maryland (2000) 229-234.
5. S.M.Kim, D.H.Baek, S.B.Kim, H.C.Rim: Question Answering Considering Semantic Categories and Co-occurrence Density. In Proceedings of the Ninth Text Retrieval Conference (TREC-9), Gaithersburg, Maryland (2000) 317-324.
6. J.L.Vicedo: Using Semantics for Paragraph Selection in Question Answering Systems, the 8th String Processing and Information Retrieval Symposium (2001)

220-227

7. A. Singhal, S. Abney and M. Bacchiani: AT&T at TREC-8. In Proceedings of the Eighth Text Retrieval Conference (TREC-8), Gaithersberg, MD, USA (1999).
8. R.Srihari and W.Li: Information Extraction Supported Question Answering. In Proceedings of the Eighth Text Retrieval Conference (TREC-8), Gaithersberg, MD, USA (1999).
9. J.L. Vicedo, A. Ferrandez: A Semantic Approach to Question Answering systems. In Proceedings of the Ninth Text Retrieval Conference (TREC-9), Gaithersburg, Maryland (2000) 511-516.
10. WordNet, Cognitive Science Laboratory, Princeton University, www.cogsci.princeton.edu/~wn
11. H.Zhuge: A Knowledge Grid Model and Platform for Global Knowledge Sharing, Expert Systems with Application, 22, 4(2002) 313-320.
12. H.Zhuge: Inheritance Rules for Flexible Model Retrieval, Decision Support Systems, 22 (1998) 379-390.
13. H.Zhuge: VEGA-KG: A Way to the Knowledge Web, 11th International World Wide Web Conference (WWW2002), Poster Proceeding, Hawaii, USA, 2002.
14. H.Zhuge: A Knowledge Flow Model for Peer-to-Peer Team Knowledge sharing and Management , Expert Systems with Applications, 23, 1 (2002).

COLLABORATIVE LEARNING BASED ON MULTI-AGENT MODEL

DAZHENG WANG ,RUIMIN SHEN,LIPING SHEN

Shanghai Jiaotong Univ.1954 Hua Shan Road, Shanghai 200030,P.R.China
E-mail:dazhengwang@sjtu.edu.cn,{rmshen,lpshen}@mail.sjtu.edu.cn

In this paper,we describe a multi-agent model called CLAM for collaborative learning on the web and propose a formal framework for learners to form groups dynamically under various conditions.And we also modified the semantic of communicative acts to enhance their power to express time and give formal specification to learner agents' intention.This learner-centered model we propose provides an easy way for learners to seek help on the web when he meets difficulties in his study

1 Introduction

In order to circumvent inherited limitations (passive, lack of interaction , etc) in teacher-centered learning , it is necessary to devise new ways for collaborative , learner-centered learning with the aid of computer networks. The new learning schema makes it possible for learner to develop characteristics such as initiative, exploration and collaboration. In this paper ,we propose our CLAM (Collaborative Learning based on multi-Agent Model) architecture for collaborative learning on the web . There are lots of reasons concerning why we choose the agent theory . First , the system is complex, distributed and difficult to capture its behavior in traditional methods . At any instant of time , there may be conditions (network breaks , absence of learner ,etc) which can not be determined in advance . Second , when a learner meets difficulties in learning he will choose to seek help from those more capable whom cannot be determined from the beginning . The learner's ability can only be judged dynamically by others during the group collaboration on a particular problem . Third , in order to model the learner's behavior to make him feel comfortable towards the system ,BDI logic provides much more convenience.

One of the most important problems in CLAM is how to form a group dynamically by learner agents through exchange of communicative acts. Though Cohen and Levesque[3] provide formal semantics to most communicative acts ,time does not explicitly appear in their logic. In the following sections , we will describe the CLAM architecture , propose a method to enhance the communicative acts with the ability to express time and model the intention of agents comprising the CLAM.

2 Architecture of CLAM

In this section ,we will describe our web learning model called CLAM which is made up of a set of agents(see Figure 1) and each one is located at a host on the web.

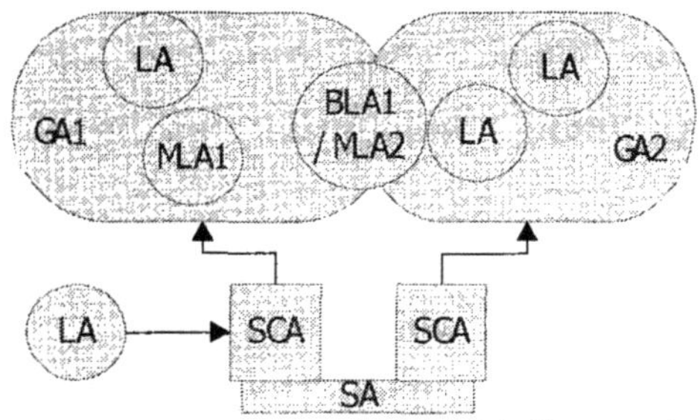

GA:Group Agent MLA:Main Learner Agent
SCA:Solution Center Agent BLA:Border Learner Agent
SA: Synchronizing Agent LA: Learner Agent

Figure 1. CLAM Architecture

The collaborative behavior of these agents is explained informally bellow:
An LA works on behalf of a learner ,on receiving a problem description from whom it will seek help on the web in the following way:

1. Sends INFORM with the problem description to the SCA who will try to find another LA registered with the capability to solve the problem .If SCA fails to do so ,the LA go to step 2:
2. Sends REQUEST to other learner agents based on its belief table and form a group with at most N agents(N>=2,N is specified by the administrator to prevent flooding which may cause unnecessary network traffic.)In this step ,the LA becomes MLA and the group is named as GA1.
3. In the group GA1,one of the LAs may meet another problem and form another group(GA2) to solve it .In this case ,the LA is on the border between GA1 and GA2 and also called BLA1 in GA1 and MLA2 in GA2.

Though the learners in the architecture have a peer to peer relationship , some of them may be more capable than others .They can publish their capabilities on the solution center where learners may find unexpected solution to their problems met in their study .This process is explained as follows:

1. After the LA of the capable learner receiving his capability description from its user ,it sends SOFFER to SCA.
2. SCA retrieves the registration information from the LA and stores in its belief table.
3. If SCA received INFORM from another LA whose problem meets the registration information ,SCA notifies the SOFFER LA and the two LAs form a group to solve the problem .And the LA requesting for help is called MLA.

In order to prevent the SCA from being the bottleneck ,there may be several SCAs bottomed by a SA. When a LA advertises its capability to one of the SCAs,the SA will keep this fact known to the other SCAs. LAs always contact those least overloaded.

3 Group Formation

3.1 Basic Concept

As mentioned in section 2,CLAM agents interact with each other using communicative acts (INFORM ,REQUEST ,etc) .Such a communication language needs a clearly defined semantics ,without which neither developers and agents can understand each other .Due to the powerful ability of joint intention theory[3,4] to characterize an agent's behavior in a group in terms of its internal state described in modal logic,linear time temporal logic and dynamic logic of action ,we have applied this theory in our CLAM architecture concerning agent communication during group formation.

In collaborative learning we should consider the time factor .A learner always wants his problem solved in a timely manner ,while the other learner he requested may not be available at the time even though she has the solution .Cohen and Levesque[3] have given formal semantics to most communicative acts ,but time does not explicitly appear in their logic .For instance ,they assume that if an agent has a PGOAL(persistent goal which is essential for group formation), then the agent believes that this proposition is not true now, but that it will be true at some time in the future. The agent will drop a persistent goal only if it comes to believe that it is true or that it is impossible .They cannot express a PGOAL toward propositions that will be true at some specific time in the future or consider situations where a proposition is true now, but which the agent believes will become false later and therefore has a PGOAL to make it true again after it becomes false .

In CLAM architecture we have modified the semantic structure of most communicative acts and conversation policies to enhance them with the ability to express time .Those basic concept for group formation will be explained bellow and detailed information can be found in a forthcoming paper.

Definition 1 Proposition with Time Interval (pti)

(1)p is a proposition ,predicate or modal formulas

(2)t1,t2 are either positive integers or positive integer valued variables and $t1<=t2$

(3)p:[t1,t2] is a pti and the composition by symbols ($\wedge, \vee$)of such pti is also a pti

Particularly ,we represent a pti by the modal operator in a modal formula and omit time interval(t1,t2) for convenience .Given a pti ,we can access its content by pti.p,pti.t1 and pti.t2. Intuitively ,when a pti is valid for p ,we may read this as "p is true only at every point between t1 and t2." Suppose the current time is t_{now}, then we say $pti.t1> t_{now}$ if p does not hold now and $pti.t2< t_{now}$ if p no longer holds .If p will never hold ,then it is expressed as $pti.t1=\infty$. From the definitions of pti ,we can see there must be some computations for time interval in case of composition .Such computations are omitted here for the reason of space.

Definition 2 Action with Time and Agent (ata)

(1)a is an action

(2) t1,t2 are either positive integers or positive integer valued variables and t1<=t2

(3) d=[t1,t2]

(4)x is the agent who is responsible for the action

(5)a:[d,x] is an ata and the composition by symbols($\wedge,\vee$)of such ata is also an ata

Intuitively ,if an ata is valid for some action a and agent x ,then x performs a during some time period d .Action that will happen next can be expressed as ata.t1> t_{now} and that has just happened can be ata.t2< t_{now}.

The primitive mental states in joint intention theory are an agent's beliefs and goals ,expressed by modal formulas as (BEL x pti) and (GOAL x pti),where x is an agent and pti follows from x's beliefs and goals. In addition to these mental states ,we also have redefined operators for actions that will happen next or has just happened .Next we will give definition to joint persistent goal which is the foundation of a group formation :

Definition 3 Joint Persistent Goal (JPG)

(JPG x y pti1 pti2) $\equiv$(MB x y pti1.t1> t_{now}) $\wedge$
(MG x y pti1) $\wedge$
([(WMG x y pti1) $\wedge$ (WMG.t2<PTI.t1)] $\vee$
[WMG.t2< t_{now}])

where PTI is:

(MB x y $t_{now} \in$ [pti1.t1,pti1.t2]) $\vee$ (MB x y pti1.t1= ∞) $\vee$ (MB x y pti2.t2< t_{now})

This definition states that two agents(x and y)have a joint persistent goal of pti1,with respect to pti2 from JPG.t1 to JPG.t2 when the following conditions hold :there is mutual belief between MB.t1 and MB.t2 that pti1.p does not hold now ,it is a mutual goal that pti1.p will be true at some time in the future, and furthermore that pti1 will remain a weak mutual goal(for x and y)until there is mutual belief that either pti1.p is already true, pti1.p will never hold or pti2.p is no longer true .A weak mutual goal (WMG)is a mutual belief among the agents that both have weak achievement goals(WAG)with regard to achieving pti1.These mental states are all formed not before JPG.t1 and not later than JPG.t2.

Definition 4 Persistent Weak Achievement Goal(PWAG)

(PWAG x y pti1 pti2) $\equiv$
[(BEL x pti1.t1> t_{now}) $\wedge$ (PGOAL x pti1)] $\vee$
[(BEL x $t_{now} \in$ [pti1.t1,pti1.t2]) $\wedge$ (PGOAL x (MB x y $t_{now} \in$ [pti1.t1,pti1.t2]))]
$\vee$
[(BEL x pti1.t1= ∞) $\wedge$ (PGOAL x (MB x y pti1.t1= ∞))] $\vee$
[(BEL x pti2.t2< t_{now}) $\wedge$ (PGOAL x (MB x y pti2.t2< t_{now}))]

This definition states that for an agent x to have a PWAG between PWAG.t1 and PWAG.t2 with respect to another agent y either the agent believes that pti1.p does not currently hold and has a persistent goal to achieve pti1,or the agent is ready to abandon the persistent goal of pti1 for one of three reasons :he believes pti1.p to be already true, he believes it to be never hold or he believes the relativizing condition (pti2.p) no longer holds .In each of the latter three cases ,the agent will have the original goal(to achieve pti1)replaced with another persistent goal ,that of creating the mutual belief of the corresponding condition with the other agent. These mental states are all formed not before PWAG.t1 and not later than PWAG.t2.

All communicative acts are redefined using above mental states augmented with time and omitted here for reason of space .A group is formed when each member has the common goal (JPG) to solve a problem and each one is bounded by a PWAG after their exchange of several communicative acts.

3.2 Group Formation in CLAM

There are two cases in CLAM when a group is formed :one is in the solution center and the other is formed by an MLA seeking help from other agents .In the former case ,we use a SOFFER followed by an INFORM[2]because the MLA sending SOFFER does not know if his offer will be accepted and the MLA sending INFORM does not know if there is a solution in the solution center ,neither agent can be sure of the outcome until the end of the conversation .In the latter case ,we use a REQUEST followed by a CONFIRM[1] because the MLA has at least the intention of communication even the other agent may not have the ability to solve the problem.

The group formed this way is very resilient because the learner agents can function successfully under adverse conditions ,including breaks of communication ,time expiration and other difficulties in problem solving process .The conversation policies augmented with the ability to express time make it possible for LAs automatically negotiate time constraints input by the learner. If the learner seeking help need a quick answer he may configure his LA to refuse those who do not meet his time requirement and turn to others to form a group. Even when the learner whom is asked for help is not available at the time ,the group can still be formed .The members may not solve the problem at once but delay it at some specific time in the future.

4 Intention Model of CLAM Agent

The BDI model [5] is a popular model for intelligent agents .It has its basis in philosophy and offers a logical theory which defines the mental attitudes of Belief,Desire, and Intention using a modal logic ,a system architecture (PRS) and applications demonstrating the viability of the model .The central concepts in the BDI model are :

Beliefs :Information about the environment; informative.

Desires :Objectives to be accomplished , possibly with each objective's associated priority/payoff ;motivational

Intention :The currently chosen course of action :deliberative

The learner agent in CLAM is specified using notation and execution model of AgentSpeak (L)[6] in which an agent consists of a belief set and a plan library .Each plan clause is of the form:

$$E{:}BEL_1 \wedge \ldots \wedge BEL_m \leftarrow H_1 ;\ldots;H_n$$

Where E is an event ,BEL $_i$ is a belief ,and each H_i is either an action or a subgoal .A goal may be either a test goal preceded by "?" or an achievement goal preceded by a "!".

The partially instantiated (some of the variables are instantiated) plans together form an intention stack and the execution model of the agent consists of the following steps:

a) The agent selects an event E (goals are also an event type)
b) The agent generates all plans with matching invocation conditions
c) From these relevant plans the agent identifies those with satisfied preconditions
d) If there are several plans ,one is chosen nondeterministically
e) The plan is added to the intention stack which is executed by popping the topmost plan and performing the first H_i .If H_i is an event then it is posted ,and if it is an action then it is executed.

In the following section ,we will model the intention of a CLAM agent in the decision scheme of forming a group .

When a SCA receive an external event from a learner agent seeking help ,it should check whether there is capable one in the solution center ,and if so it notifies the capable learner .On receiving an offer from a capable learner and if the SCA is free ,then it will register the learner and notify the SA for synchronization .The main intention model of SCA and SA is given bellow .From it we can see the registration and synchronization process is always in a low priority to save the computing resource.

```
+INFORM(x,ata,pti):
        true ←?Matched(ata , pti, y); INFORM (y, x, ata, pti)
+SOFFER(x, ata, pti):
        true ← ?Available();!Register(x, ata, pti); INFORM(SA, x, ata,
   pti)

+Synchronize(x ,ata ,pti):
true ← ?Available();Register(x ,ata ,pti);
```

The learner seeking help just provides the relevant information to his agent who will tell one SCA about this request and wait for an answer .If there is no solution from SCA then it will judge the priority given by its learner of the problem .If it is a critical one it will contact more than one learners using REQUESTALL ,otherwise it will contact only one agent using REQUEST .The learner must be cautious about this for the more request he sends to others ,the more he will pay for the requests from others .And if he has no such ability or time to answer so much requests ,then he will be isolated in the agent society when he requests later .The leaners he asks for help are selected from the history table(hist) formed during the process of cooperation .The first main part of intention model of a learner agent is given bellow:

+SeekHelp(pti):

true← INFORM(SCA,ata,pti);+AnswerReceived(SCA,ata,pti)

+ AnswerReceived (SCA,ata,pti):

~Solution(ata,pti) ∧Priority(pti)>0←

?SelectSucceed(hist,X); REQUESTALL(X,ata,pti)

+ AnswerReceived (SCA,ata,pti):

~Solution(ata,pti) ∧Priority(pti)<=0←

?SelectSucceed (hist,x); REQUEST (x,ata,pti)

Here we give a brief explanation of the building process of history table .Each agent (LA1) maintains a history table which is a 2-tuple :[IP ,Value] ,IP is the internet address of an agent (LA2) and Value is computed by LA1 during the process of cooperation according to the number of messages sent by LA2 , the satisfiability assigned by the user of LA1 towards LA2,etc.These factors are associated by a weight configured at the setup time .The Value towards LA1 is computed the same way by LA2 during the cooperation.

After a learner agent receiving a request for help from another one(x),it judges the various conditions to see whether to give such an offer. It will consider the cooperation record and relationship with x from history .If x is a good companion , the learner is available at the time and he is capable to solve the problem ,then the agent will give x a hand .Even if the learner is not free ,the agent may negotiate with x on the time requirement .On the other hand ,the agent may also refuse x if x is scored poor in history record or the problem is too difficult for the learner to solve .Following provides the second main part of the intention model of a learner agent.

+REQUEST(x,ata,pti):

Availible(ata.d)∧Score(x)>=0∧Capable(ata,pti)←

! PWAGFormed(ata,pti);CONFIRM(x, ata,pti)

+REQUEST(x,ata,pti):

~Availible(ata.d)∧Score(x)>=0∧Capable(ata,pti)←

Negotiate(ata,pti); !PWAGFormed (ata,pti);CONFIRM(x, ata,pti)

+REQUEST(x,ata,pti):

Score(x)<0∨~Capable(ata,pti)←

REFUSE(x, ata,pti)

5 Discussion

The CLAM prototype is developed in Shanghai distance learning center to provide a platform for online collaborative learning .In this paper ,we have described the CLAM architecture and specified how multiple agents may interact with each other .We have summarized the main technological issue concerning how to build a collaborative learning platform using agent theory which though is still not full-fledged yet. And we also modified the semantic of communicative acts to enhance their power to express time and give formal specification to learner agents' intention.

6 Acknowledgements

We thank Reggie Kwan and his colleagues for their critical review of previous version of the manuscript.

References

1. I.A.Smith and P.R.Cohen.Toward a semantics for an agent communication language based on speech-acts.InProceedings of the National Conference on Artificial Intelligence. AAAI Press,1996.
2. Designing conversation policies using joint intention theory I. Smith, P. Cohen, J. Bradshaw, M. Greaves and H. Holmback Proceedings of the Third International Conference on Multi Agent Systems
3. P. R. Cohen and H. J. Levesque. Rational Interaction as the Basis for Communication. In P. R. Cohen, J. Morgan, and M. E. Pollack, editors. Intentions in Communication, chapter 12, System Development Foundation Benchmark Series, Bradford Books, MIT Press, 1990.
4. P. R. Cohen and H. J. Levesque. Confirmations and Joint Action. In Proceedings of the 12th International Joint Conference on Artificial Intelligence, Morgan Kaufman Publishers, Inc., San Mateo, California, 1991.
5. M.Georgeff and A.Rao. Rational software agents:From theory to practice .In Jennings and Wooldridge chapter 8,pages 139–160.
6. A.Rao AgentSpeak(L) BDI Agents speak out in a logical computable language Technical Note 64,Australian Artificial Intelligence Institute, Feb.1996.

UBIQUITOUS E-LEARNING
– A CONCEPT OF VIRTUAL KNOWLEDGE

MATS B ANDERSSON

Media Technology and Graphic Arts, Royal Institute of Technology (KTH), Lindstedtsvägen 5, 10044 Stockholm, Sweden, tel.: +46-8-7906000, e-mail: mba@nada.kth.se or mats.b.andersson@ilu.uu.se

When attempting to communicate experiences and knowledge between people over distances in time and space we can use the abilities of information technology. With an increase in access to information resources, teaching aids and information facilities, the user can postpone learning to a moment when knowledge is needed. Learning can occur simultaneously with knowledge being used. Sometimes learning even becomes superfluous as it is replaced by technology. A problem that usually needs some specific knowledge to be solved can be solved with support from an information resource, as a kind of knowledge-on-loan. This is nothing new, a textbook can provide knowledge-on-loan. But one gets something qualitative different when one constantly can access information – one cannot walk around with a library. The user can exceed his ability to solve certain tasks in a way that is comparable to a person with such knowledge. To an observer it might look as if the user has the knowledge, here called virtual knowledge. The borderline between information and the users knowledge tends to be vague, and in many cases dependent of the viewpoint. This article will put some light on these questions and is intended to mark out a direction for further research.

1 Introduction – accessible knowledge-on-loan

In some science fiction movies the main character gets information presented in the field of vision. It seems very convenient and practical. In the motion picture *Terminator II* the leading actor, played by Arnold Schwarzenegger, easily decides what motorcycle to steal when his preferences are matched to the performance of the motorcycles. It is easy to get enthusiastic about this kind of technique, but soon some questions arise. How does the system know that he wanted information about motorcycles? Where is the information coming from and who has sent it?

A distinguishing quality of the system is that the information is accessible anytime for the user. A user can act in a similar way as a person with equivalent knowledge can do. The system will cover up the users lack of knowledge. If a moment will be repeated enough times the user might get an idea of the situation and eventually manage without the technical support. When Arnold is choosing bike for the tenth time he does not need help from the system, Arnold can do it by himself.

This kind of system is always present to the user, ready to support. One could compare it to a scaffold around a house that is under construction and not ready to stand by itself. In the pedagogical discourse that metaphor sometimes is used [6]. The support is understood from a social environment, a support sprung out of an immediate interaction with other people. The idea should be able to be extended to cover a support from a technical system.

To an external observer the situation might look as if Arnold has enough knowledge about motorcycles to make a rational decision. But as a matter of fact, the cause of the good judgement is Arnold's interaction with the system.

The network society puts new demands on people's capacity to acquire knowledge, but it can also afford new possibilities for doing so. In many cases, though, the reproduction of knowledge follows a traditional pattern, and even when information technology is used it is often used as an extrapolation – same but different. One attends a course, with a beginning and an end, and during that time one is supposed to learn the subject matter. When the course is over, the connection to it is cut.

But doesn't the upcoming technology, one may ask, with its highly accessible information resources, give grounds for completely new applications, which can adequately complement the traditional forms of knowledge reproduction? This paper aims to discuss some of these opportunities, and develop and explore a concept of virtual knowledge.

2 Some examples of knowledge-on-loan

I have used technical aid myself in order to pretend being more competent. It happens often, and once it was quite obvious. A friend of mine sent me an e-mail with a request to translate following sentence: "Bonjour, j'ai mal à la tête." I could do that, although I don't know French. I marked the text in the e-mail and copied it. Then I looked up an automatic translation service on the Internet called Babelfish [11], pasted the text into a field on the website and let it translate from French to English. The given result was: "Hello, I have a headache." I could understand the meaning of the sentence and answer the letter in a suitable way. Of course, I wrote in English and translated to French. The answering of the e-mail did not take much longer than it would if I had known French and omit using the web resource. For a long time the receiver thought I knew French, until I got tempted to reveal the truth. I don't know French but I do know how to use the website in such a way that other people think I know it.

The use of technical appliances in order to increase man's capacity is nothing new: a lever can empower man; a microscope and a pair of binoculars can help man's sight; clothes and buildings offer an improvement in protection. These kinds of amplifiers are essential in a technologically developed society and hence a significant part of the culture. Man has also been using things to support his knowledge. Maps and cooking-books have for a long time worked like stored knowledge, as a substitute for knowledge one does not have. With these tools one can work in fields one does not have any experience of. Other people's experiences of geography or cooking can be shared with a user of these supports.

A strange feeling might arise when one takes part of such knowledge, a feeling of control, exaltation and possibilities. I remember travelling as a back-packer, standing in a foreign city. The guidebook told me the hotel I was looking for was just around the corner, "but notice that the entrance might be hard to see since it is hidden by a big ugly laundry-sign", and when I approached I discovered it was just like that. One more example can be taken from a travel by car around Europe. In this case the guide was more sophisticated than a book, the map was presented on a laptop that was connected to a GPS-device (Global Position System). On the digital map [12] one could see the route of the car, the position and also display sights, petrol stations, hotels, restaurants etc. within a specified distance from the car. One goes through a foreign country but with a few seconds margin one can tell when a yellow McDonald's-sign will be showing on the right side of the road.

In these cases the support is just information, it has nothing to do with knowledge. But how should the other road-users be able to decide whether the car is piloted by experience or by a map? There is no difference to an observer. The car acts as if the driver has experience of the district. The purpose is to get to the destination, whether that is done by having experience of the district or by driving piloted by a map are just two different ways of doing it.

The new thing is not that people can take part of other people's knowledge and experience. What is new is the efficiency in the way this can be done. With information technology, the presence of this support can be almost ubiquitous. What else may Arnold be able to do with his system? Distinguish good art from bad? Do repair work on a car? Give a lecture on a subject he does not know anything about? Since an individual's knowledge is tightly connected to his/her person, and in a certain extent describes and characterizes his identity, this may generate some confusion. Who *is* Arnold?

3 A look at the virtual

Digital technologies offer new ways for communication, visualisation, information storage and simulation. One can do many more things than one could previously; in some cases it offers completely new opportunities, in other cases it might resemble traditional things. A new kind of environment, e-environment, can be set up where traditional things and phenomena can be re-created; physical things will get an electric counterpart. Some obvious examples might be (e-)mail, (e-)money and (e-)document. One has to talk about the "physical" world to avoid ambiguity, to stress that one refers to that world and not to the other one, the electric or the virtual as it is also called. The physical world has got company with what people call the virtual world. According to Negroponte [7] the first one is made of atoms, the other of bits.

But lets stop here for a while; let us make a reflection before we go on. In what sense can one say that something in the physical world has a counterpart in the virtual? Are they not completely different? How can one speak about a "counterpart"? Why is an e-document associated with a paper-document? The same term, document, is not an explanation, just a manifestation of the link.

The example is a little special; one form can be transformed into the other form, and vice versa. An e-document can be printed and become a paper-document. And a sheet of paper can be scanned to become an e-document. This kind of metamorphosis is not necessary for a virtual phenomenon to be associated with a physical one.

The link between the physical thing and the virtual counterpart seems to be based on similarities in the aims and as a result of that, similarities in functions. One can replace the other or be a good complement, such as e-mail vs. mail. Differences in features can make one of them more suitable in some cases and the other in other cases. Association between a physical and a virtual thing can also be based on appearance.

An example of the latter are those who tries to re-build a physical world in a computer generalized world, often called virtual reality (VR). With systems like DIVE [13] or program languages as VRML [14], graphical three-dimensional worlds can be presented on a monitor (or two). A block in a city, a house, a room or something else can be copied from the real world and visualized in the computer. In some environments objects can be represented auditable and tactile. It is also possible to create completely new objects, with no correspondence to reality, or illustrate a building before it is built. In the latter case the distinction between the original and the copy is not obvious [2].

The genre is dominated by a technological focus and is sometimes accused of appropriating the concept of virtual reality. It has become a little too technologically oriented (gloves, position detectors, goggles etc.). For example Steuer [8] wants to open up the definition to more interpretations. A fairy-tale and its wonderland could be included. The virtual reality can be defined as a mentally experienced world, like an imagined room.

A technically oriented definition of VR and its computer-visualized world can be regarded as an illustration of the mental world. The programmer and the author both work with VR, but they have different ways to express themselves, different ways to form the imagined world.

4 How the word virtual is being used in educational settings

The term virtual has been quite popular in the e-learning business. Let us see how the term is being used before we go in to further discussions on virtual knowledge. Quite often it seems that the virtual phenomena and the physical counterparts have, despite qualitative differences, similar purpose.

People talk about virtual university, virtual classroom and virtual laboratories etc. Students are supposed to be offered an alternative way of studying compared to what is traditional, like the activity on campus. The intention is seldom to re-create the campus environment in a literal sense, in a way the technical field of the virtual reality would do.

In some cases a learning management system is used where the students can get a personal account that offers them a digital storage, course information, e-mail and chat with other students and teachers. Quite often there is an accompanying virtual cafeteria where more informal discussions are supposed to take part (but you can never buy any coffee there).

The virtual environment is an alternative or a complement to the physical counterpart, but it is often organized in a traditional way and the main purpose is to give the student more knowledge. Written exams and knowledge tests are common parts.

4.1 A virtual university

In the year 2002, a new university was established in Sweden, the activities of which are primarily supposed to take place in a digital environment. It is called the Swedish net-university [15], but it might just as well have been called the virtual university. Information about courses and application forms will be presented on the Internet, and the students will attend lectures and seminars mainly via this medium.

The university has similarities with traditional, campus located, universities. In the first place it is all about offering access to academic courses and academic points. A certain amount of information should be taken in and graded. Students are entering the system at one end and exiting at the other with acquired knowledge and diplomas.

But there are differences as well, not that much in aim as in function. The virtual university works in a different way compared to traditional ones. This means both advantages and disadvantages. Students and teachers do not have to be at the university campus and they do not need to be active at a certain time of the day. People can communicate through technology and do not need to come together. The flexibility in time and space can make university studies attractive to new groups in society but runs the risk of making the student isolated from a social environment such as the university campus

4.2 A virtual laboratory

A second example of how the term virtual is used can be found in the laboratory environment. A laboratory lesson can be a part of an educational setting. The student gets the opportunity to gain practical experience of the subject and might get a feeling of how related parts are connected. In some situations it might be better to change the laboratory equipment to a virtual one, simulated in a computer. A laboratory experiment in real life might be too expensive, too dangerous, too difficult to access or maybe impossible to realize.

Light Studio is a production made by Swedish Television (Sveriges Television) with some international attention (it received the Emma Award [16], best interactive production in the category Business - Technical Training 1996). With this software a user can simulate different light settings in scenes for film- or TV-productions. The student can vary the kind of lamps used and their positions. The actual light setting can immediately be rendered. In this way the student can practice light settings without access to expensive equipment, actors and props. In addition, changes can be done quickly and easily.

The exercise is indeed different from doing it in real life; moving heavy light fittings, put them in good positions, making sure they have got suitable voltages and are equipped with suitable light filters, and finally look at the result in the camera view-finder. The virtual environment offers something else, but the purpose is still to give the student some experience and knowledge of light settings.

5 Virtual knowledge

We have seen two examples of how the term virtual is used in educational settings. The connection between the physical phenomenon and the virtual one are similarities in *purpose*, sometimes in function and sometimes in appearance. The main thing is to let students practice and acquire knowledge in a certain subject.

If the term virtual has some meaning in this context it should also be applicable on the type of knowledge-on-loan that was mentioned before, i.e. virtual knowledge. The *purpose* is similar – to solve a problem or complete a task. *Information technology can provide information that, when incorporated into the users action, results in an outcome that is comparable to the outcome of a person with a certain knowledge.* The solution of a problem may be of main interest; knowledge could be a key to that; learning is a way to knowledge. That is: learning is necessary for knowledge is necessary for solving a problem. (To solve a problem <- knowledge <- learning)

When people are searching for interesting applications of information technology in learning contexts (like e-learning) it is quite common with a focus on the first part in that chain – the learning. You could also go to the heart of the matter and create favourable conditions for solving the task that learning is aiming at.

The traditional view of knowledge is preventive and *just-in-case*, you prepare for a situation that might occur. An alternative view implies access to information resources but just because of that it can be supporting whenever a user wishes, learning (or its substitute) can be *just-in-time*. One activity aims at a future occasion, the other aims at the situation itself.

In some cases it can be convenient to be able to perform a task without a learning situation. Time might not exist, or interest, or motivation. Some actions have worked as a proof of knowledge. That is no more; we saw one example in the translation case where the receiver thought I knew French. One could borrow knowledge without being close to learning.

If the technological environment is right and a designed information resource is available, a user can act more skilfully with his information support than without it. There is a difference in the level of skill depending on whether a person has got support from the information resource or not, this difference in skill can be seen as a zone where the virtual knowledge originates.

6 New shapes for learning and knowledge

This has similarities to what Vygotsky [9] calls the zone of proximal development, ZPD. A child's level of mental development – experienced by an observer – can vary depending on the environment, whether there is a supporting social setting or if the child stands alone. The child will act on a certain mental development level in solitude. He/she easily gets stuck on a task, when no adults or peers can provide help or give the child a clue. In most cases the level of mental development is higher in the other situation, when people surround the child. The child can manage more tasks, just by looking at peers, by imitating, or by getting some little extra help. A child's natural environment is not in isolation but being together with others so this raise of mental level is relevant.

In a similar way one could see a person as more capable when being in a digital environment that supports different tasks, when he/she has access to information resources that can help him/her perform. A kind of ZPD but where the crucial environment does not spring from people around but from the actual e-environment the person is connected to.

Efficient information suppliers, as for example web resources, used to be rare but as the infrastructure for information technology extends it is becoming a more common part of everyday life. In some areas, access to Internet can be almost as taken for granted as access to water and electricity – or just as taken for granted as the social environment for the child.

7 Conclusion

What have been said here motivates research on accessible information resources that offer knowledge-on-loan, virtual knowledge, how such resources can be developed and what consequences might occur. Something qualitatively new can arise when information, teaching aids, and other kinds of support always are present to the user. A new kind of learning might take place. More learning is possible, because the resource is always available. But it can also result in less learning; the resource is always available, which means you can always wait until it is really necessary. Sometimes learning is not necessary at all; a technological support can help a user perform what in normal case requires certain knowledge. Why learn when you can let the technology do it for you?

In interviews I have done with people working with web resources of this character, it came out that the consciousness and thoughts about the questions mentioned are relatively moderate. People seem to prefer practical problems and problems that need to be solved in the daily work.

A lot of questions arise for further research: What kind of knowledge can fit into a system like the one mentioned? What will that demand of technology? Will a user be vulnerable, and in that case in what sense? What is a good way of designing a system that aims to give a user virtual knowledge? Who will publish information and from what perspective? Who is the consumer? Will an observer get a different view of the user and his identity, and how will it change? What can one choose not to learn?

A quite common reaction from people use to be. "Well that's good, then one can use that saved time to learn something else." Sure, that is right but one can also do something completely different; have a beer with your friends, visit your relatives, or just make love.

Maybe the school is an outdated institution. Maybe we should go back to the time before school, where learning was continuously occurring, where knowledge were shared in everyday life. At that time master and pupil acted side by side in a social environment, tomorrow's pupils might get in contact with a mediated master in an e-environment.

References

1. Baudrillard, Jean (1996) Selected writings: Stanford University Press
2. Carey, James (1992) Communication as culture New York: Routledge
3. Castells, Manuel (1996) The information age: economy, society and culture / Vol. 1: The rise of the network society Malden, Mass.: Blackwell
4. Fiske, John (1994) Media Matters – Everyday culture and political change Minneapolis: Univ. of Minnesota Press
5. Enlund, Nils (2001) Being virtually there – reality and presence in mediated learning The international Conference: Telecommunications for education and training
6. Lave, Jean (1993) The practice of learning, pp 3 – 32 in Understanding Practice. Perspectives on activity and context, eds. Chaiklin & Lave Cambridge: University Press
7. Negroponte, Nicholas (1996) Being digital New York: Vintage
8. Steuer, Jonathan (1993) Defining Virtual Reality: Dimensions Determining Telepresence Department of Communication, Stanford University
9. Vygotsky, Lev (1978) Mind in society: the development of higher psychological processes Cambridge Mass.: Harvard U.P.
10. Wertsch, James V. (1998) Mind as action New York, Oxford: Oxford University Press Caley M. J. and Schluter D., The relationship between local and regional diversity. *Ecology* **78** (1997) pp. 70–80.
11. http://babelfish.altavista.com/
12. Microsoft AutoRoute Express Europe
13. Distributed Interactive Virtual Environment, http://www.sics.se/dive/
14. Virtual Reality Modeling Language, http://www.vrml.org/
15. http://www.netuniversity.se
16. http://www.emma-foundation.org

A PRELIMINARY EVALUATION OF A COMPUTERIZED ADAPTIVE TESTING SYSTEM ON THE WEB

KENNETH WONG, REGGIE KWAN, AND JIMMY CHAN

School of Science and Technology
The Open University of Hong Kong
30 Good Shepherd Street, Ho Man Tin,
Kowloon, Hong Kong.

Email: ***kenwong@ouhk.edu.hk*** *,* ***rkwan@ouhk.edu.hk*** *and* ***sfchan@ouhk.edu.hk***

A well-designed test can always do more than assessment. Computerized Adaptive Testing (CAT) has great potential in both assessment, and in teaching and learning. The time and place bounded paper-and-pencil test is being liberated by the CAT through the use of the world wide web (WWW) technology. This transformation has opened immense opportunities in tool development and learning on the Web.

A self-pacing, immediate scoring and feedback, and time saving tool has been built based on the Rasch Model. This paper describes tries to critically evaluate the tool built. The preliminary results of the qualitative study confirmed the potential advantages of a CAT system deployed through the Web.

1. Introduction

The use of the Internet in education is making an evolution of new educational environment and in some cases revolution in creating new tools. However, much of the current testing methods still focus on conventional paper-and-pencil test (PAPT). In other words, they are bounded by *time and place*. The PAPT does not produce immediately reports and feedback. Furthermore, all examinees goes through every item in the test. Some of the questions are either too way easy or way too difficult for the assessment of some students. Having all examinees going through all and the same questions may not add any value to the process and these items provide little information about the examinee's ability level [1,2].

Computerized Adaptive Test (CAT) is a type of test in which examinees will be offered questions based on their skill level [3]. Most studies [2,4,5,6,7] find that CAT has advantages over traditional PAPT. In CAT, examinees are continuously faced with a realistic challenge, questions are not too difficult or too easy. Different questions are generated to the examinees according to their responses on previous questions. Furthermore, CAT requires fewer test items to arrive at a more accurate estimate of examinees' ability so that examinees take a shorter time to complete a test using this CAT approach. That means the CAT system could be more efficient than the PAPT. Since each examinee is potentially given a different set of test items, test security is also enhanced. CAT allows students to receive immediate feedback on their performance and examinees' performance can be tracked by using the computer to store performance data. The key for us is to ensure the CAT used fulfils the basic principles of assessment: reliability and validity [6].

To tailor test according to the ability of individual examinee, we could make CAT work like a good oral exam [7]. It first presents a question at moderate difficulty. After the answer is given, the result is scored immediately. If it is correct, the estimation of the person's ability will be higher than it was previously estimated. It then finds and presents a question that will require higher ability. If an incorrect answer is given, the procedure will be reverse. The examinee's ability level relative to a norm group can be estimated during the testing process and questions can be selected based on the current ability estimate [6]. Most CATs are based on Item Response Theory (IRT) [2,8]. The goal of IRT is to model the relationship between a person's ability level on the trait being measured by a test and the person's response to a test item or question. It uses the estimated scores to predict or explain items and the test performance.

CAT is becoming the assessment of choice in many situations. Most well-known high-stakes testing programs in United State and Worldwide have adopted adaptive testing as their current and future testing method. This is true in examinations such as CNA, MSCE, GRE, TOEFL and GMAT [5,9,10]. The test can be more efficient and shorter. Developing such a tool can facilitate on-line adaptive testing system and such a system can be deployed on a local area network or through the Internet in our case.

The long-term goal of the project was to investigate the use of the traditional multiple-choice question. We have so far developed a CAT system, accessible via the Web, which could help teachers to identify the strengths and weaknesses of different students. Therefore, instructors, as well as students, can make use of the information to help individual's learning.

2. A Web CAT System

We decided to build a prototype on an adaptive system through the Web as mentioned above. The whole system consisted of three modules: interface, adaptive testing routine and a database. The adaptive testing routine was the core module. The routine was implemented with the Rasch model [8] which is the simplest IRT model. The main functionalities of the adaptive testing routine module were: a) connect to database, b) verify the users, c) estimate the ability level and standard error based on IRT, d) select the next item, e) retrieve and update the records from the database, f) determine the stopping condition and generate the summarised reports. The target topic associated to this project was chosen from an introduction course in an information technology literacture. The target group of users were first year university students, they were assumed to be mature, intelligent and self-motivated.

The whole system was built with the following features in mind:

- students were given different problems during the test;
- a test question was selected by an item response function;
- once the system knew the estimated ability of the students, the test would stop;
- the level of ability of the students was classified according to the their performance;
- students were automatically marked and their results were summarised in a report;
- instructors were able to access an individualized or group report of the students.

3. Overall design of the system

3.1 System architecture

The architecture of this CAT system (Figure 1) consisted of three modules: a WWW Interface, an Adaptive Testing Routine, and a Database. All modules of CAT were constructed on a WWW server except the interface, which was implemented as a WWW client. The CAT system was implemented by combining the CGI and a user modelling technique. The potential users could be instructors or students.

The WWW interface module was responsible for communication between the CAT and students. It operated in conjunction with students and the CAT.

The Database contained two major records (Figure 2): the item bank and the student response record. The item bank contains all the pre-calibrated items of information. The student r

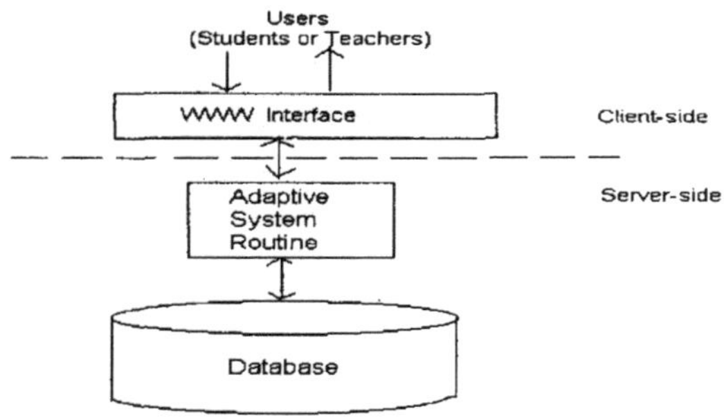

Figure 1. Computerised Adaptive Testing System

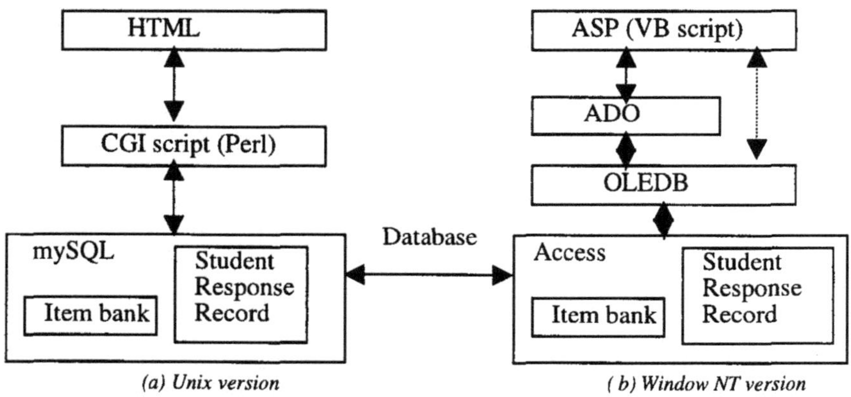

Figure 2. The hierarchy of data access in (a) Unix version and (b) Window NT version.

3.2 Preparation of Item Bank

The items presented in the item bank were chosen from the past examinations of an introductory course in information technology literature from 1997 to 1999. The questions were restricted to only one of the modules. The preparatory works were based on Umar [11]. It consisted of 62 multiple-choice questions. The item bank was of smaller size compared with a real CAT for this pilot test. All items were categorised into 5 sub-sections. All items were pre-calibrated by a software program called QUEST [12]. QUEST gave a ranking of the difficulty level of all items. It was the only information used in this system. We employed the difficulty scale unit called logits [13]. The distribution of item's difficulty level in logits in the item bank was shown in figure 3.

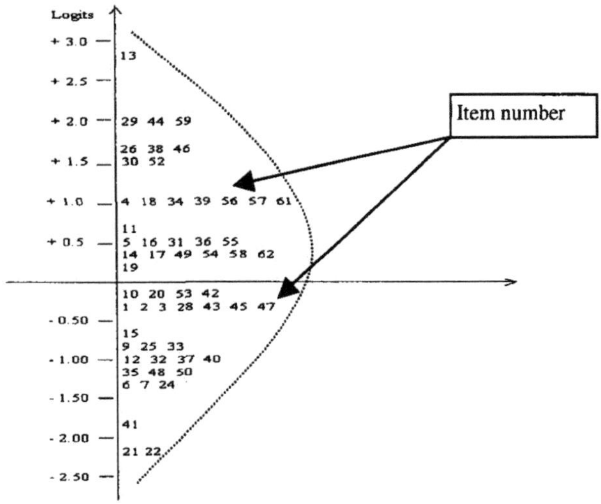

Figure 3 Distribution of item's difficulty level in logits with 62 items.

3.3 The System Flow Chart

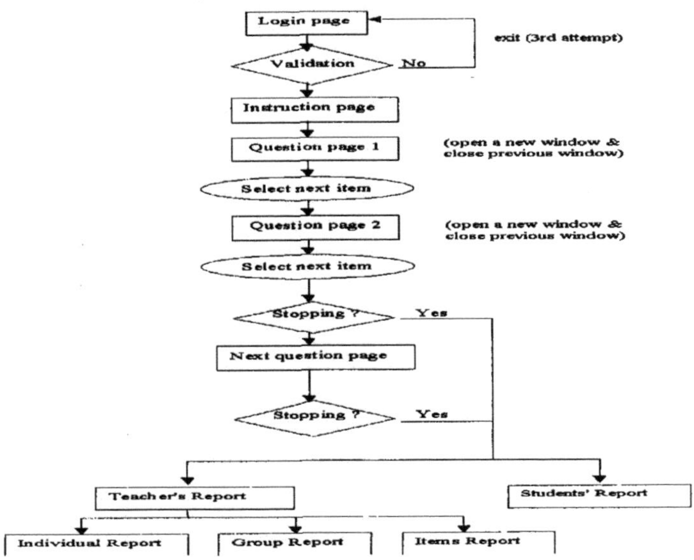

Figure 4 System Flow

Figure 4 has shown the flow chart of the overall system when a student takes the test. In CAT, examinees had no preconception of the number of questions. The stopping rules were not transparent to the examinees and were, however, a crucial factor for the CAT. The stopping rules of this system were referenced by Linacre [6]. The test would end when the standard error became less than some preset values (0.6), or when there were no more relevant questions in the item bank, or when a time-limit was reached, or when the student decided to quit the test. Then, the instant estimated ability level of the student was the final ability level of the student.

In this system, the estimation ability score of the student was used a modified PROX algorithm, which was introduced by (Cohen, 1979) and described by Linacre [14], to estimate examinees' ability level during the test. The CAT algorithm was shown at figure 5.

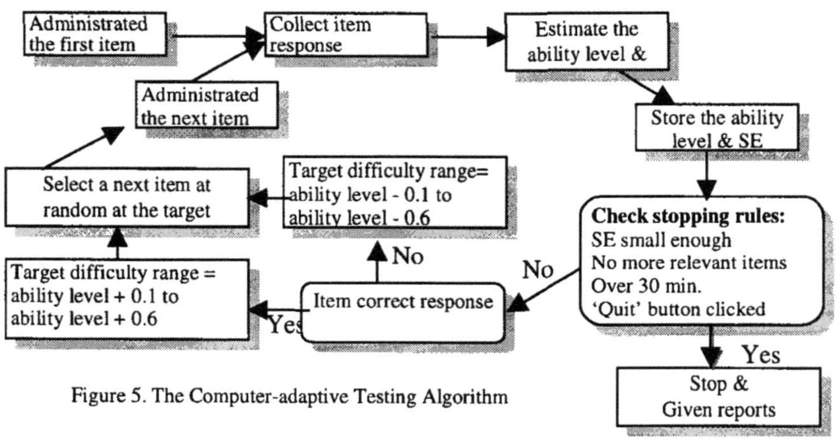

Figure 5. The Computer-adaptive Testing Algorithm

A useful estimate of student ability at any point during the test was given by accumulating the following steps:

a) The number of items administered so far = L
b) The number of right answers = R (if initial, set R=0.5)
c) The number of wrong answer = W (if initial, set W=0.5)
d) The sum of them difficulties administered = SUMCAL
e) The sum of squares of those item difficulties = SUMSQCAL
f) Calculate the mean item difficulty administered, MEANCAL = SUMCAL / L
g) A dispersion factor the spread of the item difficulties is
   DF = √ (1+(SUMSQCAL / L - MEANCAL^2)/2.89)
h) The ability estimate, B, in logits is

$$B = MEANCAL + DF * \ln(R/W)$$

i) The precision of estimate, B, is the standard error of measurement, SE,

$$SE = DF * \sqrt{(L/(R*W))}$$

j) The student ability is estimated to be in the range $B \pm SE$.

k) Stop test, if stopping rules are met.

l) Select the next item to administer in two cases:

   i) the difficulty next item, range from B + 0.1 to B + 0.6, by ascending order until find a non-administered item;

   ii) an easier next item, range from B -0.1 to B - 0.6, by descending order until find a non-administered item;

m) go to step [a]

4. IMPLEMENTATION OF THE CAT SYSTEM

Since most universities used a Unix server and Window NT server, this project was built with both versions: a Unix version and a Window NT version. There were two versions in this project: the Unix version and the Window NT version. In the Unix version, web tools such as HTML, JavaScript, Perl, and mySQL were picked. In the Window NT version, we naturally favored tools such as ASP, VBScript and Microsoft Access. The algorithm in the two versions was the same and, of course, the instruction codes were different. In the Window NT version, all pages in ASP were written with VBScript to connect records to a Microsoft Access database. In the Unix version, all pages in CGI were written with Perl script to connect records to mySQL database.

Since the aim of this system was to provide an adaptive test to the students for assessment via the Internet on which the prototype was based, the prototype was a vertical prototype [15]. It covered front pages and also back-end programmes, such as CGI program and database. The prototype was developed to cover the following features:

- Create and access to database.
- Record the date and time into the database
- Authentication on the system
- Estimate the ability level and standard error (SE)
- Selecting the best item from item bank to be the next question.
- Estimate the frequency of item being administered.
- Disallow to skip question and back to pervious questions.
- Determine the stopping rules.
- Able to provide relevant information to students and teachers.

5. CAT IN PRACTICE

To commence the adaptive test, a student had to log on the system by submitting his/her username and password. The system would verify the personal data provided by the student for authorized entry. In case of wrong data input, the system would ask the user to re-enter the data. The system would terminate when invalid trials exceeded three times. After validation, the student would enter the main instruction page. The test would wait unit the student had ready to start the test. Each question occupied the screen together with all administered items and the "get your test report" button (Figure 6). The student could quit the test either when he/she finished the test or just clicked the "get your test report" button. When a student finished the test, an immediate report would be displayed to him/her (Figure 7).

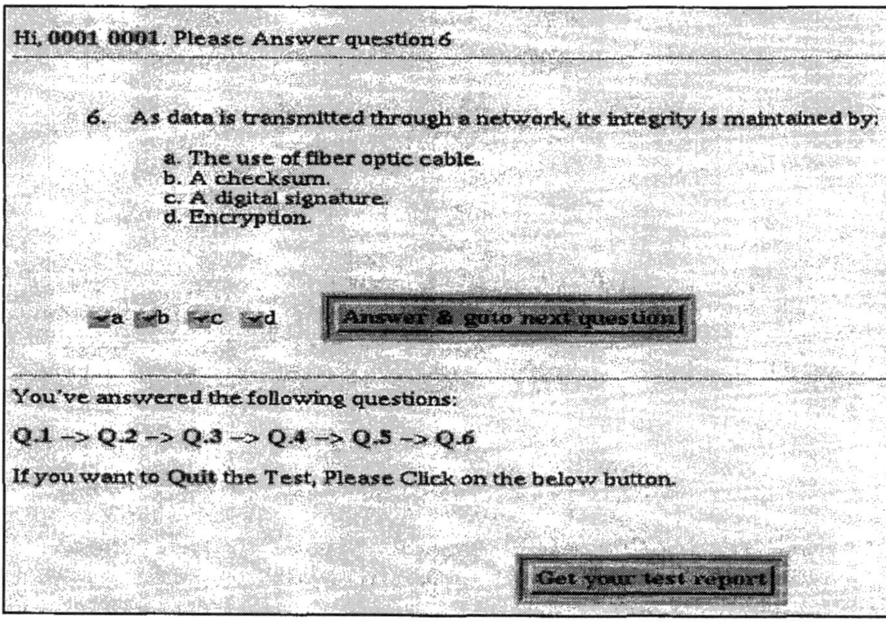

Figure 6 Question page of the system

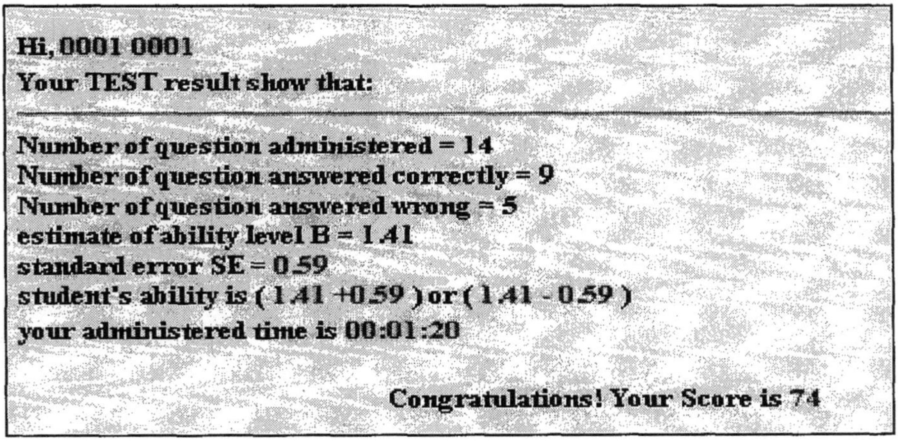

Figure 7 Summary student report of the system

Lecturers could get access to the system to review the summarized reports from the test. Similar to students, lecturers had to log on to the system by submitting their username and password. The system would verify the information of the lecturers. After validation, the lecturer would enter the main page. The main page also provided three reports for the teacher: the Student Report, the Group Report and the Item Report. An individual Student Report web page is shown in figure 8.

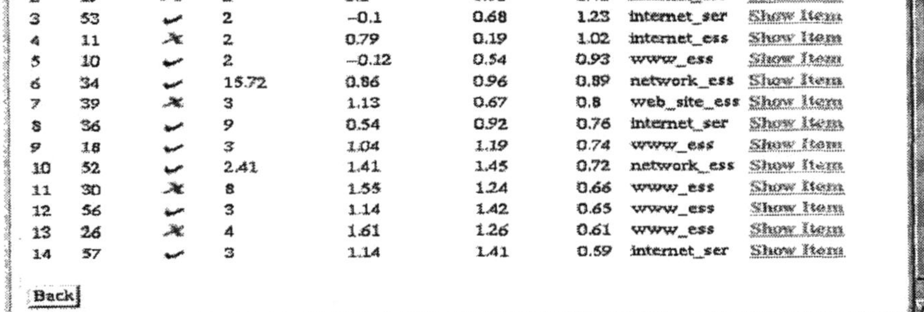

Student ID = 0001
Hi 0001 0001 , Ability 1.411117 , SE 0.5907578, Score 74

Questions Table

No	Item No	Result	Time (in Sec)	Difficulty level	ability level	SE	Sub-topic	
1	20	✓	21	-0.05	-0.05	1.73	network_ess	Show Item
2	19	✗	2	0.1	0.03	1.42	internet_ess	Show Item
3	53	✓	2	-0.1	0.68	1.23	internet_ser	Show Item
4	11	✗	2	0.79	0.19	1.02	internet_ess	Show Item
5	10	✓	2	-0.12	0.54	0.93	www_ess	Show Item
6	34	✓	15.72	0.86	0.96	0.89	network_ess	Show Item
7	39	✗	3	1.13	0.67	0.8	web_site_ess	Show Item
8	36	✓	9	0.54	0.92	0.76	internet_ser	Show Item
9	18	✓	3	1.04	1.19	0.74	www_ess	Show Item
10	52	✓	2.41	1.41	1.45	0.72	network_ess	Show Item
11	30	✗	8	1.55	1.24	0.66	www_ess	Show Item
12	56	✓	3	1.14	1.42	0.65	www_ess	Show Item
13	26	✗	4	1.61	1.26	0.61	www_ess	Show Item
14	57	✓	3	1.14	1.41	0.59	internet_ser	Show Item

Back

Figure 8. An individual Student Report page

6. FEEDBACK AND DISCUSSION

The purpose of the pilot testing was to identify potential usability problems. An evaluation method was adopted from a software usability testing method suggested by Robert Biddle [16]. The prototype of the test system needed to be examined with users. After completing the prototype of the system, the system was pilot tested.

Four students volunteered to participate in the pilot test. The participants had to complete a CAT and a traditional PAPT. The two tests were administered at two separately days to make sure that participants had not memorized the questions of the test before. In this pilot test, the PAPT was administrated a few days before the Web-based CAT test.

During the pilot test, the researchers took on the role of being the observers. Qualitative studies were conducted with the four participants to explore the perception of the participants regarding the CAT system. Based on the observation and the interviews, we found:

- most participants skipped the instruction page;
- most participants found it easy to browse pages;
- the contents, navigation and organisation of the pages were effective;
- participants spent longer on the traditional PAPT;
- participants considered the CAT system to be most useful in self-directed learning;
- participants enjoyed the interface of the CAT system; and
- participants agreed the CAT system had considerable potential in a full-blown system.

The performances of each student in both PAPT and CAT tests were indicated that CAT system was also accurate in assessing the ability of the students. We found that the CAT system was much more efficient than the traditional test. The time taken of the participants in the CAT system is above 2.5 times on average faster than the traditional test in the four cases. It was showed that the CAT had higher efficiency than the traditional test. The traditional test was more time consuming. Besides, the CAT system had other positive feedback such as security, user-friendliness, challenging, usefulness and self-paced. Nevertheless, the CAT system still had limitations such as content balance, lack of chance to review answers and some items not truly reflecting their difficulty level. All participants agreed the CAT system was a useful testing system.

This system will be especially useful in another context when an entire course is put on the Web [17,18]. Since the CAT showed more efficiency, this Web-based CAT system will be useful in pre-course competency test for students. It will give important feedback to students before they signed up for a course especially when pre-requisites are not enforced but only advisory in most OUHK courses. Such a test could help make recommendations regarding which fundamental concept or knowledge they need to work on before they take a course. Lecturers will use suitable teaching paradigms related to the students' ability. Furthermore, it can also be used as a tutorial aid, a revision aid, and integrated into courses or applied to other courses.

7. CONCLUSION

We have designed and developed a web-based tool in a CAT system. The main advantage of the Web was that a user can access the system from anytime anywhere on the Web. The CAT system is a method of assessment in which the computer selects and presents test items to examinees according to the estimated examinee's ability levels. Using the adaptive test, the system was effectively estimated the students' ability and the estimated ability was a useful indicator for teachers' reference. A prototype of the system was established and was pilot-tested. The feedbacks from users were positive and encouraging. CATs such as this one can easily be employed in other courses for assessment or as a learning aid.

8. FUTURE WORK

The current system only handles plain text multiple-choice questions. There are other areas that we intend to explore a multi-media CAT, and to incorporate CAT with electronic tutoring system in our distance learning programs. The research team is currently developing a competency test using this CAT system on the Web to aid students in course picking. It is part of a Web-based advising project for non-traditional distance learning students under an open entry system.

REFERENCES

1. Dixon, H., *Introduction to Computerized Adaptive Testing (CAT) for Placement Testing,* Indiana University - Purdue University Indianapolis (IUPUI) (2001). Available: http://assessment.iupui.edu/MTF/Cat.html
2. Rudner, L.M., *An On-line, Interactive, Computer Adaptive Testing Mini-Tutorial,* ERIC Clearinghouse on Assessment and Evaluation (1998). Available: http://ericae.net/scripts/cat
3. Description of the Computer-Based TOEFL Test, torfl.org (2000). Available: http://www.toefl.org/descbcbt.html
4. *Frequently Asked Questions about Computer-Adaptive Testing (CAT),* Center for Advanced Research on Language Acquisition, The University of Minnesota (1999). Available: http://carla.acad.umn.edu/CATFAQ.html

5. *Testing Theory*, Testing Information, Education, Novell, Inc. (2000).
Available: http://www.novell.com/education/testinfo/theory.html
6. Linacre J.M., *Computer-Adaptive Testing: A Methodology Whose Time Has Come*, Memo#69 Iom Research Memoranda, Institute for Objective Measurement, Inc. (2000). Available: http:// rasch.org/memo69.htm
7. *Windowsgalore*, Adaptive Testing, Certification and Skills Assessment Group, Microsoft, Inc. (2002). Available:
http://www.windowsgalore.com/cert/adaptive_testing/index.htm
8. Lord, F.M., *Applications of item Response Theory to Practical Testing Problems*, Erlbaum, Hillsdale, New Jersey (1980).
9. Microsoft, *Testing Innovations*, Training & Certification, Microsoft Co. (2001).
Available:
http://www.microsoft.com/traincert/mcpexams/faq/innovations.asp
10. Educational Testing Service, United State.
Available: http://www.ets.org
11. Umar J., *Item Banking*, in Educational Research, Methodology, and Measurement, Edited by John P. Keeves, p. 923 (1997).
12. Adams, R.J. and Khoo, S.T. , QUEST: An Interactive Test Analysis System. Victoria, Melbourne: ACER (1994).
13. Keeves, J.P. and Alagumalai, S. (1999). *New Approaches to Measurement*, in Masters, G. N. and J. P. Keeves (Eds). Advances in Measurement in Educational Research and Assessment, Pergamon, 23- 48.
14. Linacre, J.M., *Individualized Testing in the Classroom*, Advances in Measurement in Educational Research and Assessment. Editors: G.N. Masters and J.P. Keeves, New York: Pergamon, p.186-194 (1999).
15. Nielsen J. *Usability Engineering*, Academic Press/AP Professional, Cambridge, MA, (1993).
Available: http://jthom.best.vwh.net/usability/vertical.htm
16. Biddle, R., Usability Testing and Human Ethics home page, MCS, VUW, (2000).
Available: http://www.mcs.vuw.ac.nz/comp/research/usabtest/
17. Kwan, R., *Authoring Multi-media Teaching and Learning Material on the Web*, AAOU (Asian Association of Open Universities) 99, Vol II (pp 119-130), Beijing, China (1999).
18. Kwan, R., *Using the Web to Conduct A Laboratory*, WebNet Journal, Vol. 3, No. 4, 45-49 (2001).

Patterns of Web Based Learning in the Semantic Web Era

ANDREW K. LUI
School of Science and Technology,
Open University of Hong Kong,
30 Good Shepherd St., Homantin, Hong Kong
Email: alui@ouhk.edu.hk

S. C. LI
Department of Education Studies,
Hong Kong Baptist University,
Kowloon Tong, Hong Kong
Email: sandyli@hkbu.edu.hk

The emergence of the Semantic Web presents immense opportunities and challenges to the education industry. The second-generation web environment promises to offer a metadata framework for effective querying and intelligent tools for knowledge reasoning and inference. It is now regarded as an ideal platform for the implementation of E-Learning, an increasingly prominent style of learning. This paper identifies various web based learning scenarios that will thrive in the Semantic Web era. Three representative patterns will be shown. Each of these patterns would satisfy a characteristic learner group, sustain learning, and add values to web learning resources. The identification of all these patterns would enable tertiary institutions and other E-Learning providers to be more aware of possibilities and threats.

1. Introduction

Web based learning is entering into a significant phase of development with the emergence of the Semantic Web [2]. The Semantic Web is the second-generation web being advanced by the W3C[1]. The key new feature is the potential of intelligent processing and knowledge derivation through automatic interpretation, integration and reasoning of web resources. The presence of machine process-able metadata with web resources provides the semantic information required in the process. Comparatively the current web is merely a repository of information, but the Semantic Web promises to be a global knowledge repository. The imminent evolution of the environment has already induced exciting new web-based learning styles.

Future web-based learning scenarios will conceivably involve the notion of E-Learning. The core themes of E-Learning include learner-centric, automatic customization, and cost effectiveness. The learners could set the agenda of what and when to learn. The worldwide E-Learning industry is expected to hit US$23 billion by the year 2004 [7]. In due course, we will not only see technological advances but also fierce competition between E-Learning providers. We suggest that the future learners will choose from a number of different E-Learning styles, as the E-Learning providers attempt to offer services that better matches the needs of learners. Some learners may desire a just-in-time solution

[1] World Wide Web Consortium, Semantic Web, http://www.w3c.org/2001/sw/

to their problem, while others may want more interactions with the instructors and fellow learners. Each variation of E-Learning scenario will offer something different in learning experience and attract different types of learners.

The aim of this paper is to identify key web-based learning scenarios in the Semantic Web era. We will present three representative patterns of web-based learning scenarios. Each of the patterns intends to capture the essential features that characterise the class of scenarios it represents. We will also show that Semantic Web is capable of supporting the implementations of these future web based learning scenarios.

We suggest that the understanding of future web-based learning scenarios would be of particular significance to tertiary institutions. In the past, the adoption of web in instruction and learning had been purely the effort of individual enthusiasts[21]. This is very likely to change in the Semantic Web era. Tertiary institutions, in particular, will take an active role in setting out the agenda of web-based learning. With dwindling public funding, tertiary institutions are already looking for opportunities in E-Learning. To these institutions, the early identification of key web-based learning patterns in the Semantic Web era could mean better business position. The Semantic Web has not come yet, but its emergence has already bought challenges and opportunities.

2. E-Learning and the Semantic Web

The importance of semantic metadata to the reuse and content packaging of web resources is well documented in and out of the E-Learning community[4][19]. Metadata (or data about data) can be seen as a label that is put onto a learning resource for description. Before automatic content understanding becomes a reality, metadata offers computers an easy glimpse into the knowledge present within the learning resource. Properly indexing the metadata will allow the learning resources to be searched, located, and then packaged into courses.

A metadata standard for E-Learning is essential so that learning resources could be shared and interoperable applications could be built. A number of education technology organizations have proposed standards such as IEEE-IMS-LOM[10] and ADL-SCROM[1]. After a period of development, most of these standards have converged to cover a similar set of information including the technical, pedagogical, relational, and knowledge domain details of a learning resource. The aim is to narrow down the gap between different standards and hope to introduce some level of interoperability between different E-Learning communities.

These standardisation efforts share several common weaknesses in their approach. First, the desire to search metadata efficiently often compels the setting up of a central repository of learning resources. The resulting monolithic system will be un-scalable and inflexible[24], an extreme contrast to the open and flexible nature of the web. Also, the metadata schema is standardized but the metadata content is deemed to be subjective [18]. Introducing formal semantics may not work with the democratic nature of the web, and that a universal standard will even be less acceptable. The last and possibly the most fundamental weakness is related to the use of XML2 documents for the metadata in most E-Learning standards. The structure of XML, together with XML Schema for defining the syntax of XML documents, is fundamentally hierarchical or tree-like (see Figure 1). A hierarchical structure may be sufficient for indexing; but it is not a sufficiently expressive representation. For instance, we cannot combine two trees arbitrarily to form a greater body of knowledge. This inflexibility of representation restricts the more intelligent types of E-Learning applications.

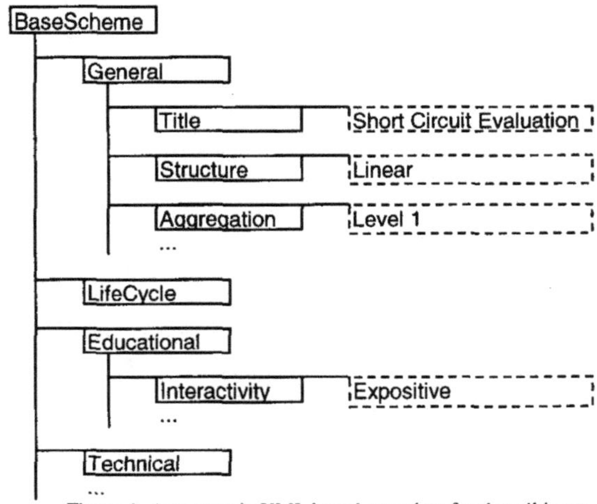

Figure 1. An example XML based metadata for describing a learning resource

Enter the Semantic Web. The vision of the Semantic Web is to allow labeling of anything about any web resource. The Semantic Web opts for an open and expressive language for the purpose in Resource Description Framework (RDF) [17]. The metadata would appear as a set of statements written in RDF, and each statement denotes a predicate between two entities: a subject and an object. For example, in the context of C programming, a RDF statement could express "type part-of variable" (see Figure 2). The predicate part-of connects the subject type and the object variable.

An interesting feature of the Semantic Web is that web resources can be readily integrated to form an expressive network of knowledge. The subject-predicate-object format of RDF statements is a simple yet powerful building unit. A set of RDF statements can be combined to form a concept of knowledge graph, with the predicates as edges and the entities as the vertices. We could foresee that an

[2] eXtensible Markup Language. http://www.xml.org

intelligent tool could readily combine a distributed set of RDF statements into a knowledge map for reasoning and inference.

The Semantic Web offers a solution to address the issue of subjectivity. Given that anyone can say anything about anything by creating RDF statements. Two parties on the Semantic Web may use two different sets of vocabulary probably for the same set of ideas in a subject domain. The Semantic Web proposes the use of ontology for resolving the different sets of vocabulary. There is no universal definition of the term ontology, but in our context it is a document that describes a standard set of vocabulary of concepts and the taxonomy in a subject domain[8]. It is envisaged that the Semantic Web will be populated with ontology documents, which provide the ingredient for intelligent tools to connect and resolve sets of vocabulary. There already exist interesting developments on ontology platforms for the Semantic Web such as OIL3[5] and OntoBroker[3].

There are now evidences to show that the Semantic Web is capable of hosting E-Learning. A small sector in the E-Learning community has attempted implementation using Semantic Web related technologies. We have found that the approaches are diverged and would thus lead to different web based learning styles.

[22] describes a scenario of E-Learning that is mainly driven by demand of solving problems at hand. The learning process will be inexpensive, personalized, and dynamic. Using an ontological approach, learning resources are automatically selected, annotated, and integrated into a personalized course.

The KMR4 group at the Royal Institute of Technology at Stockholm suggests a

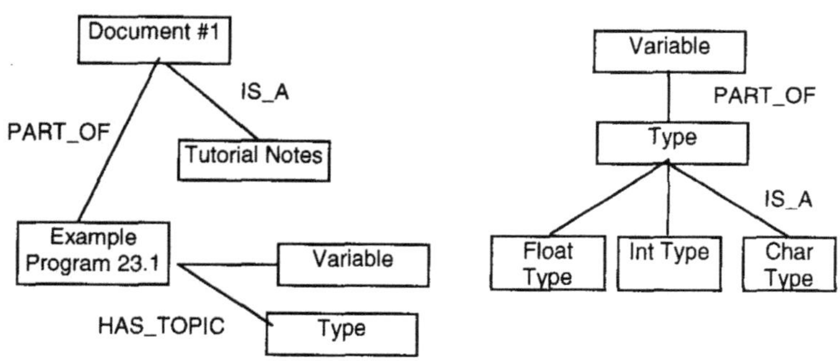

Figure 2. An example RDF for describing a learning resource (left) and concepts in programming. Note that the two graphs can be integrated usefully.

broader view of E-Learning in the Semantic Web era[20]. Their E-Learning scenarios includes not only the reuse, annotate, and extension of learning

[3] Ontology Interchange Language.
[4] Knowledge Management Research (KMR) group

resources. Other scenarios such as learner tracking, monitoring, and collaboration are also suggested. The group is also involved in the project Edutella[16], focusing on a RDF based infrastructure for sharing and querying learning resources in a web environment.

Based on the observation and study above, we are able to identify key E-Learning scenarios in the Semantic Web era.

3. E-Learning Patterns in the Semantic Web Era

Patterns are useful in communicating solutions in their essence[6] and this approach has been applied usefully in describing instruction and learning scenarios. We have identified the following three patterns of E-Learning scenarios. The patterns are partially derived from the notion of the Teacher-Resource/Learner-Rights pattern described in[14].

- **Problem Solving Pattern.** Allows learners to search for reusable resources for solving the problem at hand.
- **Coordinated Learning Pattern.** Enables the incorporation of an instructional design strategy into an E-Learning scenario
- **Learning Community Pattern.** Facilitates a learning community to evolve and flourish.

We describe each of the three patterns in details. We will follow the UML5 based modeling technique by [12] and describe the patterns graphically. Also, such patterns should capture the following characteristics of E-Learning scenarios.

1. The *roles* played by the instructor and the learner.
2. The *interactivity* between the instructor and the learner.
3. The *motivation* that drives the learning.
4. The viability of the *economy*.
5. The key enabling *technology*.

3.1 *Problem Solving Pattern*

The intent of this pattern is to allow learners to search for reusable resources for solving the problems at hand. There is an increasing concern that learning must be relevant to the context of the business. Timely, quick and cost-effective learning is desired. This pattern satisfies the requirements by resource reuse, effective location of required resources, and reducing the interaction between the instructor and the learner (Figure 3).

[5] Unified Modelling Language.

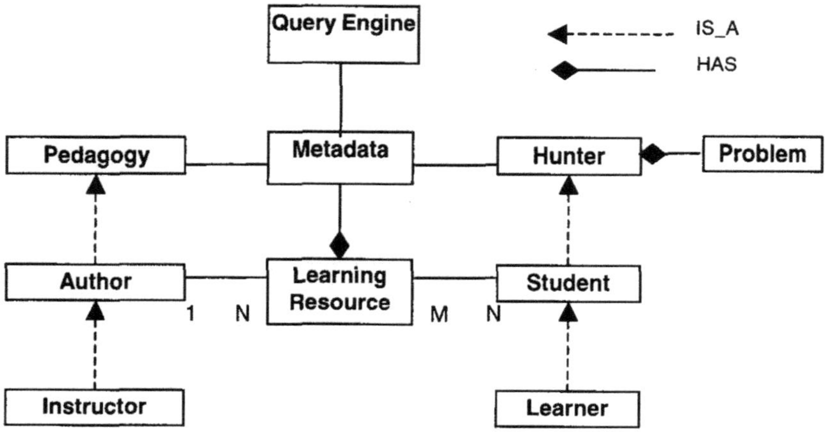

Figure 3. The Problem Solving Pattern

There is no direct connection between the Instructor and the Learner. The Instructor produces Learning Resources as an author and the Metadata of the resources with a pedagogical capacity. In some cases the Instructor could obtain Learning Resources from other sources and supplement with Metadata. The Learner acts as a Hunter to look for a solution of the Problem at hand, and studies the Learning Resources located by the Query Engine.

The pattern is cost-effective given a possible large Student-Learning Resource ratio through reuse and that each instructor would produce a number of learning resources. The motivation for learning is driven by the need to solve problem. The learner would initiate the learning process by searching for solutions and then asking for customised learning resources. The pattern facilitates an always-available learning system that the learner can join and leave readily.

The main technology required in this pattern is a metadata querying service. Metadata service is a core and arguably the most matured technology being developed in the Semantic Web. There are also a number of prototypes based on some E-Learning standards.

3.2. *Coordinated Learning Pattern*

The intent of this pattern is to incorporate an instructional design strategy into an E-Learning scenario. Instructional design strategy is not rigorously considered in most E-learning scenarios. Research work has highlighted that instructional design theory is also salient for the reuse and automatic integration of learning resources. This pattern values the participation by the Instructor to provide instructional design input (Figure 4).

Instructional design strategy may be incorporated in the following areas of the pattern.

- The instructor could express the expert's views on the structure of the subject domain using ontologies. The learner (or his/her agent) could use the ontologies as a scaffold to guide the subject topics and the selection of learning resources.
- The instructor could create context defining learning materials, such as the prescriptive linking material described in [23], and annotations to attach to the learning resources.
- The instructor could provide consultation on learning strategy to the students through the web. A direct connection exists between the Instructor and the Learner. The communication channels would include emails, discussion forums, and the plain old telephone.

In this pattern, learners are usually registered within a course administrative structure. This allows the instructor to identify the learners in consultations and personalised assistance. Administrative support is also needed in the implementation of some instructional design elements (e.g. assessment).

The motivation for learning is mainly interest-driven. The learner would simply have an interest in a certain subject area and so embark on the learning journey. For the interest to sustain, however, the inspiration of the instructor is important. Having a course structure in this pattern also make certification possible. Learning could be driven by the desire of recognition by an institution, from a you-did-it certificate to a degree.

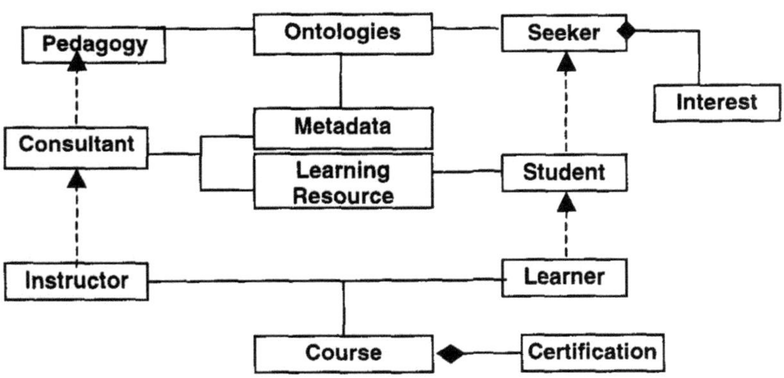

Figure 4. The Coordinated Learning Pattern

The pattern would operate with an increased participation of the instructor and interaction between the instructor and learners. Although it would mean higher cost than the Problem Solving pattern, the more interactive learning style could warrant a higher learning service fees.

The key technology here is ontology management. A number of non-trivial ontology application prototypes have been created and studied for the Semantic Web, including SHOE[9], OIL, and OntoBroker.

3.3. *Learning Community Pattern*

The intent of this pattern is to facilitate a learning community to evolve and flourish. The learners work together and explore one or more subject areas. A Learner is expected to play several roles including Student, Consultant, Expert, and Librarian. A learning community is formed based on the collaboration in setting out a learning strategy and communicating the knowledge acquired. This pattern values the co-construction of knowledge through interactions (Figure 5).

The Instructor is not explicitly present in this pattern. An institution instructor could however reveal as a Learner playing a role. To other learners in the community, the instructor could just be somebody who is more knowledgable and experienced. The learners have absolute freedom in suggesting a new subject area to explore, and no instructor here would set a boundary.

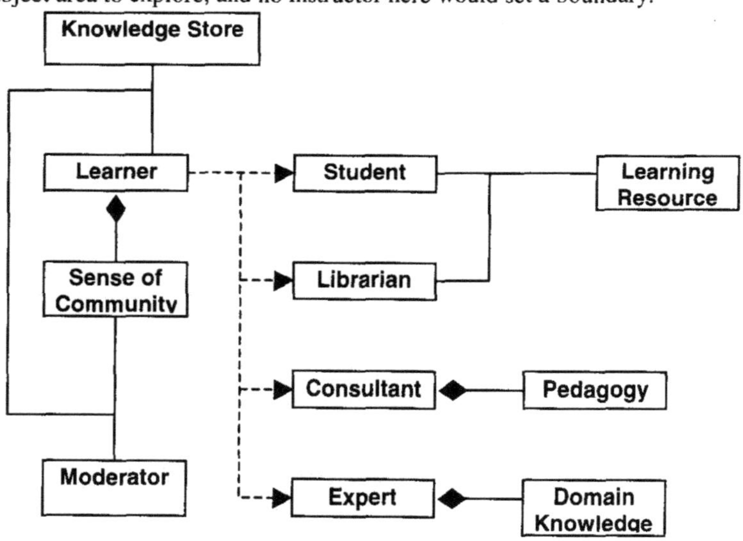

Figure 5. The Learning Community Pattern

The learning process will happen when the learner takes up the four roles. As a Student, the learner seeks out learning resources in the Semantic Web and self-studies them. As a Librarian, the learner refers community members to learning resources and organises the knowledge own by the community. As a Consultant, the learner suggests learning strategy and provides reflective questions to the community. As an Expert, the learner shares the understanding of knowledge and suggests solutions to problems.

Learners are motivated by a sense of community that brings along self-satisfaction and self-realisation. However, the sense of community is rather fragile that can take lots of effort to achieve (e.g. making contributions to the community) but can break down easily (e.g. learners lurk and do not participate). This pattern would require the members in the community to take up all four roles. For learning to sustain in this pattern, tremendous sense of responsibility and social interaction skill is demanded. We suggest that a Moderator, who manages the community, can partially address these requirements. The Moderator would use tools to monitor the rate of participation of the community members.

The cost of operating this pattern is mainly due to the Moderator and the tools for managing the Knowledge Store and the community in general. We envisage that a Moderator service could be set up so that the learners interested in this pattern could register with a small fees. The Moderator will help organising the knowledge store and provide other services such as regular updates on new learning resources on the web.

There is an interesting potential with the knowledge accumulated within the community. If the learners have done a good job, the knowledge store will contain original ideas, useful perspective on certain subject areas, and practical comments. The knowledge store could then be made available to other E-Learning systems to promote knowledge sharing. This sharing of knowledge beyond the community may have interesting implications on the economy of E-Learning and new applications.

Knowledge management tools will be the key technology used in this pattern. Although there are already many knowledge management tools such as concept map builders, document repositories, and discussion forums, the Semantic Web offers these tools in a truly open and distributed environment. Some tools have already been built such as Annotea[11] for managing distributed annotations, Conzilla[15] for managing personal knowledge and distributed content, and the ontology management tools mentioned above. The technology is currently still immature, but the potential is clear. As stated in [2], "... if properly designed, the Semantic Web can assist the evolution of human knowledge as a whole".

4. Discussions and Conclusion

The following table summaries the characteristics of the three patterns.

Table 1: Key characteristics of the three patterns of E-Learning scenarios

	Problem Solver Pattern	Coordinated Learning Pattern	Learning Community Pattern
Key Activity	Query for suitable learning resources	Explore and study suitable learning resources within a subject domain	Research, share, and discuss knowledge.
Interactivity	Indirect	Supported	Core activity
Cost Factors	Learning resource and Instructor-Learner ratio	Instructor participation	Moderator, collaborative tools
Motivation	Solving Problems	Interests/Recognition	Sense of Community
Learner Skill	Able to ask the right questions	Able to interact with the instructor and draw up a learning strategy	Able to direct a community discussion

More than one pattern may be incorporated into an E-Learning service. For example, the Coordinated Learning pattern, for example, can be augmented with the Problem Solver pattern for the querying of suitable learning resources. Such mixtures of services could be presented to the learners seamlessly.

On the other hand, there is a competitive edge for an E-Learning service provider to support more than one pattern. Operating these patterns of E-Learning scenarios will enable the establishment of *value-adding chains*. A value-adding chain of learning resources would be conducted as the following multi-stage process. The learning resource can gain value with additional knowledge added to it (Figure 6).

1. The authoring of learning resource. Cost from modest (eg. text based tutorial-notes) to very expensive (eg. multimedia and interactive presentations).
2. The annotation of the learning resource *content* with metadata. The learning resource gains value if it is found to address suitable problems. The query engine needs accurate metadata, so that the learners can find the query service satisfactory.
3. The annotation of the learning resource *context* with metadata. The learning resource gains value by being composed suitably into a course.
4. The annotation of the learning resource by a community of learners. The learning resource has been discussed in a learning community and gains value by comments from a range of perspective.

The value-adding chain for learning resources highlights the salient role of instructors with domain expertise. In the Semantic Web era, the value of instructors in E-Learning will not diminish. While institutions like the MIT make learning materials on the web for free, the project fact sheet states that " ... cornerstone of the learning process at MIT is the interaction between faculty and students in the classrooms, and amongst students themselves on campus"[13]. We suggest that the same can be said of virtual classrooms and campus.

In this paper we presented three representative patterns for E-Learning in the Semantic Web era. The patterns intended to capture the essential features that characterise classes of scenarios. We analysed each pattern on the roles of the instructor and the learners, the interactivity between them, the motivation factor in learning, and the economical viability. We also described briefly on the technologies of Semantic Web that are related to the E-Learning patterns. We suggested that these patterns could indicate potential opportunities in the E-Learning industry.

References

1. ADL Technical Team, Sharable Content Object Model (SCORM) Specification 1.2, ADL, Department of Defense, USA, Oct. 2001.
2. Bernes-Lee T. et. al, The Semantic Web, Scientific American, 284(5): 34-43. May 2000.
3. Decker, S., et. al., Ontobroker: Ontology based Access to Distributed and Semi-Structured Information, in Meersman, R., Tari, Z., and Stevens, S., eds, Semantic Issues in Multimedia Systems, Kluwer Academic Publisher, Boston, 1999.
4. Dornfest, R., and Brickley, D., The Power of Metadata. http://www.openp2p.com/pub/a/p2p/2001/01/18/metadata.html , Jan 2001.
5. Fensel, D., et. al., OIL: An Ontology Infrastructure for the Semantic Web, IEEE Intelligent Systems, 16(2):38-45, 2001.
6. Gamma, et. al. , Design Patterns - Elements of Reusable Object-Oriented Software, Addison Wesley, 1994.
7. Goodridge, E.,, Slowing Economy Sparks Boom in E-Learning, InformationWeek.com, Nov 12, 2001.
8. Gruber, T.R., Toward Principles for the Design of Ontologies used for Knowledge Sharing, Int. Journal of Human Computer Studies, 43(5/6):907-928, 1995.
9. Heflin, J., and Hendler, J., A Portrait of the Semantic Web in Action, IEEE Intelligent Systems, 16(2):54-59, 2001.
10. IEEE LTSC, IEEE Learning Technology Standard Committee. IEEE LOM Working Draft 6.1, April 2001
11. Kahan, J., et. al. Annotea: An Open RDF Infrastructure for Shared Web Annotations, in Proceedings of 10th International Conference on World Wide Web (WWW10), Hong Kong, May 2001.
12. Naeve, A. The Garden of Knowledge as a Knowledge Manifold - a Conceptual Framework for Computer Supported Subjective Education, CID-17, TRITA-NA-D9708, Department of Numerical Analysis and Computer Science, KTH, Stockholm.
13. MIT OKI, MIT OCW Fact Sheet, http://web.mit.edu/ocw/ocwfactsheet.html.
14. Naeve, A., The Knowledge Manifold – An Education Architecture that Supports Inquiry-Based Customizable Forms of E-Learning, in Proceedings of the 2nd European Web-Based Learning Environment Conference (WBLE 2001), Lund, Sweden, Oct 2001.

15. Naeve, A., The Concept Browser – a New Form of Knowledge Management Tool, in Proceedings of the 2nd European Web-Based Learning Environment Conference (WBLE 2001), Lund, Sweden, Oct 2001.

16. Nejdl. W., et. al., Edutella: A P2P Networking Infrastructure Based on RDF, in Proceedings of the 11th World Wide Web Conference (WWW2002), Hawaii, USA.

17. Nilsson, M., The Semantic Web: How RDF will change Learning Technology Standards, CETIS, Sept 2001.

18. Nilsson, M., et. al., Semantic Web Meta-data for e-Learning - Some Architectural Guidelines, in Proceedings of the 11th World Wide Web Conference (WWW2002), Hawaii, USA.

19. O. Lassila , Web Metadata: A Matter of Semantics, IEEE Internet Computing, 2(4):30–37, July 1998.

20. Palmér, M., et. al., E-learning in the Semantic Age, in Proceedings of the 2nd European Web-based Learning Environments Conference (WBLE 2001), Lund, Sweden.

21. Sheely S., et. al., Building the Web Interactive Study Environment: Mainstreaming online teaching and learning at the University of Western Sydney, Australian Journal of Educational Technology, 17(1):80-95, 2001.

22. Stojanovic, L., et al., eLearning based on the Semantic Web, World Conference on the WWW and Internet, Orlando, USA, Oct 2001.

23. Wiley, D.A., Connecting Learning Objects to Instructional Design Theory: A Definition, Metaphor, and Texonomy, In D.A. Wiley (ed), Instructional Use of Learning Objects, Association of Educational Communications and Technology.

24. Wilson, S., The next big thing? – Three Architecture Frameworks for Learning Technologies, CETIS, Aug 2001.

PART THREE Tools

Improving the Design of an Online Self-Assessment Tool Utilizing Confidence Measurement

Graham Farrell[1] and Ying Leung[2],

[1] School of Information Technology
Swinburne University of Technology
Melbourne, Australia
gfarrell@swin.edu.au

[2] Department of Information & Communications Technology,
Hong Kong Institute of Vocational Education,
Tsing Yi,
New Territories, Hong Kong.
yleung@vtc.edu.hk

Abstract. There is an increasing reliance on corporate training centres and educational institutions to deliver their programs via the Internet or Intranet. The success of such programs is dependent on the marrying of Internet technology, information systems, human computer interaction and educational strategies while catering for the needs of the individual student. This research investigates and evaluates the refined design of an innovative approach to an online formative assessment tool that permits the participant to choose their correct response and register their level of confidence in their choice. The tool provides enriched, granulated feedback to the students assisting them along the learning path.

1 Introduction

Educational institutions supplying quality education globally, at a reasonable cost and with the additional convenience to the recipient, is seen to be an appealing option to the prospective student. Flexibility and portability is fast becoming a requirement of a successful educational program. Students often find themselves in the situation where they are unable to participate in the traditional mode of delivery, and pursue options that best fit their busy work schedule.

Assessment plays a critical role in the educational process as a means of both grading and supplying valuable feedback to the students. The embracing of technology as an integral part of the delivery of education has increased the requirement for effective assessment systems to be available to the student, encouraging self-assessment at all stages of the learning experience. It is accepted wisdom that testing for the purpose of feedback should be an integral part of the sequence of learning activities rather than an interruption to that sequence [1].

Traditionally both formative and summative methods of assessment have been reliant on the instructor to supply the feedback. With the ever-increasing demand to constrain delivery costs, resulting in increased student staff ratios, unintentional delays in supplying feedback to the students can occur to the disadvantage of both the student and the instructor. As a result often the most valuable feedback occurs at the final stages of the learning path, generally too late to be of great value to the students' learning process and providing only limited feedback to the instructor. This situation tends to benefit primarily the group of students participating in the next scheduled delivery of the unit. To maximize the effect and value of the feedback, it must be instantaneous; this is an inherent characteristic of online assessment tools due to the nature of the encompassing technology. The formative assessment feedback cycle should occur early, and then constantly throughout the duration of the learning experience.

Doebbert emphasizes the need for students to develop skills in managing and controlling their learning with the utilization of technology, assisting in the process as they travel the educational path [2]. Accordingly we are interested in looking at approaches to assessment that help to place control of the learning in the hands of the student.

This paper investigates the design refinement of an innovative formative assessment tool, Multiple Choice Questions Confidence Monitor (MCQCM), using internet technology. The self-assessment tool is based on the traditional Multiple Choice Questions. However it utilizes a method permitting the students to register their level of confidence for each of the options available. The package instantly generates a score that aims to reflect the students' level of understanding of the topic being considered. This paper also discusses the initial design considerations and the pilot program that followed. It then describes the consequential redesigning of the system to maximize its effectiveness. The objective of the project is to develop a self-assessment system that provides enriched feedback to both the student and the instructor in order to benefit all those associated with the learning process.

2 Formative Assessment

Black and William use the term "Assessment" as referring to the group of activities undertaken by both teachers and students in assessing themselves, providing both grades and feedback to modify teaching [3]. They state "*such assessment becomes formative assessment when the evidence is actually used to adapt the teaching to meet the students' needs*". It is generally accepted that summative assessment is a tool that whilst providing feedback has the primary objective of supplying a grade for the student.

Black and William also refer to the learning environment as being a "Black Box", with the familiar aspects of input, being pupils, teachers, parents and resources, with the consequential outputs being pupils with advanced educational standing [4]. It is within this Black Box that they see the role of Formative

Assessment critical in the transformation of the student's educational standing, contributing to the raising of the national standards.

Black and William observe that pupils are too often " *content to get by* " [2]. Perrenoud suggests that a solution would be for the instructors to "reconstruct the teaching contracts to counteract these acquired habits" with the inclusion of formative assessment as a key component of the learning process [5].

Many of the programs offered by learning institutions are becoming increasingly aware of the benefits of shifting the responsibilities of learning into the students' hands. As the Guidelines for the Teaching of Educational Psychology in Teacher Education Programs suggests, educators addressing the "*growing problems of school dropouts, low-levels of academic achievement, and other indicators of school failure are arguing for more learner centered models of schooling*" [6]. The guidelines recognize the importance of "Meta-cognitive learning", which concentrates on "thinking about their own thinking". This includes the critical components of "self-awareness,.. self-inquiry,.. self-monitoring and self-regulation", promoting high levels of commitment, persistence and involvement in learning.

The guidelines further recommend the curriculum be designed to include components that "*practice meta-cognitive strategies, including reflective self-awareness and goal setting*". In addition they state that assessment tasks should foster self-appraisal and self-regulated learning.

The amended instruction resulting from formative assessment is critical to the success of the learning experience. It is an accepted opinion that instruction and formative assessment are not just strongly linked but are inseparable.

3 Multiple Choice Questions and the Online Environment

The general acceptance of the multiple choice question (MCQ) formats as both a formative and summative assessment tool has seen them extensively utilized in traditional education. The ease of their adaptation to the Hypermedia environment produced fully integrated and automated systems, supplying instant feedback to students with suggested direction for further study.

MCQs offer an excellent method of assessing the students' knowledge in areas deemed as either right or wrong. However, what about the "shades of gray" or fuzzier areas? Diamond and Forrestor define knowledge as asking the question "What do you know?" followed by the meta-question of equal importance "How sure are you of the answer to the question about what you know?" [7].

Davidoff recognizes the need for a more thorough approach in assessing students in the medical arena [8]. He suggests that a system designed to recognize "incomplete or partial knowledge", permitting the student to "hedge", would be greatly beneficial to the learning process. He further states that much of the medical knowledge is "incomplete, ambiguous and conflicting" and that the standard MCQ testing method does not facilitate or reflect the students' level of knowledge and their confidence in that level of knowledge. One of his main concerns is that MCQs recognize and reward those areas of knowledge that is either right or wrong, encouraging guessing and often leading to overconfidence, and he considers "mis-calibrated confidence" in medical education equally as concerning as lack of knowledge. The scoring of MCQs has long been a point of discussion with serious consideration been given to various scoring models. Pollard and Clarke produced a series of scoring techniques designed to eliminate guessing utilizing complex scoring algorithms aiming to produce a reflection of the real understanding that the student has of the topic [9].

Brown and Shuford proposed an MCQ calibrated scoring system "that encouraged honesty", designed to reflect the level of confidence in choosing the answer whilst severely penalizing the participant if they answered incorrectly. The primary objective of this scoring system is to identify students that are either overconfident or under confident [10].

Klinger [11] and Paul [12] both designed testing tools where the student nominated a position in areas joining the apexes in a triangular shape. Each of the apexes represented the three optional answers. The students would then receive a score based on a logarithmic scale aimed to reflect their knowledge.

Farrell and Leung consider that these tools, although effective, could be difficult for the student to use and that the scoring mechanisms were too complex [13].

The research of Pollard [14], [15], [16] demonstrated the advantages of developing a scoring system that aims to reflect the students' understanding of the subject while Paul [12], Brown and Shufford [10] and Klinger [11] all have demonstrated variations on systems designed to capture a numerical representation of the students' level of knowledge.

The combination of previous research with the rapid development of the Internet as a means of delivering education and assessment encourages the designing, testing and evaluation of formative assessment tools that incorporate scoring systems aimed to reflect the true knowledge of the student.

4 The Original MCQCM Self-Assessment Tool

The MCQCM self-assessment tool, proposed and developed by Farrell and Leung [13], is based on the traditional Multiple Choice Questions format, consisting of a stem and four options, as recommended by Kehoe [17], and Frary [18]. The MCQCM is scalable to permit a variation on the available options.

The original MCQCM tool was required to:

- Permit more than one correct answer. This encourages the student to consider all options separately and not to identify what they consider to be the single correct answer and ignore the rest.
- Permit the instructor to word the options to closely examine the areas of study, eliminating the need to use easily recognizable distracters.
- Force the student to consider all options carefully, increasing their exposure to associated areas within the topic.
- Produce a score aimed to reflect the students' understanding of the concept being considered in each question.

The MCQCM utilizes a simple linear scoring technique, which is easily understood by the student, giving them control of the tool. This scoring technique is also designed to reflect the students' level of understanding. The students are placed in the position where they must clearly state their level of confidence, knowing that they would be proportionally penalized for an incorrect choice and proportionally rewarded for a correct choice.

The original design of the MCQCM is shown in Fig 1.

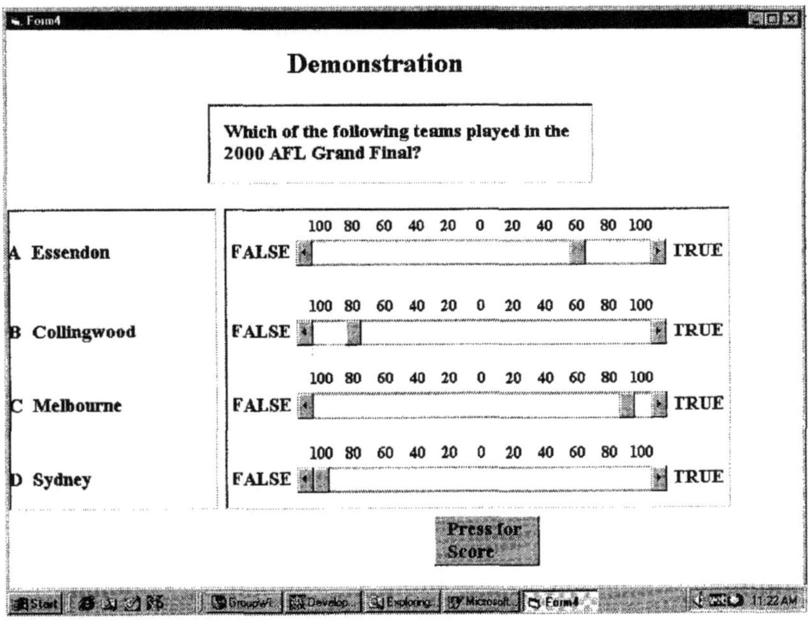

Fig. 1. The original design of the MCQCM showing the demonstration screen used as part of the training

5 Review of Pilot Study for the Original Design

Farrell and Leung performed a pilot study aimed at evaluating the functionality of the MCQCM [13]. The pilot study consisted of an initial introductory session where the six students responded to a general knowledge question. Following this the students completed a formal topic test whilst being observed.

During this pilot study it was observed that all of the students completed the test without any major operational problems. The simple scoring system was well received. The students considered the MCQCM easy to operate and the method of scoring appeared to encourage risk taking, resulting in the students manipulating the MCQCM to their advantage. Furthermore, all of the subjects stated that they understood the feedback, as it clearly reflected their responses. They also agreed that that the feedback would assist them in deciding their study path to improve their understanding of the topic. However, the students did express the following concerns.

- They were not comfortable with the interface due to the lack of familiarity.
- They were not used to identifying both the correct and incorrect options.
- They found it difficult to register their level of confidence for all of the options, not just the correct one(s).
- They were not able to use the slide bar freely.

The students increasingly used the sliding bar to register their confidence and confirmed that the feedback and consequential score was both comprehensible and helpful for further study direction.

Instructors also acknowledged the value of the tool with its enriched feedback in assisting the direction of instruction to meet the needs of students. The tool appeared to produce a refined set of results reflecting the students' level of understanding. They considered it as a useful, decisive tool to modify the direction of instruction to the benefit of both the students and the instructor.

Some students registered a concern about the decision-making process required which they found confusing. This was not apparent during the running of the test but surfaced during the discussion that followed.

The area of concern appears with the following question. Is the choice of the option being either 'true' or 'false' dominant in the participant's mind? Having the confidence sliding bar as the primary source of identifying if the option is 'true' or 'false' could be confusing to the student. This is because normally the student would prefer firstly to identify if the option is 'true' or 'false' before registering his/her level of confidence. Furthermore, because the confidence sliding bar is used to perform two specific functions, selecting the answer and registering the level of confidence associated with it, there may be misinterpretations in using the sliding bar. For example, in stating that you are 80% sure the option is 'false' (Fig. 2a), is it the same as stating that you are 20% sure the option is 'true' (Fig. 2b)? Therefore, there are potential problems with this design.

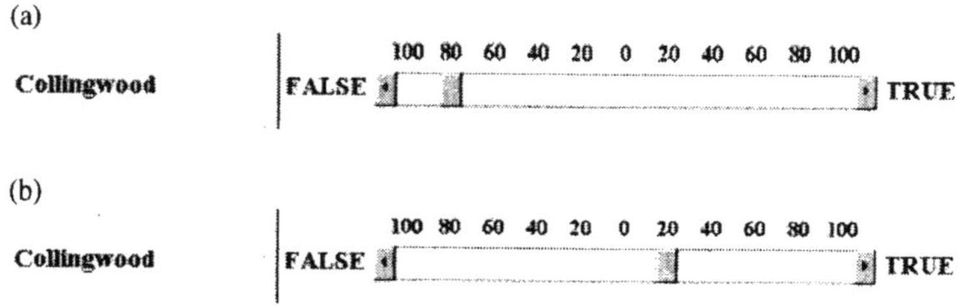

Fig. 2. a) 80% sure the option is 'false', b) 20% sure the option is 'true'

6 Justification for Redesigning the MCQCM

In addressing this problem we must refer to one of the most influential concepts formulated in modern psychology, being Albert Bandura's theory on Self-efficacy Expectations [19]. Bandura's work focuses in the belief of our capabilities to successfully perform a given task or behaviour which influences behavioural choices, performance and persistence. Bandura states that self-efficacy can be increased through performance accomplishments. He considers this to be the major influences of behaviours and behaviour change. He further states that low self-efficacy expectations within a domain can lead to avoidance while an increase in self-efficacy will result in an increase in the learning activity. He considers intervention can increase the self-efficacy expectations and specifies four sources by which self-efficacy expectations can be modified. Two of these are of particular interest in our area of study. The first is that experiences of success will be beneficial to the learner. The second is the awareness of physiological arousal, such as anxiety, with the behaviour or task is seen as a co-effect of self-efficacy expectations, where an increase self-efficacy should result in a decrease of anxiety. Importantly to our study the reverse also applies, a decrease in self-efficacy leads to an increase in anxiety.

Betz and Hacket extensively used the concept of self-efficacy expectations applying it to career psychology and counseling [20]. They ultilized a questionnaire format that retains Bandura's original notion of the level ("yes/no") versus the strength (confidence) of self-efficacy. Their developed technique requires the participant to commit to an answer first. Once committed the individual is required to clearly state their level of confidence in that answer. Fullarton also utilized the same method of testing when investigating the effects of gender on confidence in mathematics [21]. Her technique required the student to identify the correct answer and then to register their level of confidence in the choice.

This is the very crux of the situation that we found ourselves facing. We felt that by adopting the above technique in asking the student to firstly commit to an answer before stating their level of confidence eliminates the possible confusion in the process. As Bandura has identified the idea of stating a "level" to be followed by a "Strength" (confidence) of self-efficacy gives a clear, unambiguous picture of the students' response [21].

7 The Revised Design of MCQCM

As a direct result of the observations and the discussion of our pilot study, we redesigned the MCQCM. The MCQCM is still based on the MCQ format with the student required to consider all of the options, given that there could be one or more correct options. It is felt that this produces a more granulate set of results for analysis by requiring the student to identify not only what they consider to be correct but also what they consider is incorrect. The initial questions are displayed with the stem and the options with True and False buttons at the end of each option. (See Fig. 3)

The sliding bar that is designed to register their confidence will only appear once the student has chosen True or False for the option. This controlled environment ensures that the student is led through the testing procedure with minimal confusion. (See Fig. 4)

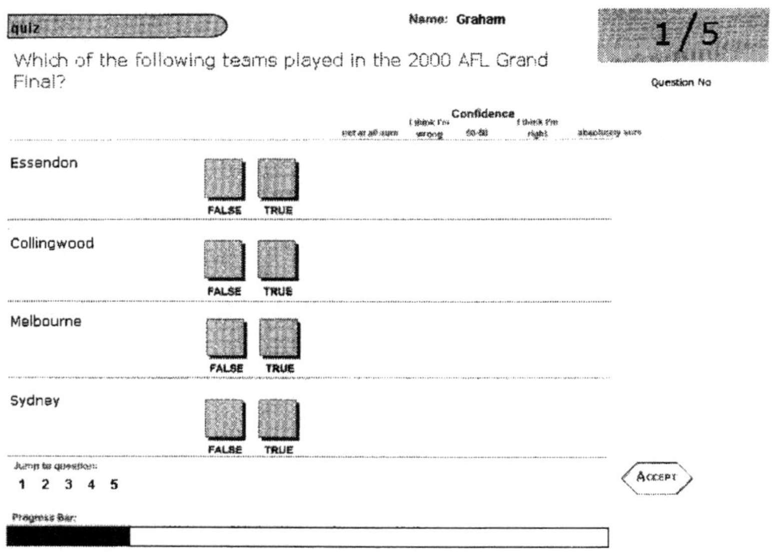

Fig. 3. The redesigned MCQCM demonstrating the requirement to first commit to the True or False option

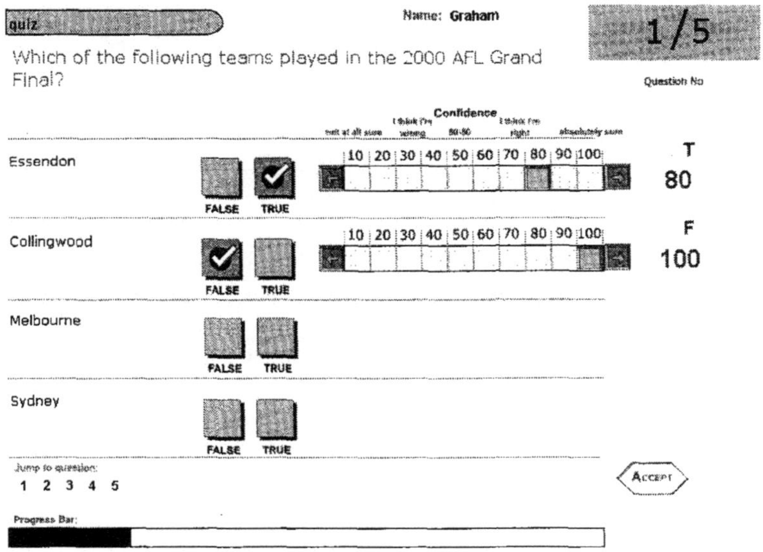

Fig. 4. The sliding bar appears only when the student commits to True or False. The scoring mechanism remains the same, and is specifically designed to give valuable feedback to the student whilst building their confidence.

8 Further Work

We intend on conducting a series of tests to evaluate the MCQCM as part of the delivery program of subjects presently being offered. The tests will be performed across different institutions for various subjects. The data produced will be analyzed to evaluate the effectiveness of the tool as part of the students' learning path.

In particular we would like to investigate if the tool is biased towards a particular learning style, either the extraverted individual or the introverted. We are also interested in investigating if the effects of this tool on gender.

We also identified that a tool like this could also be utilized as a measurement of marketing effectiveness and Web security risk applications. Figure 5 illustrates an application of the MCQCM to evaluate the effectiveness of an advertising campaign for the games industry. The level of registered confidence reflects the relative success of the advertising campaign in brand recognition. We further intend on creating similar tools using the same technology for application in these fields.

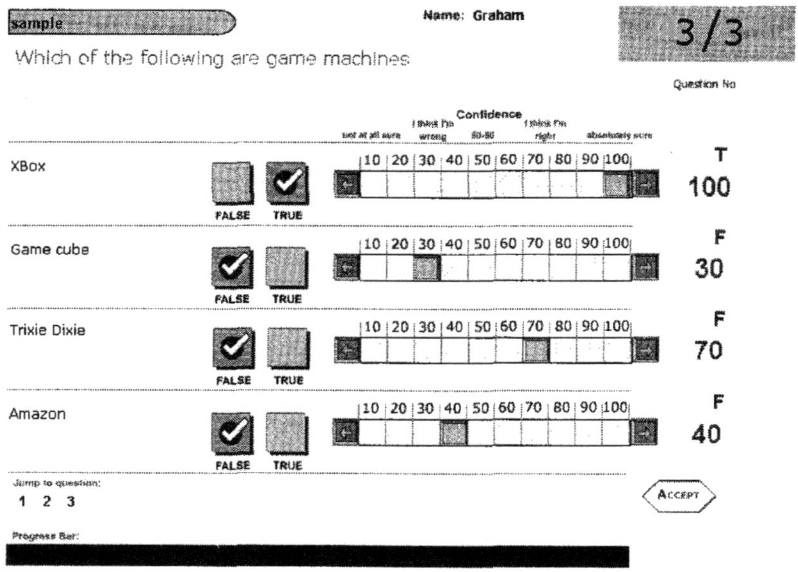

Fig. 5. Application of MCQCM to a marketing strategy evaluation

References

1. Principle and Standards for School Mathematics: National Council of Teachers of Mathematics - Standards 2000 Project Chpt 2 (2000)
2. Doebbert J (1999): Benchmarking the Learning Environment (Technology). National Centre of Research in Vocational Education (Copa & Ammentorp press) Chpt 5 http://vocserve.berkeley.edu/abstracts/MDS-1108/MDS-1108-CHAPTER-5.html
3. Black, P and William, D: Assessment and Classroom. Learning Assessment in Education, Vol 5 March P. 7-74 (March 1998)
4. Black, P and William, D: Inside the Black Box: Raising Standards Through Classroom Assessment. Phi Delta Kappan October 1998· Volume 80· Number 2 P 139-149 (1998) http://www.pdkintl.org/kappan/kbla9810.htm
5. Perrenoud, P: Towards a Pragmatic Approach to Formative Evaluation. Assessment of Pupils' Achievement: Motivation and School Success (Amsterdam: Swets and Zeitlinger) P92 (1991)
6. Learner-Centered Psychological Principles: Guidelines For The Teaching Of Educational Psychology In Teacher Education Programs http://seamonkey.ed.asu.edu/~gene/TEPSIG/apa-principles.html (1995)
7. Diamond GA, and Forrester JS (1983): An Epistemologic Model of Clinical Judgment. Am J Med 75: P129-137
8. Davidoff F (Feb 1995): Confidence Testing- How to Answer a Meta-Question. American College of Physicians Observer http://www.acponline.org/journals/news/feb95/conftest.htm

9. Pollard, G and Clark, D: An Optimal Scoring System of Multiple Choice Competitions and an Analysis of Candidates Responses Under Two Different Methods of Scoring. Mathematics Competitions Vol 2 No 2 P33-36 (1989)
10. Brown TA and Shuford EH (1973): Quantifying Uncertainty Into Numerical Probabilities for the Reporting of intelligence. Defence Advanced Research Projects Agency Report R-1185-ARPA. Santa Monica, Calif., Rand Corp
11. Klinger, A: Experimental Validation of Learning Accomplishment. Frontiers in Education. Technical Report No. 970019 (1997)
12. Paul, J: Improving Education Through Computer Based Alternative Assessment Methods. People and Computers Vol 9 (1994)
13. Farrell, G and Leung, Y: Designing an Online Self-Assessment Tool Utilizing Confidence Measurement. Conference Proceedings IFIP 8.4 WG (2002) [in press]
14. Pollard, G: Scoring in Multiple Choice Examinations. Math. Scientists Vol 10 P93-97 (1985)
15. Pollard, G: Scoring to Remove Guessing in Multiple Choice Exams. Math Education Science Technology Vol 20 No2 P 33-36 (1986)
16. Pollard, G: Further Scoring Systems to Remove Guessing in Multiple Choice Examinations. Mathematics Competitions Vol 2 No 1 P 27-43 (1993)
17. Kehoe J (1995): Writing Multiple Choice Test Questions Practical Assessment, assessment and evaluation ERIC Clearinghouse on Assessment and Evaluation. Vol 4 (9) http://ericae.net/pare/getvn.asp?v=4&n=9
18. Frary R (1995): More multiple-choice item writing do's and don'ts. Practical Assessment, assessment and evaluation ERIC Clearinghouse on Assessment and Evaluation. Vol 4 (11) http://ericae.net/pare/getvn.asp?v=4&n=11
19. Bandura, A: Self-Evaluation and Self-Efficacy Mechanisms Governing the Motivational Effects of Goal Systems. Journal of Personality and Social Psychology Vol 45,No 5, P 1017-1028 (1983)
20. Betz, N and Hackett, G: Manual for the Occupational Self-Efficacy Scale http://seamonkey.ed.asu.edu/~gail/occse1.htm 5/6/2002
21. Fullarton, S: Confidence in Mathematics: The effects of gender. Geelong: Deakin University National Centre for Research and Development in Mathematics Education (1993)
22. Bandura, A: Self-Efficacy: Toward a Unifying Theory of Behavioral Change. Psychological Review. Vol 84,No 2, P 191-215 (1977)

REFACTORING THE APPLICATION INFRASTRUCTURE FOR BUILDING OPEN-DISTANCE -LEARNING WEBSITES IN THE GERMAN LITERATURE AND LANGUAGE DOMAIN

ALEXANDER SCHATTEN, MARIAN SCHEDENIG, A MIN TJOA

Institute for Software Technology and Interactive Systems, Vienna University of Technology, Favoritenstr. 9-11/188, 1040 Vienna, Austria
E-mail: {schatten, schedenig, tjoa}@ifs.tuwien.ac.at

Growing interest in german literature initiated two succeeding projects to provide content about "Austrian literature round 1900" and "Austrian Exile-Literature since 1933" as well as the technical infrastructure for content management and publication. This infrastructure is platform independent and based upon open standards like XML and mainly on open source libraries and tools. Publication is done to multiple formats like HTML and PDF from the same sources. From the first project to the second project it turned out, that standards and tools were subjected to significant changes, as well as experiences from the first project led to new concepts in the second project. Hence a complete refactoring of the application-code from the first project was performed. The experiences of this multi-step process is the main focus of this article.

1 Open Distance Learning - Literature in Internet

In the past years a steadily growing interest in german literature was experienced. Hence the department of german literature and language science of the University Salzburg initiated two open-distance learning projects in cooperation with the institute for software technology and interactive systems of the Vienna university of technology. This paper describes the technical aspects of these projects, mainly focused to the refactoring steps between the two succeeding projects.

The first project, "Literatur in der Wiener Moderne" (Literature round 1900) was started in Spring 1999 and finished in summer 2000 [8], with the (technical) goal to create a content management and publication system build with open standards beeing highly flexible in the publication process. The second project "Exilliteratur" (Exile-Literature) was started immediately after the first project and ended in spring 2002.

The first project now has about 600 registered users and more then 100 exams made by students, with a focus not only to students in Austria, but also to eastern countries like Russia, Croatia, ... The information provided by this project turned out to be a valuable and accepted source for students in different countries interested in this specific area of literature. The second project will start the "public phase" in the next month, so no practical experiences are available yet.

2 Literature Projects

2.1 *Basic Concepts*

The content is based on statical created html pages for main navigational purpose or few special features. The main content is managed in a content management sytem published automatically using templating mechanisms.

The automatically generated information is structured mainly into lectures, articles and multimedia elements (images, original texts, video, urls, ...). Where lectures are bigger in size then articles and contain the "main information" to learn from. Articles are additional information; for example articles about authors, or specific "side-topics". From the first to the second project both categories have been extended. While "articles" meant information about authors in the first project, different types of articles (extensible) are available in the second project. Also different types of lectures are available in the second project. This data is provided twofold: for easier online reading in html "chunks" and for printing in portable document format (PDF).

Besides the automatically generated information there are additional (statical created) sections like special prepared topics in "museums" or a "walk" through famous literature coffe houses in Vienna.

Keywords are registered during the entering of the information, not by automatical indexing mechanisms. As a consequence, the keywords are of very high quality and provide a valuable additional access schema for users.

In the second project "interactive elements" as well as new multimedia types (video, audio) have been added. The interactive elements allow students-interaction with the system by answering different types of questions. A deeper understanding of the lectures is expected by the use of this new feature.

2.2 *Cooperation*

The project successful cooperation was a a demanding task by many reasons. Not only the communication between different "scientific cultures" namely information technology, german literature and language science and design needed time and professional engagement on all sides. Moreover the teams were dislocated: Literature and Language Scientists are located mainly at University of Salzburg, Graz, but also in Vienna, information technology and design is located in Vienna.

Good project management, and the efforts on all sides to communicate even difficult tasks in a way, that all project members are able to understand the consequences, as well as using all possible communication facilites leaded to successes in both projects.

2.3 *Focus of Projects*

The Open Distance Learning Project "Literature round 1900" was the initial project and build the foundation of cooperation and concepts as described above.

The Online-Project "Österreichische Exil-Literatur seit 1933" (Austrian Exile-Literature since 1933) is dealing with emigration and exile in the 20th century. The projects aim to present qualified material anbout the topics to students and to the interested public in general. The educational material of this project is a foundation for approaching this topic in higher schools as well as in universities and education for adults.

Especially for the open-distance-learning, interactive elements are designed to provide the possibility of a deeper interaction for the students with the material. Working with these interactive pages are also a part of the evaluation process in examinations.

Part of the open-distance-learning project is also a cooperation with other universities for students to make exams about the exile-literature topic (e.g. universities in Innsbruck, Debrecen, Vechta, Leiden, St. Petersburg, Rijeka, VU Amsterdam).

2.4 *References*

The literature projects can be found under: http://www.literaturepochen.at (which is the main site). It has to be notified, that the main part of the information is in German.

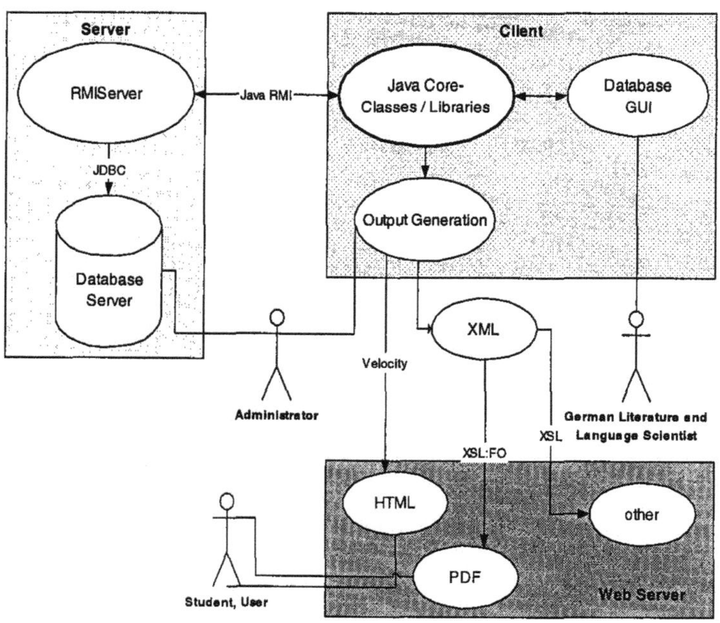

Fig 1. Conceptual Overview over the Content Management System

3 Used Technology and Experiences

3.1 Relational Database Management System (RBDMS)

Data is stored in RDBM systems. This turned out to be a useful approach to ensure the flexible access to the information and the integrity of the complex data structure. Moreover the modular approach allowed the easy move from a desktop database system in the first project to a RDBM server in the second project. We decided to use an open source database server (Interbase).

3.2 Java

Platform independent use of all parts of the application was a goal in both projects. The use of the Java programming language turned out to be a good decision by many reasons: First of all it was possible to run the applications and libraries on Windows clients as well as on Linux server systems. Additionally a huge pool of (mainly open source) tools and libraries are available (e.g. the Apache pool) which facilitated the implementation of several parts of the application. Finally Java allows good object oriented design and development of stable and very performant applications that run on different target platforms.

Connection between the different system parts (database, GUI-client server communication) was performed using standard Java protocols like Java Database Connectivity (JDBC) and Remote Method Invocation (RMI).

The data is published out of the database, partly using XML as mentioned later. These steps are performed using Apache java-xml parser, xslt and xsl:fo libraries and template engines [5].

3.3 Client / Server Architecture

In the first project the user interface was part of the desktop database, which turned out to be fine for rapid-prototyping, but a hard to maintain implementation for productive use. Consequently also the user interface was rebuild in the Java language, which allowed the re-use of libraries needed for different parts of the project. Moreover also the user interface is platform independent running on Windows, Unix and MacOS systems.

3.4 XML

The use of XML [4] is an essential part since the beginning of the first project. There are multiple reasons, why choosing XML proved to be a good decision. First of all, the produced content is extremly valuable also in future, honestly seen, eventually more valuable then the technological infrastructure. By transforming the complete information into XML a future use also in completely different systems will be possible, hence the survival of the content should be guaranteed.

Moreover using XML as intermidiate format gives us the flexibility for publishing different output formats as described below [7].

3.5 Template Engines

The production of html is done using template engines. This allows the easy integration of sample html documents produced by the designer into the production system. Moreover, exchange or modifications of the design is possible also very late or even at the end of the production cycle.

3.6 Output Format

As mentioned already the two main output formats (for production use) are html (for on-line learning) and portable document format (PDF) for printing the information.

In research versions even other output formats were tested. The use of XML as intermediate format allows flexible and easy production for other systems, like open e-book or version for other mobile clients like PDAs. Test-productions for the rocket e-book were performed using XSL transformations and basically worked good. However, e-book formats were not yet integrated into the production version, as no significant impact is seen in the market (and even worse, different formats are available) and the students could be more confused by this option.

The "raw xml" format could be offered directly or in (xsl) modified version in future editions for data exchange purpose or web services (library systems...), if necessary or desired.

The complete system is illustrated in Fig.1.

4 Refactoring Revisited

4.1 "Wiener Moderne" to "Exile"

The development of content management and publishing system for this type of open distance learning project turned out to be a phase of multiple refactoring steps. There are many reasons for this process. First of all: the technologies used from the beginning (XML, XSL, template engines) developed very fast, requiring adaptations and re-builds. But more important: the literature projects are among the first projects of this type as well as the cooperation. This required some time to find out the best solutions for the aimed goals and find the right interaction mechanism for the users and for the german literature and language scientists. An easy user interface to enter the data was necessary, the design had to be flexible, and different output formats were required, beeing open for future developments (as described above).

Not only did the technology change, also the size of the second project increased compared to the first project. For example: the second project had the double amount of lectures compared with the first one, additional interactive elements, ...

Just to give a brief quantitative overview about the size of the second project. It contains about 600 articles, 40 lectures, more than 3000 keywords, nearly

5000 multimedia elements (this includes URLs and literature references, but also more than 650 images and about 40 videos and 120 audio files). From this "raw" data about 40 pdf files and nearly 12.000 html files are generated.

After experiences with the first project, several extensions were desired:

- Adaptions in many parts of the infrastructure to fulfill the needs of the new project.
- New interactive elements, to allow interaction of students with the system.
- A client server architecture for better data management and hence a new user interface to enter the content.
- A new design for the second project.
- Additional Multimedia Elements (video, audio, ...).

4.2 Client / Server Architecture

The first project was based on a desktop database, which had some advantage in terms of rapid prototyping, but big disadvantages in data-safty, security and flexibility. In the new project a client/server architecture was selected. This allowed the separation of user interface and data, which has many advantages:

- Multi User capability
- Backup of Data is easier and straighforward on the server side.
- Generation of Output is more flexible.
- Update of User Interface is easier, as a clean separation between data and User Interface is done

4.3 Template Engine

When the first project was started, we decided to write an own template mechanism for HTML production, with the requirement, that it is easily possible to use html-stylesheets produced by the designer as template for production of the html output. After finishing the first project several open source projects showed up, that implemented other even more powerful template mechnisms.

The experiences showed, that this approach was very useful for our system, as it allowed easily to cooperate with the designer, who supported the technicians with sample html files, which then could easily be transformed to templates for html production.

On the other hand, our template engine turned out to be not flexible enough for the second project. As beeing "standard" conform was always a design goal, we decided to switch to the Apache Velocity [2] template mechanism.

This library is powerful and flexible. It is not only a "simple" template mechanism that allows to "set variables" in a html template, but even allows to use java objects inside the templates. So the "template itself" can call java classes and e.g. database classes to get data. This allows a manifold use of this system. Lately one of us suggested a system, where the complete html generation process could be template-driven, not application driven. This might be a future extension, or part of a future refactoring step.

4.4 XSL

The development of Extensible Stylesheet Language (XSL) standards [1] and even more important xsl tools between 1999 and 2002 was a significant one. This had consequences considering our new project: Not only all xmp parser libraries had to undergo main updates, we also decided to use XSL formatting objects (FO) language for PDF production. In the first project no useful FO processors were available, so we implemented a multiple step PDF generation using an IBM alphaworks library to generate LaTeX out of XML, then PDF out of LaTeX. Though the results were pretty good, the libraries were flawed and the generation process needed manual work, which was off course not desired.
Currently an open source formatting objects processor is available in the Apache XML project (FOP) [3]. Though FOP is also in an early stage, the functionality is sufficient for our purpose. The consequence is a much better integrated and flexible product as a combination of XSLT and XSL:FO can be used to generate the PDF documents. This is possible automatically without the need to do manual interactions.

4.5 Documentation

Documentation of the new application is done using javadoc for sourcecode documentation and UML (unified modeling language) for a system overview.

4.6 Compatibility between Projects

Refactoring steps often have consequences in terms of compatibility to old data. This is true especially in our case, as we did not only make a refactoring of the initial project applicaiton, but also extended it in many ways. So every new feature had to be reviewed in terms of compatibility with the old data and goals of previous work. This sometimes conflicts with the ideas of the new project manager, and compromises have to be worked out. Currently work is done to update the "old" data and templates for working with the new system.

4.7 Refactoring Steps – in a Nutshell

Especially in research project, when it is not always precisely clear in which direction a system will evolve, it sometimes is a good decision to redo complete systems, or a least big parts of it, also to increase the quality of the design after experiences with previous version. This was what we decided to do after beginning the second project. Nearly every single stone of the first infrastructure was turned and refactored.

The process could be seen as a multi-step approach towards a system useful for many cultural open-distance-learning projects:

- The first project started as a learning phase, not only in technological sense, but also, and maybe most important, in terms of cooperation between different cultures of science.

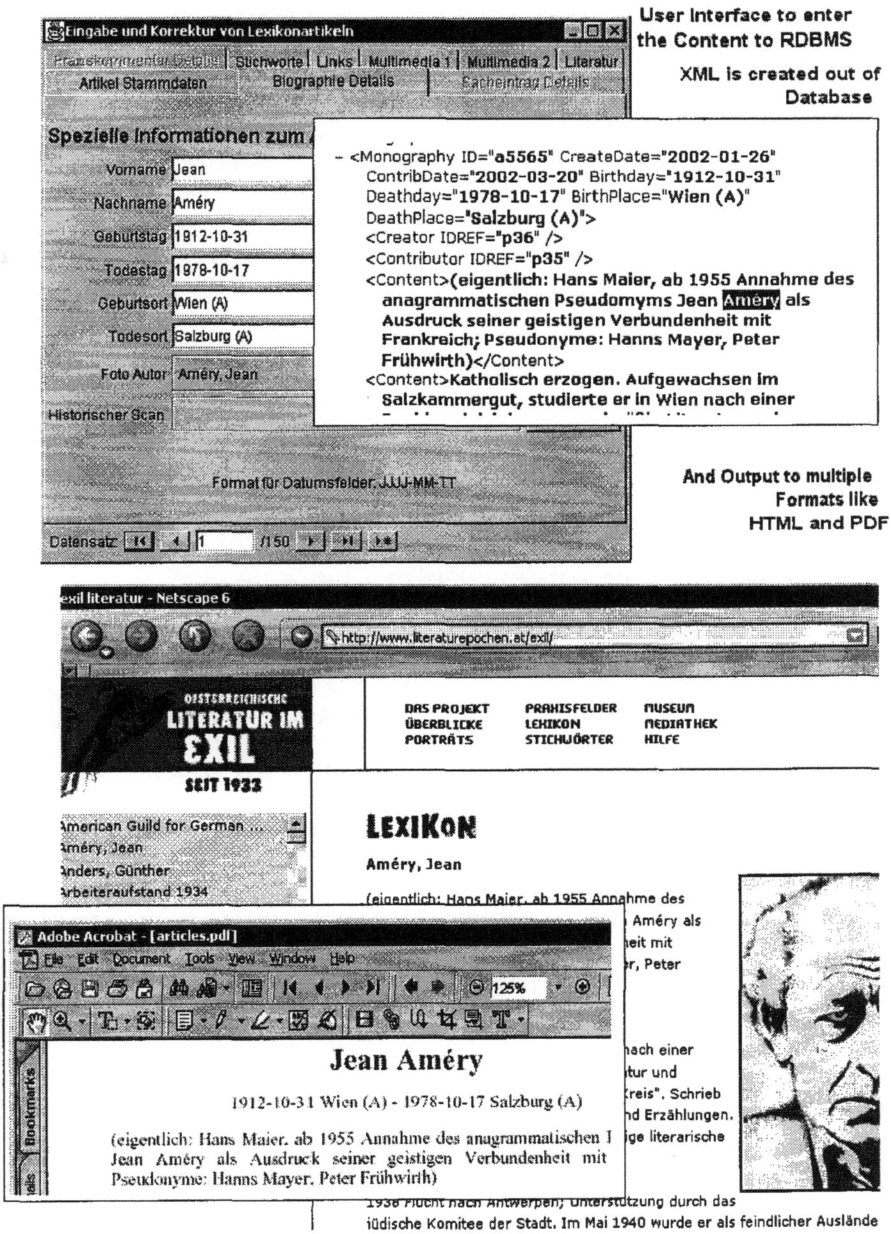

Fig 2. Illustration of the Publishing Process

- In the first & second project there was off course an inception and production phase.
- The start of the second project was used as turning-point. All parts of the system were discussed, following the experiences with the first system, and a complete refactoring was performed as described above. The quality of the new system hence is improved in many ways compared with the first version(s).
- As a (preliminary) last step, additional specific refactoring is desired for a new project allowing to add flexibility in some parts of the publication and fixing several issues in the Client/Server system, which is a new part since the second project.

References

1. Adler et al. (2001), XSL (XSLT and XSL:FO W3C Recommendation) http://www.w3.org/TR/xsl/
2. Apache Jakarta Velocity Project: http://jakarta.apache.org/velocity/index.html
3. Apache FOP (Formatting Object Processor) Project: http://xml.apache.org/fop/index.html
4. Bray, Tim and Sperberg-McQueen, C.M. (1996), Initial XML draft, http://www.w3.org/TR/WD-xml-961114.html
5. Connolly, Dan (1997), Extensible Markup Language (XML), http://www.w3.org/XML
   Sun (1999), JavaTM Technology, XML: A Perfect Match, http://java.sun.com/xml/
6. Harold, Elliotte Rusty, XML Bible, IDG Books (1999)
7. Leventhal, Michael and Lewis, David and Fuchs, Matthew, Designing XML Internet Applications, Prentice Hall PTR, Upper Saddle River (1998)
8. Schatten, A. and Tjoa, A Min and Zelewitz, K. and Stockinger, J. (2000), Austrian Literature Moving to Cyberspace - A Framework for Building an Open Distance Learning Website using Platform Independent Standards Like XML, *ED-Media Conference Montreal 2000*

THE DESIGN AND IMPLEMENTATION OF VIRTUAL LABORATORY PLATFORM IN INTERNET

WANG JIANXIN[1,2] CHEN SONGQIAO[1] JIA WEIJIA[2] AND PEI HUIMIN[1]

[1]*Department of Computer Science, Central South University, Changsha 410083, China*
[2]*Department of Computer Eng. & IT, City University of Hong Kong, Kowloon, Hong Kong*
E-mail:jxwang@mail.csu.edu.cn

With the development of the modern long-distance education, it is very important to study the virtual laboratory, which is a key part of the long-distance education resource. This paper introduces the project of architecture and implementation of the virtual laboratory platform to overcome the shortage of the current virtual laboratory. It also illustrates the key design and implementation technologies of its server and client in details. There are some new features in our virtual laboratory platform: (1) It is base on the general virtual laboratory and use component to provide the concrete fscilities to construct laboratories in various domains. (2) It provides visual tools to design experimental process. (3) It introduces and creates the object of experimental process dynamically, and just downloads relative implement documents and resource documents according to the requirements of the clients. As the result, it will resuce the flow of network. (4) It uses multithead technique to improve implement efficiency. (5) Laboratory equipments, such as algorithms and instruments, can be developed with component design to improve the development efficiency, to reuse the software, and to expand the function of virtual laboratory easily. (6) It uses Java in client, so it is independent of platform, Safe and strong. (7) It makes use of CORBA to integrate various objects and to accomplish distribute process.

1 Introduction

With the development of Internet, a profound reformation on education mode have been motivated by modern long-distance education. The Internet is now extensively used as connectivity and reference tool for commercial, personal, and educational purposes. In education, the Internet opens a variety of new avenues and methodologies for enhancing the experience of learning as well as expanding educational opportunities [1]. The remote education based on Internet has become a important education mode in many unversities and middle schools. The China Ministry of Education has granted more than thirty colleges to develop modern remote education. Developing remote education need abundant resources, such as course teaching contents, virtual laboratory and so on. There are many web sites which provide learning software for some courses [2]. How to provide a remote learning platform was discuessed in [3,4].

Virtual Laboratory (VL) can be classified into two categories acording to its role. One is to provid remote controlling methods for real instruments to do some experiments[1,5]. Another is to provid virtual instruments for users to do experiments in remote way [6]. In this paper, we mainly discuss how to design a platform for the later virtual laboratory. Due to the cost of the experimental laboratories, the new teaching methods and the remote education, the virtual laboratory with virtual instruments has increased steadily in recent years.

VL provides the students learing in anywhere and anytime with a convenient expriment enviornment. Many famous universities, such as Oxford and Carnegie Mellon, have established their VLs. Some VLs have opened to users through Internet. In Oxford's chemical information industry center, students are allowed to develop their chemical experiment through Internet. In Carnegie Mellon U, students can conduct their circuit properties analysis in VL. Some products of VLs mainly provide certain subject's experiments by which students can conveniently study or do some research. But this products have some great shortages, such as interaction, extendsion, reuse of software. For examples, the students can not define their own experiments, can not add some experiment devices developed by themselves to the laboratory, so that many of the devices can not be reused. In order to solve these problems, we propose the architecture of VL platform. In the architecture, the experiments devices are provided by the way of components. The main goals pursued in our research and implementation were:

- Users can self-design experimental processes. They can select appropriate virtual instruments to construct an experiment.
- Users can insert some virtual instruments, which were designed by themselves into the laboratory for experiments.
- The platform provides a user-friendly interface.
- The platform can provide an interface with some other experimental tools, such as Matlab.
- The platform is security, efficiency and flexibility.

The rest of the paper is organized as follows. In section 2, the architecture of our VL is proposed. Section3 describes the design and implementation of the system in www server and Section 4 discusses the design and implementation of the system on client side. Section 5 concludes the paper.

2 The Architecture of Virtual Laboratory

According to the goals in our research and implementation and the experimental features (such as digital image processing, digital signal processing, digital communication principle, computer network technology and so on), the architecture of VL based on Internet was proposed in Figure 1.

The architecture of a VL falls into two parts: server and clients. The server mainly contains: the OLE automation interface with Matlab which uses Matlab computing engine; COM components supplied by the third part; CORBA sever components written by using Matlab library. Clients are Java Bean containers and Java Bean components. These components fall into two types: one is running in server by using server component object; the other is running in the client directly.

Based on the architecture, the virtual laboratory platform can be implemented. Some components should be design in one course. Then by assembling these components, the experiments can be done in the VL platform.

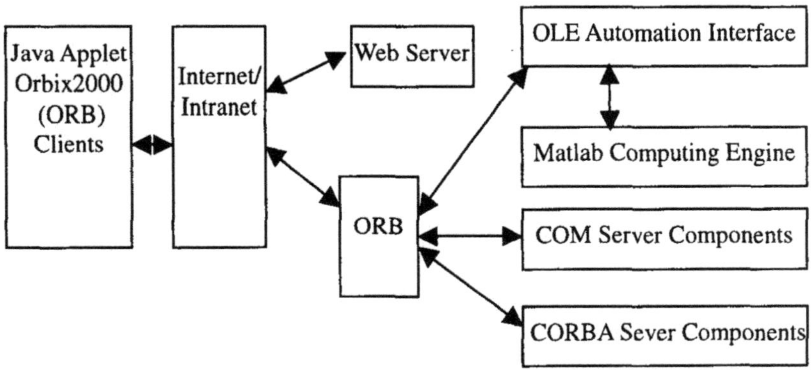

Figure 1. The architecture of virtual laboratory.

3 Implementing the Server

Because there are many local VLs, which are designed in Matlab, we use Matlab to act as the server computing engine to interpret the implementation of OLE automation interface. Matlab is one of the important tools for virtual instruments and computing now, which provides a great amount of function packages including digital image processing, digital signal processing, signal emulation, artificial intelligence, pattern recognition and so on. Matlab also provides strong, simple script language and c/c++ or other languages' interface. In general, there exist three methods to use Matlab.

1. In Matlab integrated environment, we can write Matlab script language program and run the program directly.
2. By using the OLE automation interface provided by Matlab, we can call the Matlab in C++,VB or others. Matlab will activate auto automatically and run the script language program, then return the result to the requesters.
3. By using C/C++, Fortran or other languages interface, we can call the Matlab library function, and then compile to executing file. This first method is not fit for sever computing engine in virtual laboratory.

The second method is not efficient by the reason of Matlab running the script language program. On the other hand, this method is very simple. The third method is the most efficient, but writing the program is more complicated than the others methods. Matlab provides a tool by which you can transform Matlab program to C/C++ program. The tool may simplify the process of writing programs. But such codes may not be understood easily, and bring many difficulties on how to modify them. In the implementation, the second and third methods were used. If the virtual instruments is used frequently and requires high running speed, the third method should be used. In the second method, users who are familiar with Matlab may submit their Matlab script program through client components, so that they can use the function of Matlab in the virtual laboratory.

By using CORBA (Common Object Request Broker Architecture), the Java applet can communicate with CORBA sever components written in C++ language, COM components and OLE automation interface in the client of VL. CORBA is an industrial criterion defined by OMG, which are used to realize the communication among different type of objects and distributed process. CORBA provides the distributed computation application with a program interface and module which are independent of platforms, program languages, network protocols, which make it more fit for the new distributed application and system integration. Because of the existence of COM, OMG define their interaction architecture between COM and CORBA. In the system, the server COM components (including automation) are mapping to CORBA object by the way of bridge. The bridge is used to map client requests into aim object and issue the information transparently.

COM (Component Object Module) is a kind of object model, which issue components. COM also defines the interaction criterion among components, and provides the necessary environment in which components run. A great number of components have been supplied as COM/OLE, for example, in this system, Matlab computing engine has been offered as a component. Thus a CORBA client can accesses the components transparently, consequently, reducing the workload in the system development substantially.

4 Implementing the Client

Components and object-oriented technologies are used for the implementation of client for VL, which are programmed in Java language and offer users with applet program embed in HTML files. So the VL is independent of platforms, safe and scalable. Only with the browser that supports Java, one can do the experiments in the VL. On the client side, the VL is designed as a common platform on which users can perform their experiments including digital image processing, digital communication system, digital signal processing and so on. Moreover, the experimental instruments for each course are offered as components. The VL has many properties, such as creating components object dynamically, setting the object properties, calling the object methods, responding the object events and providing the communication approach among components. So users can do their experiments by assembling these components. To realize these functions, the main technologies were used in the implementation of client in the virtual laboratory as follows.

4.1 The reflection technology in Java

Reflection is a feature in the Java^{TM} programming language. It allows an executing Java program to examine or "introspect" upon itself, and manipulate internal properties of the program. For example, it is possible for a Java class to obtain the names of all its members and display them.

While the client of the virtual laboratory runs in Internet, so the number and size of the files that are transported in Internet will influence the running speed.

With the increment of instruments, the number of the transported files may increase greatly. On the other hand, many downloaded instruments may not be used in the user's experiments. To avoid downloading these instruments, the instrument is encapsulated as independent Java Bean components with single function. This also can reduce the size of single instrument. By using the reflection in Java and the design mode of object plant, Java Beans container is constructed and object is introduced, loaded and created dynamically. Take the advantage of these technologies; users can simply download the necessary instruments for their experiments. The system is also open and scalable. Users may insert their own experiment instruments to the laboratory with the registered function provided by the VL.

4.2 Multi-thread technology

A thread is a path of execution through a program. Single threaded programs have one path of execution, and multi-threaded programs have two or more paths of execution. Single threaded programs can perform only one task at a time, and have to finish each task in sequence before they can start another. For most programs, one thread of execution is all you need, but sometimes it makes sense to use multiple threads in a program to accomplish multiple simultaneous tasks [7].
The advantages of multithread is following:

1. The user's interface will be more flexible. During the experiment need to process a great number of calculation or transport data files with great size, a single thread program will bring a lot of problems. For example, the system may not be able to respond client requests in time and get the running information or break running experiment off with single thread. However, multi-thread programming can solve these problems.
2. Improving the running speed. Considering distributed process, multiprocessor system, multi-thread program can let the unrelated devices run in the same time, so that save the computing time.
3. Displaying the dynamic process of data transportation such that many communication ports send signal to each other at the same time in network simulating experiment and oscillograph receives multi-signal in digital communication experiments.

4.3 XML technology

XML, Extensible Markup Language, is a text-based markup language for defining what information is as opposed to how it looks. In addition, XML is platform independent. The Java™ programming language and XML combined complement the portability of both technologies. In the VL, XML is used to save parameters of system and components, such as instruments provided by the system and classic experiments and so on. XML is structural and scalable, so that XML can be very useful to establish complex data model and to define the new marks. There is an example of the XML description of one instrument in Figure 2.

4.4 Plug-in

With the fast development of Java language, JDK (Java Developer Kit) updates very fast. Now, the edition of JDK is 1.3, but JDK 1.4 is released soon. However, the development speed of browser is slower than JDK. In order to run Java programs in these browsers, SUN has offered their resolving scheme. JVM (Java Virtual Machine) of higher edition embeds into browsers as plug-in. In this way, JDK codes may run in browsers of lower edition. For example, in our VL, JDK1.3.1 is used. In order to run these codes in IE or NetScape6.0, users must install the homologous plug-in. By using plug-in, a single buffer can be allocated for Java Applet, which is different from the buffer of the browser. Thus, the buffer content will not be replaced with other files such as html files. In this way, we can avoid downloading Java Applets repeatedly.

```
    ...
    <Class>
     <URL>CSU:/GetImage</name>
     <label>Get Image File </label>
     <Description>Get Image File, please input your file
name(URL format) in the "imageFile" parameter. The
device may read the file. Now the device only supports
JPEG and GIF format</Description>
     <Property>
      <Name>imageFile</Name>
      <Label>imageFile</Label>
      <Description>threshold value one</Description>
     </Property>
     <Method>
      <Name>readImage</Name>
      <Label>readImage</Label>
      <Description>read image file, output 24bit colorful
image
      </Description >
     </Method>
```

Figure 2. An example of the XML description of one instrument

5 A virtual lab for digital image processing

It is very difficult to learn the algorithms of digital image processing. The aim of this virtual is to provide the processing result of any algorithms, which will help people to master these knowledge quickly and effectively. The lab provides many standard algorithm components for showing the processing result. It also provides an interface that can be used by users to add the components designed themselves. The users can assemble these components that are provided by the lab and themselves. Then the users can quickly test a new digital processing algorithm and these properties make the lab more flexible and creative. Figure 3 shows the main interface of the lab. Figure 4 gives the interface of the output, which is the result of filtering experiment.

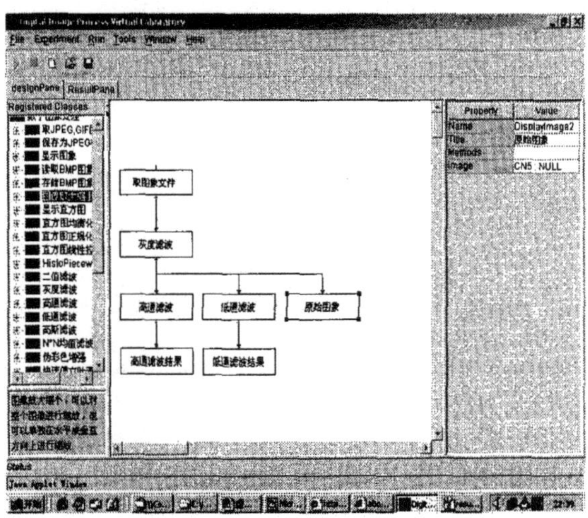

Figure 3. The main interface of digital image processing lab.

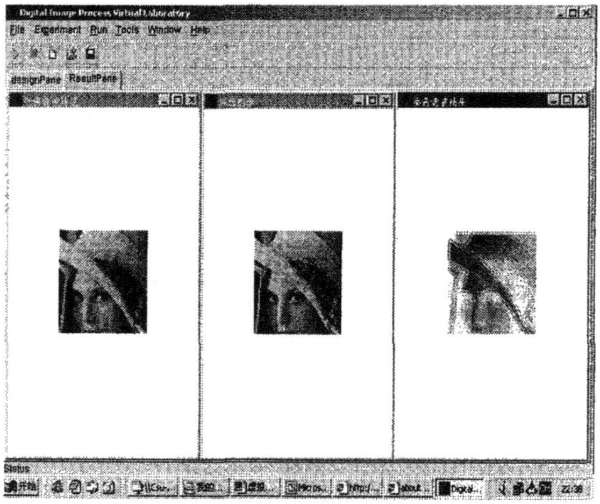

Figure 4. The processing result interface of filtering experiments.

There are the following functions in the lab:

- Design and run their experimental flow according to the requirement of users.
- Read and save the their experimental flow.
- Register user's component in the lab, which can expand the lab easily.
- Online help, which helps users to design the experiment flow and use the lab.
- Online classroom, which provides a web page for learning the course of digital image processing .

6 Conclusion

The development of remote education has played an important role in the whole world. Moreover, virtual laboratory based on Internet is the key on improving the remote education. In this article, the architecture of virtual laboratory based on Internet has been studied, and the main implementation scheme is discussed. The virtual laboratory has a good interaction ability, expansion, scalability, reusing components and independence of platforms.

There are some new features in our VL platform: (1) It is based on the general VL and use component to provide the concrete fscilities to construct laboratories in various domains. (2) It provides visual tools to design experimental process. (3) It introduces and creates the object of experimental process dynamically, and just downloads relative implementation documents and resource documents according to the requirements of the clients. As the result, it can resuce the flow of network. (4) It uses multithead technique to improve implementation efficiency. (5) Laboratory equipments, such as algorithms and instruments, can be developed with component to improve the development efficiency, to reuse the software, and to expand the function of virtual laboratory easily. (6) It uses Java in client, so it is independent of platform, Safe and strong. (7) It makes use of CORBA to integrate various objects and to accomplish distribute process.

We reliazed a virtual laboratory for digital image processing based on the platform, please visit the web site: http://202.197.66.180. We are currently building a virtual laboratory for digital communication based on the platform.

References

1. Chi Chung Ko, Chen, B.M, et.al. .A web-based virtual laboratory on a frequency modulation experiment. IEEE Transactions on Systems, Man, and Cybernetics, Part C: Applications and Reviews, 31(3): 295-303, 2001.
2. http://www.csu.edu.cn/CAI/network.html.
3. R. Pascoe. Introducing WWW technology into tertiary teaching: A personal perspective. in *Proc. North American Web Conf.*, Fredericton, NB, Canada, 1997.
4. J. Rosenblum and E. Healy. Developing an educational intranet. in *Proc. North American Web Conf.*, Fredericton, NB, Canada, Oct.1996.
5. F. J. Gomez, M. Cervera, J. Martinez. A World Wide Web based architecture for the implementation of a virtual laboratory. Proceedings of the 26th Euromicro Conference, 2000, pp: 56 –61.
6. A. Ferrero, V. Piuri A simulation tool for virtual laboratory experiments in a WWW environment. *IEEE Transactions on Instrumentation and Measurement*, 48(3): 741-746,1999.
7. http://developer.java.sun.com/developer/technicalArticles/Threads/applet/index.html.

INCOM: A COLLABORATIVE TOOL FOR DISTANCE LEARNING

K. M. NG, S. J. WONG AND Y. L. WONG

Department of Computing and Mathematics
Hong Kong Institute of Vocational Education (Chai Wan)
E-mail: ylwong@vtc.edu.hk

S. C. NG

School of Science and Technology
The Open University of Hong Kong
E-mail: scng@ouhk.edu.hk

The recent emergence of Internet technology changes the study life of people. Interactive e-learning will become popular in the decade. In this paper, we introduce an interactive collaborative tool for distance learning – InCom. InCom is a server-based system designed to provide instant messaging services, flexible control and easy administration for online distance learning applications. It relies on open architecture based on Jakarta Tomcat Server, Apache web server and Java Technology. Its functions include instant whiteboard and instant chat for future development of virtual classroom, online tutorial and online synchronous discussion forum so as to facilitate both online teaching and learning purposes.

1. Introduction

The concept and implementation of distance learning is changing with time and place. By allowing the use of text, graphics, audio, animation and video, internet has become an ideal media for distance learning [1]. The recent emergence of Internet and multimedia technology changes the study life of people. Online and distance learning through the web will become popular in the decade. Collaborative technologies such as messaging, document conferencing, chat system, multipoint videoconferencing, virtual classroom and online tutorial help create an interactive learning environment between students and instructors at different locations in a real-time situation.

In [2,3], the authors introduced a multimedia distance learning tool which enables online education through the internet – Learn@Net. Learn@Net is a server-based distance learning system designed to provide centralized, flexible control and easy administration of online distance learning applications. Its functions include virtual classroom, assignment handler, course material browser, discussion forum and online chat room so as to facilitate both online teaching and learning through the WWW. Nowadays, several common web-based learning systems providing similar functions are available in the market [4,5]. In this paper, a collaborative learning tool – Instant Communications (*InCom*) is introduced to enable instant messaging service [6] in synchronous distance learning environment. The system includes an interactive whiteboard and interactive chat environment for use in communicating in many forms of media.

It can be suitable for delivering online tutorial meetings and online discussions for distance learning.

This system, InCom, is a 3-tier web application which provides online instant messaging service between users by using java client programs. The client and server applications can be installed on different operating systems at anywhere. The whole system is divided into front-end and back-end portions. The front-end system is user interface, while the back-end system includes the application logic written in Java language. The server database is built on top of MySQL, Jakarta Tomcat Server and Apache web server.

Not only that InCom provides text-based communications, it also provides whiteboard to let users express in a more direct and effective way like the face-to-face discussion. It is extremely helpful in presenting difficult concepts such as mathematics and science subjects. This tool can greatly enhance the ability to explain mathematical concepts, or any concept for which a teacher would use a blackboard in the classroom.

Traditional chat room retrieves messages by transmitting the whole list of messages from the server to the clients. It is not efficient to traverse thousand messages on each request. In our system, message includes text, graphics and object; a message can be a string, a circle, a rectangle or etc. We use a technique which allows traversing only the changed messages. As a result, higher software performance, lower network usage, and higher flexibility to manipulate message are achieved.

2. Intended Users

- System administrators will be responsible to manage and maintain all aspects of the learning system such as users access rights, student registration and course registration.
- Instructors will be able to communicate through InCom with their students which in turn assists student learning using built-in collaborative tools.
- Students will access the system through the client program. They can benefit from the system by going through vigorous synchronous discussion with their instructors and fellow students.

3. General description of functions:

1. Registration
   1.1 User registration
      An on-line form is provided for users to register.. The user can use this system after registration.
2. Retrieve user information
   2.1 Update user information

Changing the personal information can be updated at any time through webpage.

2.2 Change password

Student can change password inside webpage.

3. Changing look and feel

MacOS, CDE, Metal, Windows look and feel are provided. An user may select his/her favorite interface.

4. Message Type

The types of messages can be classified as public message, private message and urgent message.

4.1 Public message

There is public message server. It allows every user to see the same message.

4.2 Private message

Each user maintains a list of users to whom the private messages are sent.

4.3 Urgent message:

Users can send urgent messages to other user.

4.4 Message alert

When an urgent message arrives in, the system uses a special sound or dialog box to alert the user.

5. Message Storage

Chating message can be saved on web (refer to output screen section).
Users can read the saved file through the webpage.

6. Drawing board

As a simple drawing board, it provides the standard drawing picture function.

6.1 Selection of a color from a color palette

6.2 Drawing different shapes such as rectangle or circle, straight line, and also free hand drawing

6.3 Moving, modification, rotation, or deletion of any objects drawn.

7. Administration tools:

It is used for maintaining the database and the user account:

7.1 Retrieve (Add new/update) data

Information in the database can be retrieved or updated, according to the users' requests.

8. Plug-in download

We will provide the link to the latest version of JRE (Java Runtime Environment).

4. System Architecture

Figure 1 shows the class (object) diagram of the system, which will be described in details in this section.

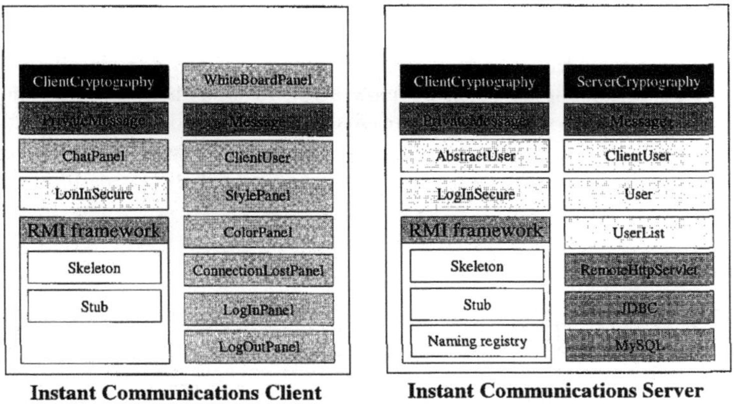

Figure 1: Partial Class Diagram of the Instant Communications (InCom)

RMI framework

The stub and skeleton

The Remote Method Invocation (RMI) framework (as shown in Figure 2) consists of a stub and a skeleton class, which are generated by `rmic`, a tool available in the JDK.

Figure 2 shows the steps of method call from the client to the server using RMI. The client sends a request to the server by invoking a method in the remote object – the server. The call will be passed directly to the stub, which marshals the input call parameters and handles all the details of communication setup to the skeleton. The skeleton is another class that resides on the server, it will accept the incoming call and unmarshal the parameters, it will then make the actual method call at the server side. The return value of the actual method will be sent back to the skeleton and then to the stub. It will in turn pass back to the client as if the method is called locally.

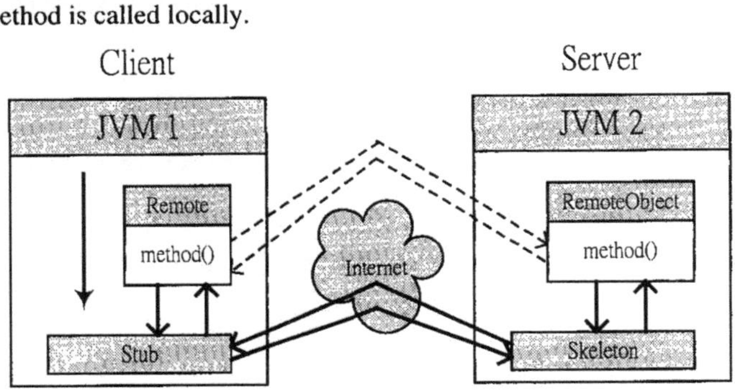

Figure 2: The Client and Server Model

Marshaling, delivery, and unmarshaling

The autogenerated client stub and remote object skeleton contain all the code involved in serializing details of a remote method call, dynamically invoking the remote method and serializing the results back to the caller. To perform data marshaling, they use a customized `ObjectOutputStream` class; delivery is performed over TCP/IP socket connections, and unmarshaling is performed with a customized `ObjectInputStream` class.

Naming registry

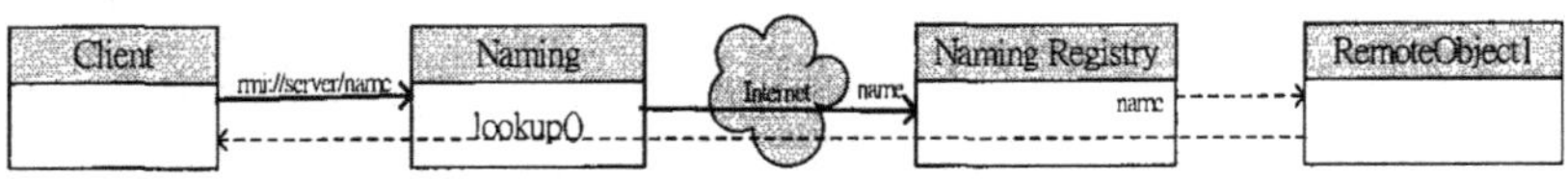

Figure 3: Naming Registry Lookup

Remote object must be registered with a naming service that allows clients to locate where it is running. The client connects to a naming registry and asks for a reference to a service registered under a given name. The naming registry then returns a remote reference to the object listed under that name.

When an object registers itself with the naming registry, it specifies a name under which it should be listed. Clients can then use the `java.rmi.Naming` class to obtain a remote reference to the object from the registry. The object is simply identified with a URL containing the host name on which the naming registry is running and the name under which the object is listed.

RemoteHttpServlet is a subclass of HttpServlet. RemoteHttpServlet provide basic RMI facility. Any servers that wish to use RMI can build top of it. Programmer doesn't need to rewrite the same code to let RMI works.

The commonly accepted way to run an RMI registry server is with the standalone Java program `rmiregistry`. However, it is easier and more efficient to let the RemoteHttpServlet create the registry itself. By starting one servlet container, both web service and rmi service will also start. The first servlet that needs the registry can create the registry. And, by starting the registry within a servlet, the registry runs using the same JVM as the servlet. That makes it possible to use just one JVM for the server, all of its servlets (the remote objects), and the registry.

AbstractUser is a super class of User and ClientUser. It provides basic definition of a user.

User class is used by server side only and it is subclass of AbstractUser class. If the client wants to have user information, he/she should ask ClientUser object. User class provide many information that system need to know such as current country in stage. Private matter personal information must not be able to view by third party. So ClientUser should be used instead.

ClientUser class provides information that is required in communication session. When chatting or playing with white board. It provides less information than User class, but it provides both enough information for user and protects user information from third party.

UserList make database communication simpler. Server doesn't need to talk to database directly. Server just need to know it is talking to a list of user, and doesn't care how to store data and retrieve data.

LogInSecure class make user log in to a system with higher security. It makes use of ClientCryptography to encrypt password. Then RMI help this operation. LogInSecure is use once and throwaway. When LogInSecure is received at server side, it make use of ClientCryptography to decrypt password. And server retrieve password from User object or database and decrypt it be ServerCryptography.

ClientCryptography is similar to ServerCryptography. They both have encryption and decryption method. If the key used by the client is same as the server, it is very dangerous. Client may be view server detail data. At this stage system use two different class. But it can be use one class instead, if higher classes encryption can be use such as RSA (Rivest-Shamir-Adleman).

ServerCryptography please refer to ClientCryptography.

Message is an abstract topic here. It can be a chat message, white board circle, a red line, etc. It is a basic element for communication channel to pass on.

PrivateMessage is similar to Message. It contain one more element receive user. This allow server to identify this message is a private message for someone else. This enable user to communicate with many user privately.

JDBC technology is an API that lets you access virtually any tabular data source from the Java programming language. It provides cross-DBMS connectivity to a wide range of SQL databases. Server makes use of this to communicate with MySQL database.

The ***MySQL*** database server is the world's most widely used open source database. Its ingenious software architecture makes it extremely fast and easy to customize. This is the central of user data and their relevant data.

The following part describes mainly the GUI components of the client.

StylePanel is a panel or frame that allow user to choice his own favorite frame such as cool frame, cute frame. And download appropriate frame from server, load it into client desktop.

ColorPanel which provide a color panel for user to choose colors.

LogInPanel is a panel allow user to type their username and password, and pass it to LogInSecure object for server authentication. If success plays a sound let user know.

LogOutPanel give a user interface for logging out the system.

ConnectionLostPanel is used by client and server. It can tell that the communication channel is lost. Connection lost can be detected by client itself or indicate by server when server want to shut down.

ChatPanel is a panel or a small window that make client to chat publicly or privately. The text color can be change by using ColorPanel, background color also can be change.

WhiteBoardPanel is a window that make client to draw publicly or privately. This provides many shape, many color.

5. Maintain session and Distribution of messages

When an InCom Client (Both Chat and Whiteboard) connects with the InCom Server (which using RemoteHttpServlet). The server will maintain a client in its list (remote reference in the term of RMI), it should drop client (remote object reference) from list when the client is logout or connection lost due to network error. The server can detect which client connection is lost (in programming when an exception is thrown).

The server needs to know what message belongs to which user. A public message or private message is used depending on the user's selection. It distributes messages and keeps a huge number of whiteboard objects. Users can play whiteboard with each user, a whiteboard can carry many objects. Imagine ten users connected to a server, one user is communicating with other nine users privately. Nine private whiteboards and one public whiteboard (in client WhiteBoardPanel) will be created.

6. InCom – Output screens

Figure 4 shows the startup screen of InCom client system.

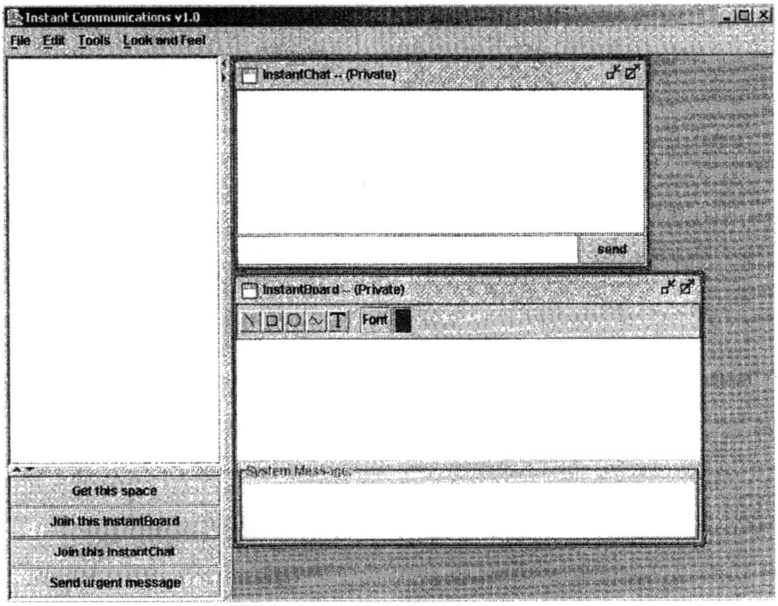

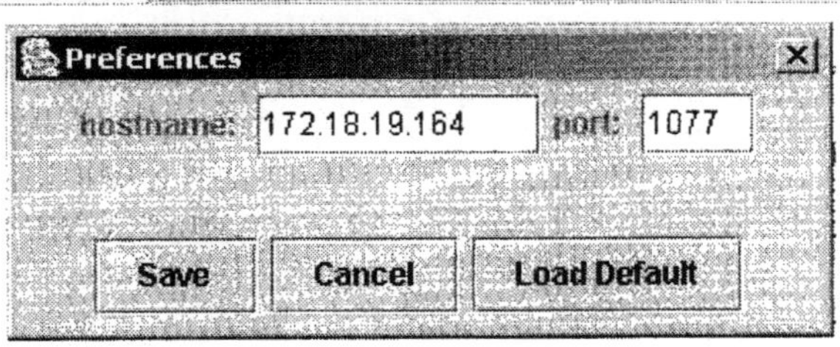

Figure 5: Preference dialog

To connect the server, the user can choose "Join public space" from the file menu. And a login dialog box will be shown as Figure 6. The "Space name" is optional for indicating the private communication on other InCom client system.

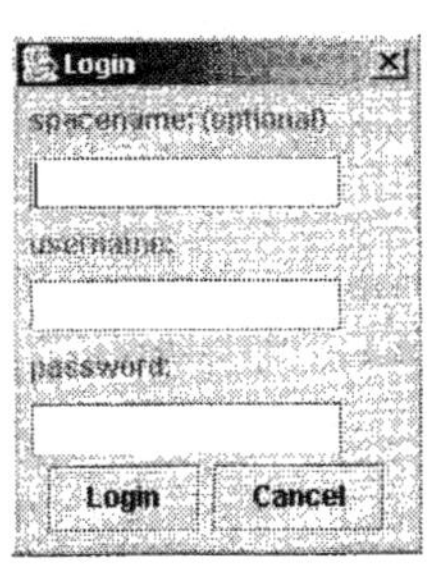

Figure 6: Login dialog

If the user is successful in connecting to the server, the following message will be displayed.

Figure 7: Welcome dialog

Instant Chat:

It is a text-based communication tool for talking with others in typing words. All the chat content can be saved on the web according to the user's choice, as shown in Figures 8 and 9.

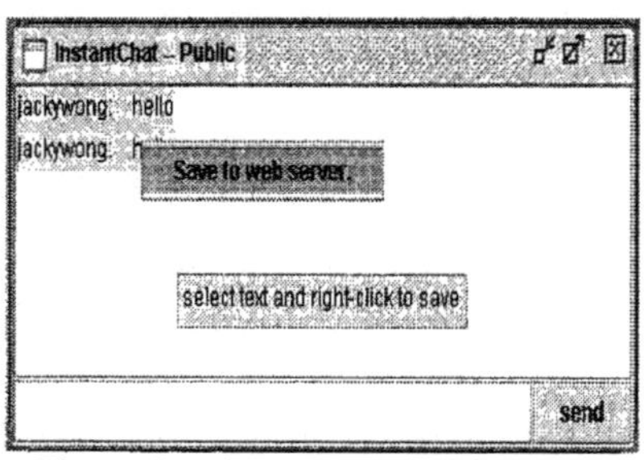

Figure 8: select text and right click to save to web

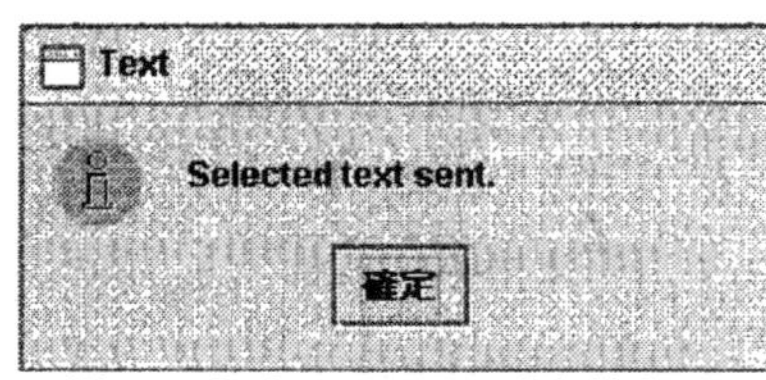

Figure 9: Save successful dialog

In this system, user can click "Change personal information" to edit your information. Also, user can click the file name to see what you have saved or select the row for deleting unused message content.

Instant Board:

InCom provides simple drawing functions for the user to draw picture.

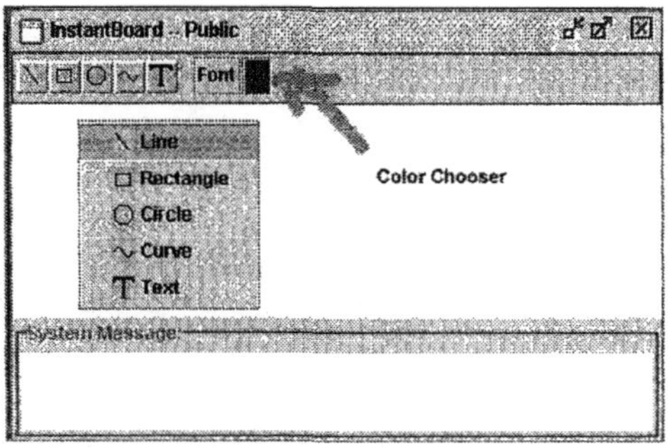

Figure 10: Drawing board.

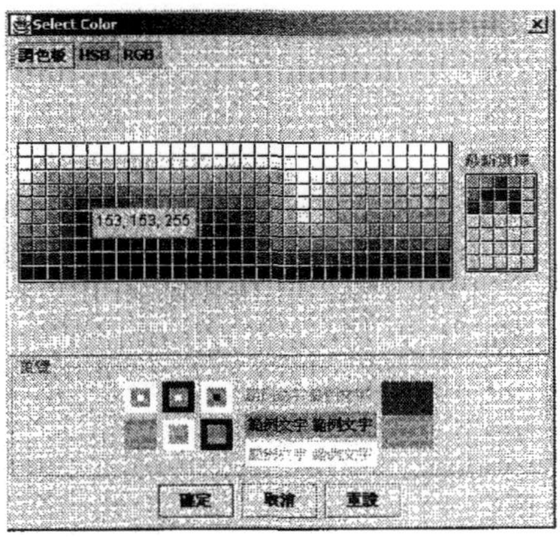

Figure 11: Color Chooser

Other than drawing functions, we also provide "Move", "Rotate" and "Delete" functions to edit the drawing object. To use these functions, the user firstly moves the mouse pointer to the object, which he/she wants to do editing, until it is highlighted. Then right-click the mouse will show the pop-up menu like Figure 12a for the user to select action. At last, the object can be dragged until the action is finished.

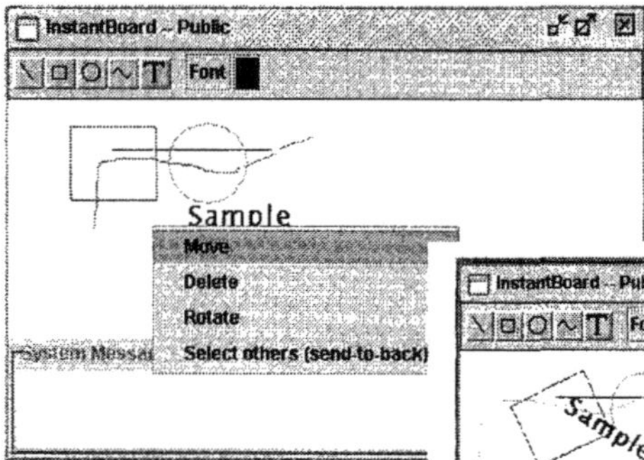

Figure 12a: Before editing

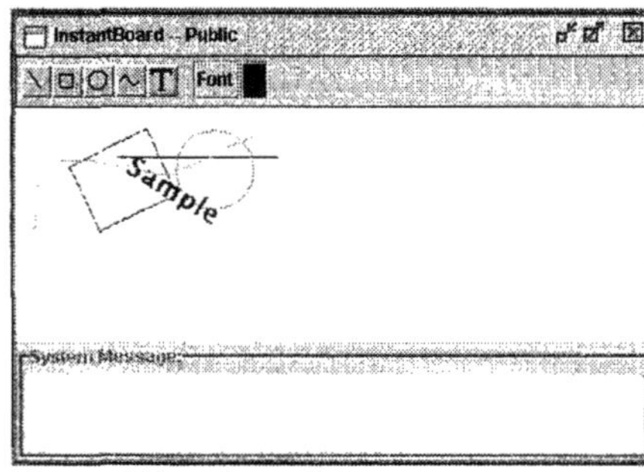

Figure 12b: After editing

At the bottom of the board, there is a system message area that shows any error message from the InCom server.

Urgent Messages:

User can send urgent message to any of the users in the board, as shown in Figure 13.
Other functions such as private communications with private board and chat are also provided in InCom.

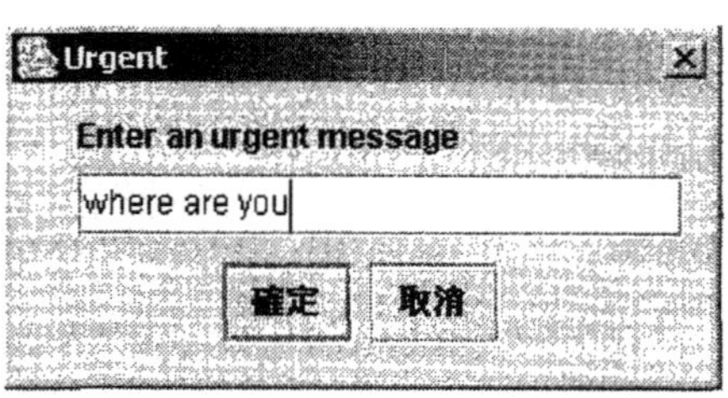

Figure 13a: Jacky sends an urgent message to Keith

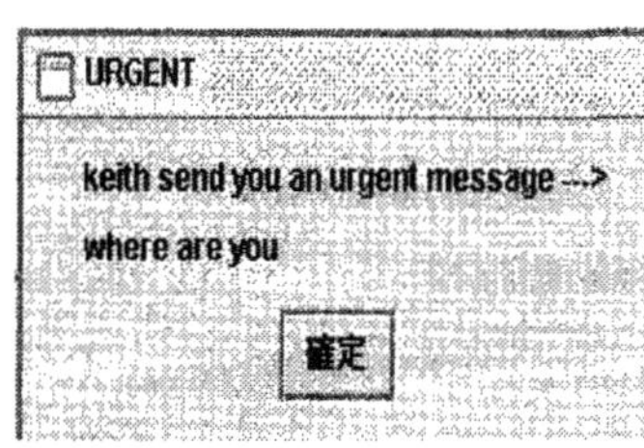

Figure 13b: Keith receives an urgent message.

7. Conclusions

An interactive collaborative tool – InCom has been developed to enable the users to learn at anytime and anywhere. The system relies on the open architecture based on Jakarta Tomcat Server, Apache web server, JAVA Technology and SQL. The system involves communication tools such as instant board and instant chat which can be used for online synchronous tutorial meetings for distance learning to be taken place on the web.

References

1. S. Adhvaryu and I. Balbin, "How Useful is Multimedia on the WWW for Enhancing Teaching and Learning?", *Proc. of 1998 International Conference on Multimedia Computing and Systems (ICMCS'98)*, Austin, USA, June 28 - July 31, 1998.
2. S. C. Ng, C. M. Ng, H. W. Tsang and L. M. Hung, "Learn@Net: An Integrated Multimedia System for Distance Learning", *Proc. of the 3rd International Conference on Computational Intelligence and Multimedia Applications (ICCIMA'99)*, New Delhi, India, 23-26 September, 1999, pp. 479-483.
3. H. W. Tsang, L. M. Hung, and S. C. Ng, "A Multimedia Distance Learning System on the Internet", *Proc. of the 1999 IEEE International Conference in Systems, Man and Cybernetics (SMC'99)*, Tokyo, Japan, 12-15 October, 1999, vol. II, pp. 243-246.
4. Murray W. Goldberg and Sasan Salari, An Update on WebCT (World-Wide-Web Course Tools) - a Tool for the Creation of Sophisticated Web-Based Learning Environments , *Proceedings of NAUWeb '97 - Current Practices in Web-Based Course Development*, Flagstaff, Arizona, June 12 - 15, 1997.
5. http://www.bu.edu/webcentral/research/courseware/about.html
6. R. Batchelder and D. Smith, "Instant Messaging: The Sleeping Giant", August 2001, http://www3.gartner.com/DisplayDocument?id=338943&acsFlg=accessBought

PLATO - PLATFORM FOR LEARNING AND TEACHING ONLINE

WILLIAM Y.M. LEE AND H.-ARNO JACOBSEN
Department of Electrical and Computer Engineering
University of Toronto
10 King's College Road, Toronto, Ontario, M5S 3G4, Canada
leewi@eecg.toronto.edu | jacobsen@eecg.toronto.edu

It is common that each course at a university has its own web site for managing course materials and communicating with students. However, the people, mainly instructors, who develop the course web site, tend to provide different interfaces and functions depending on their needs and web development skill. The Platform for Learning and Teaching Online (PLATO) is an online course management system, which aims at providing a uniform interface and hands-on functions for constructing various course web sites in a simple and customizable manner.

1. Overview

Nowadays, it is commonly expected that courses and lectures offer a web site which serves as central information-hub for collecting, disseminating, and managing course related information. This does not stop at universities, but will likely proliferate across all institutions of learning. Moreover, with the rise and the wide accessibility of sophisticated web development tools, the functionality such web sites offer, will likely increase, and with this increase, will the expectation of their users.

The OpenCourseWare project at MIT [1], for instance, has as one of its objectives "to make the materials from virtually all of its courses freely available on the World Wide Web for non-commercial use..."

The Platform for Learning and Teaching Online (PLATO), under development at the University of Toronto, aims at meeting the objective of supporting courses and lectures with a highly functional web-site, that is easy to use by all participants (students, assistants, and instructors).

The development of PLATO underlies two primary objectives. The first objective emphasizes the design and development of a generic, customizable, and user-friendly web-based learning and teaching infrastructure, which can be used and adapted to administrate various courses at universities, so that uniformity of the interface and functionality among different course web sites can be achieved. After initial trials in various courses, PLATO will be distributed over the Internet and managed as an open source project.

Currently, PLATO offers the following functionality. For all users: automatic registration of users (based on pre-loaded IDs, e-mail addresses, or restricted to a particular domain of email), a message board differentiating between different user categories (student, assistant, instructor), and an announcement mechanism; for assistants and instructors: e-mail-list management functions, secured mark database to store, display, and modify students' marks, and functions to display aggregated mark information; for instructors: definition of marking schemes, system administration and system monitoring, and authoring and automatic evaluation of surveys.

The second objective aims at developing a controllable research infrastructure, which will be used for experimentation under real-world conditions. There are several different research directions for this endeavor.

First, the goal is to better understand how to build, maintain, and deploy large web-based systems. In the development stage we are particularly interested in experimenting with automated testing strategies to ensure the quality of the code base of our system. These strategies involve the actual script code – including the server-side scripting language and client-side scripting, – the database, and the web server. Due to the distributed nature of web-based systems, their interactive and GUI-based nature, and the more fragile languages used (untyped scripting languages), this problem is far more severe than the well-explored testing strategies for non-distributed and less interactive systems. Second, problems we will investigate in this context are online upgrade of the running system (deploy patches and bug fixes), system self-monitoring, and peak load management of the PLATO site. Third, PLATO will be used to observe the behavior of users in web-based systems and study their reaction to artifacts posted on the site (e.g., color, size, and shape of advertisements etc.)

The paper is organized as follows. In Section 2 we briefly discuss related projects. In Section 3 we discuss the PLATO system in greater detail and show some of its features. In Section 4 we describe the setup and usage of PLATO.

2. Related Projects

The design and implementation of a Web-based Learning System (WLS) is not a simple and easy task. WLS developers are expected to face technical difficulties; some of the most common ones are the production of multimedia information, efficient information retrieval, reuse of existing pedagogical material and management of communication between the users [2]. These issues are addressed in various research projects. One of these projects is ARIADNE which is a European project that defines, implements and tests methodologies for the proper use of telematics-based solutions for academic education and certain types of corporate training [3]. Another information framework, MATILDA, separates the information domain from the application one. The purpose of which is to promote information reuse and provide a 'filtered' identification of information structure [4]. In addition, World Wide Web Course Tools (WebCT) [5,6] is a full-featured product which can be used under the Unix operating system. It is used widely in many universities because of the user-friendly interface and relatively strong pedagogical components. Another related project is Blackboard CourseInfo which supports authoring and evaluating of interactive quizzes. While most

PLATO features can be found in one of the above cited systems, none of the above systems could support our second key objective.

3. System Architecture and Implementation

3.1 *Overview of PLATO Functions*

PLATO possesses many functions, which are very useful and convenient for managing a course. Students are required to register and log on the system before viewing personal and critical course-related information, and each login session time is limited for security reasons. The registration can be limited by preloaded IDs, emails or a particular domain of email. When a user logs in, his/her priority will be automatically detected to define his/her limited access to the system. It has a message board allowing students to post opinions and ask questions. Figure 1 shows the multicolored highlight of different messages according to the users' priorities on the message board. An announcement section is particularly for instructors, organizing announcements according to date and time. It has a secured mark database system to store, display, and modify students' marks and the marking scheme. Students can view their individual marks and also aggregated mark statistics for comparison as in figure 2. A survey function is available to instructors to easily set up an online survey for students' response, (e.g. anonymous assessment of difficulty of a lecture), and to display the resulting statistics numerically or graphically as in figure 3. A mailing list function is available to teaching assistants and instructors to send emails to individual students or pre-defined groups of students at once (e.g., only to section 1 of the course, or to a number of students managed by a particular TA). The table of contents is configurable without interfering with any scripts, e.g. see Figure 4. Files can be uploaded by instructors directly through the system and links can easily be set up in the table of contents. The instructor can set the visibility of links, that is he/she can allow certain pages to be accessed without logging into the actual site. Instructor can also do other system-monitoring tasks, such as changing priority of a user, canceling the registration of a user, or shutting down the web site (only instructor or administrator can log in afterwards) for maintenance or upgrade.

3.2 *Implementation*

PLATO is a web system built around a secure web server, a database server, and a script-interpreting engine. The software tools used to develop the system are the

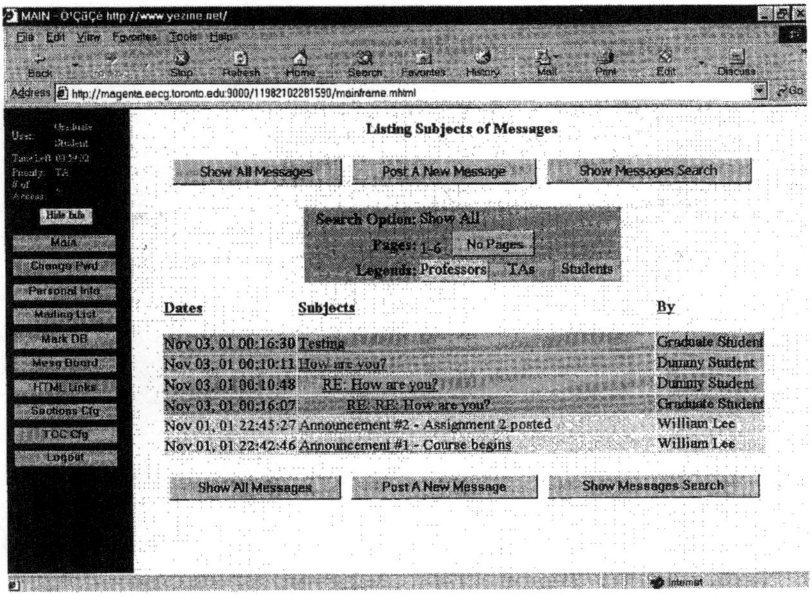

Figure 1. Message board with priority highlights

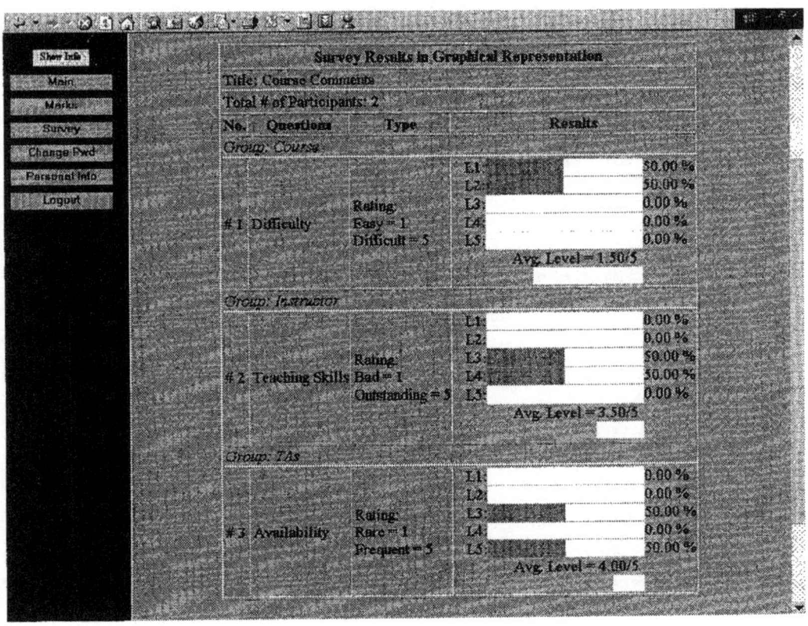

Figure 2. Graphical representation of survey results

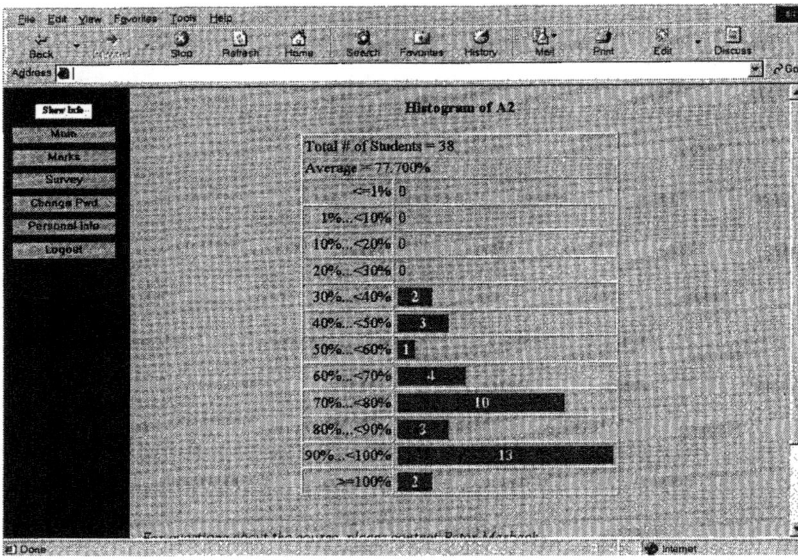

Figure 3. Aggregated mark statistics and average of an assignment

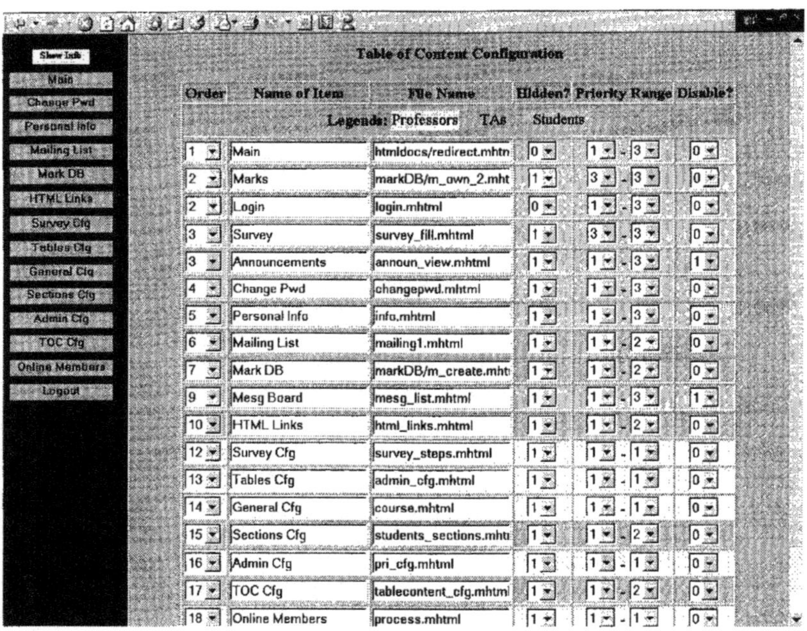

Figure 4. Configurable table of contents

Apache-SSL web server, the mSQL or MySQL database server, and the Meta-HTML CGI engine. Figure 5 illustrates and briefly explains the conceptual architecture of PLATO. Currently, we operate PLATO under Linux (it can easily be ported to Solaris and Windows). All tools used in the development of PLATO are available as open source, a key development requirement.

The Apache web server is the heart of the entire system since every single

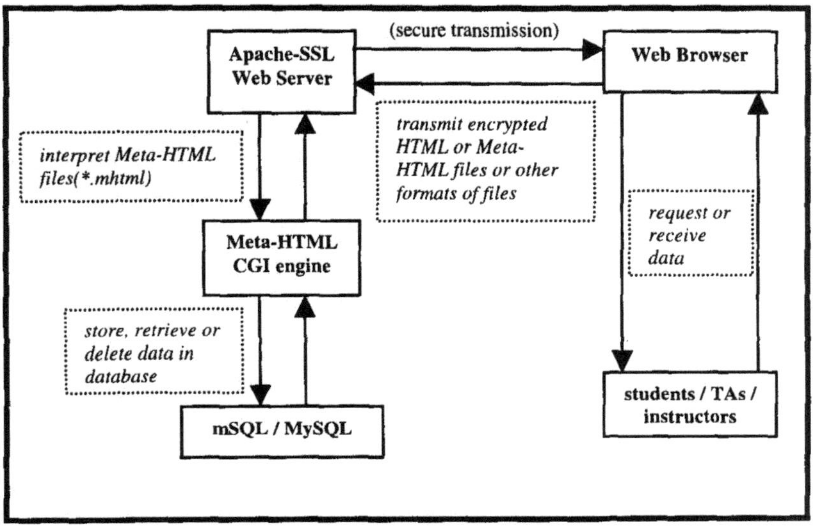

Figure 5: Conceptual Architecture of PLATO

document or action has to be processed through this server. The web server will invoke the Meta-HTML CGI engine to further process the specific documents. Apache web server is very stable and robust but it does not provide a secure transmission of data, thus OpenSSL has to be combined with Apache and the combination is called Apache-SSL. Apache-SSL web server incorporates the use of secure socket layer (SSL). SSL provides 128-bit encryption of the data being transmitted over the Internet between the client and server sides. Thus, when users send or receive confidential information, such as address, password, or mark, to or from the web server, other people are not able to view the important information for illegitimate use.

Meta-HTML is a server-side web programming language managing the layout of web pages as well as the interactions between the client and server. HTML is a static layout description language so it cannot handle the dynamic change of web page layout according to different needs. Meta-HTML is used to customize the web page layout and display the required data on the pages in a predefined or customizable format. All documents of extension ".mhtml" are to be processed by the Mata-HTML CGI engine. The Apache web server can easily be configured to invoke the engine to interpret the Meta-HTML documents when they are requested by users. The engine will generate the corresponding HTML tags for a web page and Apache will return the resulting web page to the clients. Moreover, Meta-HTML has the capability of communicating with different kinds of database servers, such as mSQL, MySQL and Oracle. Meta-HTML can retrieve the required data from the database and organize them in a manner predefined by the programmer or customized by the users. It can also store the received data into the database, as well as create and destroy tables and databases.

The chosen databases for PLATO are mSQL and MySQL. mSQL was chosen initially due to its simplicity. MySQL is more powerful in supporting transactions and concurrent database access. The database server has a set of databases and tables storing and organizing data for the web servers and clients. mSQL and MySQL support a high number of simultaneous transactions and fast searching, storing and retrieving of data. Meta-HTML acts as a bridge between the database and client, and can easily be configured to communicate with mSQL and MySQL during Meta-HTML installation. Since PLATO is mainly used by schools, research groups or academic organizations, mSQL and MySQL are sufficient to provide stable and efficient transfer of data (e.g., instances of PLATO will not have to support more than 500 users, which can be considered as absolute maximum).

3.3 *Project Status*

PLATO is fully functional and supports all of the above described functions. We are currently validating our prototype in three courses with a total of 450 users. In this stage we are mostly concerned with the acceptability of the system by different user groups, to identify problems, and to improve the functionality of the system. Upon successful completion of this stage we will proceed with the other objectives outlined in the overview.

We are currently working on the automation of regular tests on a web system. HttpUnit is a free, open source Java API for accessing web sites without a browser, and is ideally suited for automated unit testing of web sites [7]. We are employing HttpUnit to implement the automated tests on PLATO. After running the automated tests, developers or testers can immediately view the reports and then make corrections accordingly, thus saving tremendous amount of time and effort. Another issue that we are exploring is system self-monitoring. We will modify PLATO to keep track of statistics regarding the performance of the system. For example, PLATO will record the average number of people logging into the site each day and the average length of their login sessions. We will also have PLATO to periodically email those statistics to the site administrator, and to display the results in histograms on the web site.

4. Setup, Maintenance, Upgrade and Self-monitoring of PLATO

4.1 *Setup of a New Instance of the PLATO Site*

Proper installations of Meta-HTML engine, mSQL or MySQL database server, and Apache-SSL web server have to be completed before creating a new course web site via PLATO. After the source files of PLATO are loaded, setting up a course web site involves setting the priority of different users (instructors and assistants), configuring the functions that different user groups may be allowed to use (e.g., disallow the use of the message board, for instance), as well as authoring the content of the site and creating the corresponding links.

4.2 *Maintenance of PLATO*

Administrators and instructors have access to all kinds of functions and data in PLATO. Some highlights are to delete any unwanted messages in the message board, post announcements, shut down the web site for maintenance, and view any data stored in the database.

A PLATO developer conducts the automated tests and interprets the reports, after changes to the code base. The developer will accordingly fix the reported problems.

4.3 *Automated Test and System Self-monitoring of PLATO*

We are currently working on a mechanism for online upgrading the running PLATO system with new revisions of individual site components (this feature is under development).

Secondly, PLATO will be able to record statistics regarding its throughput and performance. The statistics could be the average number of users and the average speed of download from PLATO per day. They will be presented in a graphical format on the web site. Also, PLATO can raise alarms due to the occurrence of unsafe states. For example, when the number of simultaneous users exceeds the preset maximum, PLATO will immediately send an email to the site administrator.

5. Conclusion

PLATO aims at simplifying and standardizing the development of course web sites at universities. This simplification and standardization will save the time of instructors in web site construction as well as provide a consistent interface and functionality of course web sites for students.

After experimenting PLATO in a course[1] at the University of Toronto, the feature that received most concern from instructor and students was the mark database. Instructor was cautious about the difficulty of mark entry and security of the mark storage when dealing with a large number of students. Students were

[1] Computer Networks (CSC458F) in Computer Science department with about 100 students

concerned about the privacy of marks and aggregated mark statistics for comparisons. The employment of MySQL, Apache-SSL and Meta-HTML completely take care of these issues.

There is future work that can be extended from PLATO. We will experiment PLATO with separation of concerns to separately manage, the Meta-HTML code, from the content, and the server side JavaScript support to make system more easily maintainable. We will also provide a test framework for automated testing of site's dynamic functionality. The issue of automated testing is extremely important, due to fragile nature of web-development languages in general. Additional ideas are to add subscription support such as allowing users to subscribe to certain messages being posted in the message board, as well as to integrate message board with net-news and e-mail clients.

References

1. "MITOpenCourseware", 2001 Oct 24, [cited 2002 Feb 15], http://web.mit.edu/ocw/.
2. Karacapilidis, N., Abou Khaled O., Pettenati M.C. & Vanoirbeek C. (2000). Developing Higher-Order Skills with the MEDIT Web-based Learning Environment. In *Educational Technology & Society* 3(1), 1436-4522.
3. Forte, E. N., Wentland Forte, M. K., & Duval, E. (1996). ARIADNE: a Framework for Technology-Based Open and Distance Education. In *Proceedings of the 7th EAEEIE International Conference on Telematics for Future Education and Training*, June 12-14, Oulu, Finland, 69-72.
4. Lowe, D. B., & Ginige, A. (1996). MATILDA: a framework for the representation and processing of information in multimedia systems. In *Proceedings of the 3rd International Interactive Multimedia Symposium*, January 21-26, Perth, Australia, 229-236.
5. Goldberg, M. W., & Salari, S. (1997). An Update on WebCT (World-Wide-Web Course Tools) - a Tool for the Creation of Sophisticated Web-Based Learning Environments. In *Proceedings of NAUWeb-97: Current Practices in Web-Based Course Development*, June 12-15, Flagstaff, Arizona.
6. Goldberg, M. W., Salari, S., & Swoboda, P. (1996). World Wide Web Course Tool: An Environment for Building WWW-Based Courses. *Computer Networks and ISDN Systems*, 28 (7-11), 1219-1232.
7. "HttpUnit", [cited 2002 Feb 16], http://httpunit.sourceforge.net.

A WEB-BASED PLATFORM CLP FOR COLLABORATIVE LEARNING

Mao Xiaoguang and Qi Zhichang
Department of Computer,
National University of Defence Technology,
Changsha, Hunan, China, 410073
Email: xgmao@nudt.edu.cn and qzc@nudt.edu.cn

IT companies pay a lot of attentions to experience than before. Different from traditional education, IT training emphasizes the ability of problem-solving, design and project activities rather than concept knowledge. Accommodating themselves to new conditions, education organizations turn to the methodology of collaborative learning. In the paper, a self-controlled social-similar web-based platform CLP is provided for the training of persons satisfying the requirements from information industry.

Key Words. Web-based Platform, Collaborative Learning, CSCL

1 Introduction

Nowadays IT companies pay a lot of attentions to experience. One of the most important reasons is to save training expenses. Naturally, academies take over the training business. IT training emphasizes the ability of problem-solving, design and project activities rather than concept knowledge, which the theory of collaborative learning is quite suitable for. On the contrary, traditional education always teaches well-established facts, which is far away from the question-centered, collaborative style of real science practice, especially in cyberspace.

Collaborative learning deals with instructional methods that seek to promote learning through collaborative efforts among students working on a given learning task [9]. Collaboration is a philosophy of interaction and life style. A collaborative learning system concentrates on refining and integrating the learning process and the subject knowledge of the students with the help of the collaborative associates. The promise of collaborative learning is to allow students to learn in relatively realistic, cognitively motivating and socially enriched learning contexts, compared to other tutoring paradigm like socratic learning, discovery learning, integrated learning, etc. [10]

Effective collaborative learning requires computer-supported environment to enliven and enrich the collaborative learning process, to create more realistic social contexts, which will increase effectiveness of the system, to provide a more natural learning habit. Through the environment, associates share their perspectives, experience, insights, and understandings, and also cooperate to solve much more complex problems. With the help of such learning style, learners can come to more sophisticated understandings than they could do on their own [1].

In the following sections, after the analysis of the main characteristics of collaborative learning, the authors describe the architecture and design of a platform CLP which enables collaborative learning based on web.

2 Collaborative Learning

Collaborative learning is the process whereby each member contributes personal experience, information, perspective, insight, skills and attitudes with the intent of improving the learning accomplishments of others [6].

Depending on the type of collaborative tasks to perform, Computer-supported collaborative learning (CSCL) could be employed to address concept learning, problem-solving, design and project activities. [8] gives five elements in collaborative learning:

- positive independence. Learners need to believe that they are linked with others in a way that ensures that they all succeed together.
- interaction promoting. Associates help and encourage each other to learn by explaining what they understand, by gathering and sharing knowledge, and by cooperating.
- individual accountability for the group's work.
- social skills. Teamwork skills includes conflict management, group behavior, leadership, and decision-making.
- self-evaluating. The effectiveness of learning process will be evaluated continually.

Collaborative learning can be exciting for learners because they must become actively engaged. That is why collaborative learning may be more effective than the typical lecture modes where learners are often treated like passive 'vessels' to be filled with information.

Another advantage is the socialization that collaborative learning promotes. Collaborative learning creates a learning community, helps learners gain needed interpersonal and small group skills. It helps create a shared identity among learners and instructors as well as creating learner networks and relationships that will last a lifetime[7]. The enemies of education are isolation, loneliness, anxiety, and failure. Learners absorb more when they are doing things they enjoy. The learner who learns best is the one who organizes, summarizes, elaborates, explains, and defends [11].

3 Architecture and Design of CLP Platform

The primary objectives of computer-supported system for collaborative learning are: providing the opportunity to participate in and enjoy the benefits of cooperative learning without having to coordinate meeting times or come to campus; providing a more technologically enriched collaborative environment than is possible in a traditional face-to-face classroom; providing much more methods enabled by advanced computer technologies.

Our approach to promoting and supporting collaborative learning is based on a variety of cooperated approaches. The platform CLP consists of the following components: version controller, group configuring, text-based communicating, multi-media whiteboard and knowledge learning engine. Such facility can enable learners enhance their high-level skills much more effectively than competitive or individualistic learning environments [6].

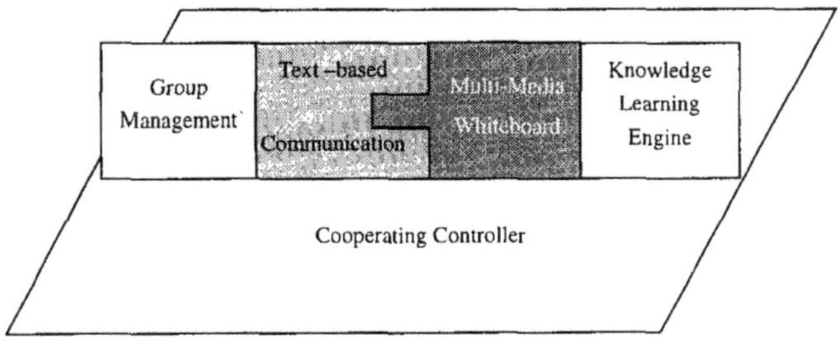

Fig. 1. The architecture of CLP platform for collaborative learning

3.1 Group Management

While learning is ultimately an individual enterprise, the support of a group working towards a common learning objective can produce improved learning by each member of the group [6]. The group reorganization is elementary to achieve the casual atmosphere which is quite important to learning efficiency. Informal learning group, forma learning group and study groups [4] can be maintained here.

Informal groups can be organized at any time in a society of any size to check on students' understanding of the material, to give students an opportunity to apply what they are learning, or to provide a change of pace. Formal learning groups are teams established to complete a specific task, such as perform a lab experiment, write a report, carry out a project, or prepare a position paper. Study groups are long-term teams (usually existing over a whole course) with stable membership whose primary responsibility is to provide members with support, encouragement, and assistance in completing course requirements and assignments. The larger the class and the more complex the subject matter, the more valuable study groups can be [4].

3.2 Knowledge Learning Engine (KLE)

The major obstacle to collaborative learning in education is the lecture tradition to which most of us have become bound [6]. Opponents of collaborative learning typically complain that it abandons the lecture, which arguably is the most effective means of information transmission. The mechanism of KLE gives an opportunity that collaborative learning system not only can co-exist with lecturing, but can even be built around lectures.

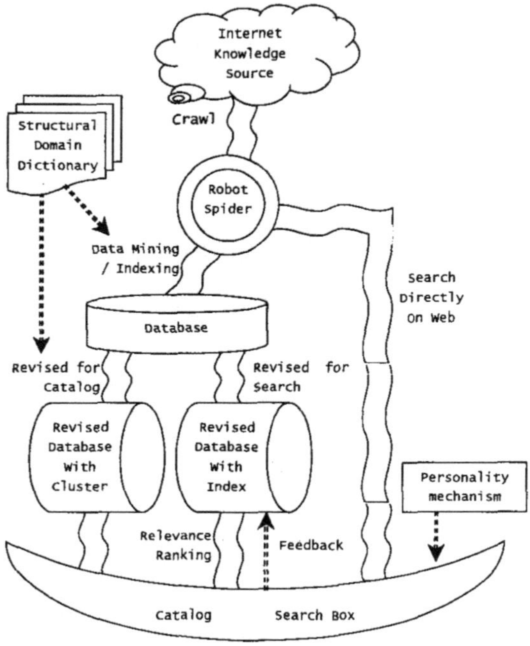

Fig. 2. Knowledge Learning Engine

KLE is an education-domain-based internet search engine, which consists of internet search engine, knowledge mining, knowledge clustering, structural domain dictionary, education source list. Crawling through education sources, KLE analyzes fetched information, clusters useful knowledge (include documents, lectures, videos and etc.) with the help of structural domain dictionary. The learner can search the knowledge-base constructed by KLE, or just search step-by-step guided by the knowledge catalog, which is similar to the catalogic search style of Yahoo.

3.3 Version-controlled Text Communication (VTC)

VTC is essential to project activities, such as documenting and programming, and problem-solving. Group members work together to address challenges: planning, analyzing, designing, programming, debugging and discussing. Except version controller, synchronized text communication is not fresh [3]. Cooperative documenting and programming will be controlled by the version controller running in a server. The lock system enables authors exchange yet continue their documenting or programming works.

3.4 Multi-Media Whiteboard (WMW)

Web-based WMW offers key collaborative method for remote education. The media includes: figure, audio, video, image, text, file, stream and etc. Synchronization between WMWs of the same group is maintained automatically. Members in the same group have full group-awareness for synchronous work.

The system of WMW has already been implemented and used by students to finish their project tasks in the courses such as software engineering, programming language and etc.

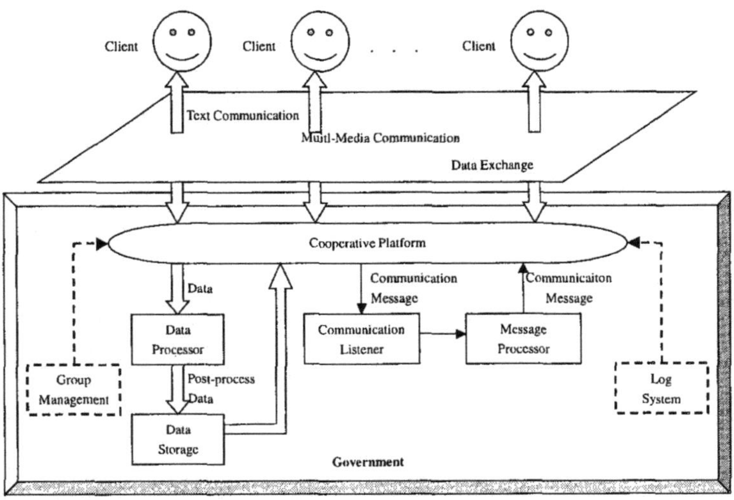

Fig. 3. Collaboration within the virtual society

4 Discussion

The field of CSCL is booming recently. As a result, a number of systems are being developed [10][5]. E-mail, computer mediated conferencing systems are mostly used to support their group work and to communicate with one another.

Compared to above system, CLP platform presented in this paper bears the following advantages:

- CLP is constructed according to mentor-apprentice fashion instead of teacher-student one. As to IT training , the former is superior to the latter.
- Knowledge learn engine combines both traditional learning and collaborative learning patterns.
- CLP provides learners with virtual education society rather than virtual classroom or chat room.
- Mechanism of version control enables tasks such as project engineering.

As opposed to former computer-supported learning systems, skills can be learned unconsciously from collaborative documenting, project process, cooperative programming, problem solving and etc.

- Instead of Client/Server, Browser/Server architecture is adopted in CLP. Learners can learn, cooperate and share knowledge on the platform at a distance freely, only web browser is needed.

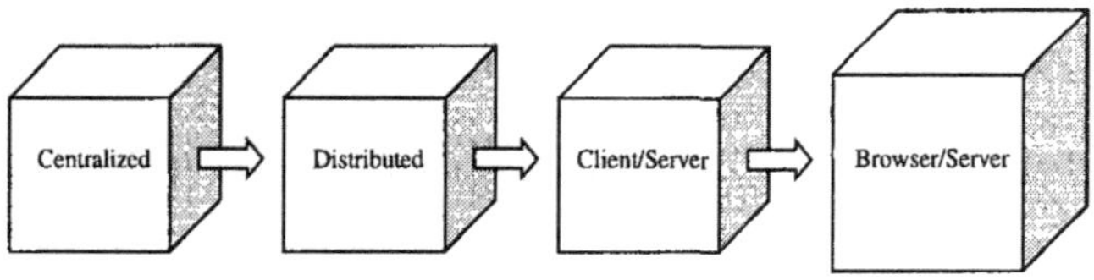

Fig. 4. Progress of system architecture

- JAVA is the main programming language of CLP, which results in a distinct character of CLP: CLP can shift from platform to platform with freedom.
- Advanced techniques supporting cooperative actions have been designed into CLP.

This paper is a report on work in progress. Although much has been accomplished, much still remains to be done. We present the entire architecture to show the final configuration that we expect to be available for collaborative learning.

References

1. Barrows, H.S. How to design a problem-based curriculum for the preclinical years. Springer, 1985.
2. Cicognani, A. Concept Mapping as a Collaborative Tool for Enhanced Online Learning. Educational Technology and Society 3(3), 2000.
3. Cerratto, T. and Rodriguez, H. Studies of computer supported collaborative writing. Implications for system design. Fifth International conference on the Design of Cooperative Systems. Saint Raphaël, France, 2002.
4. Davis, R.G Tools for Teaching. Jossey-Bass Publishers. 1993.
5. Dufner, D., Kwon, O. and Hadidi, R. Web-CCAT: A Collaborative Learning Environment for Geographically Distributed Information Technology Students and Working Professionals. Communications of the association for Information Systems. 1999.
6. The Instructional Design for the New Media (6) project. http://www.rcc.ryerson.ca/learnontario/6/main_page/about.htm.
7. Johnson, D.W. and Johnson, R.T. Cooperative learning: where we have been, where we are going. Cooperative Learning and College Teaching. Vol 3, No. 2, Winter, 1993 .
8. Johnson, D. W., Johnson, R. T. and Smith, K. A. Active Learning: Cooperation in the Classroom, Interaction Book Company, Edina, MN, 1991.
9. Janet L. Kolodner and Kristine Nagel. A Collaborative Learning Tool in Support of Learning from Problem Solving and Design Activities. In Proceedings of the Computer Support for Collaborative Learning (CSCL) 1999 Conference, C. Hoadley & J. Roschelle (Eds.). Stanford University, Palo Alto, California. Mahwah, Lawrence Erlbaum Associates, 1999.

10. Kumar, V.S. Computer-Supported Collaborative Learning: Issues for Research. Eighth Annual Graduate Symposium on Computer Science, University of Saskatchewan. 1996.
11. Smith, K.A. Cooperative learning and problem solving. Cooperative Learning and College Teaching. Vol 3, No. 2 Winter. 1993.

A PLATFORM FOR VIRTUAL LABORATORIES

W. A. HALANG
Fernuniversität,
Faculty of Electrical and Computer Engineering,
58084 Hagen, Germany
E-mail: Wolfgang.Halang@FernUni-Hagen.de

P. TANG
Guangdong University of Technology,
Computer College,
729 East Dongfeng Road,
Guangzhou 510090, China
E-mail: rachel@gdut.edu.cn

The concept of a distance teaching laboratory is presented. Based on the widespread availability of personal computers and telecommunication networks as well as on utilising multimedia technology, this is an innovative approach for the automation of laboratory practicals as constituent of university teaching, and for both the spatial and temporal separation of students and experimental rigs and experimentation, respectively. An environment for the design of digital circuits was developed as the first realisation of the concept. A number of further experiments is in preparation.

1. Introduction

The main didactical components of university curricula are lectures, exercises, laboratory practicals, and seminars. In distance teaching universities, lecture notes and corresponding exercises are sent to the students' homes, where the notes are studied and the exercises elaborated before being returned for marking and correction. Traditionally and still to a large extent, self-study course texts and exercises are shipped in form of printed material to the students, who return their feedback by mail as well.

Recently, distance teaching universities have begun to replace printed by electronic media. Thus, for instance, the Faculty of Electrical and Computer Engineering of Fernuniversität strives to transform all its courses to multimedia form. Such courses can be distributed on CD-ROMs emulating traditional shipment, or via communication networks leaving the initiative to obtain material to the students. Electronic mail appears to be the most appropriate means for returning exercises, and video conferencing has already been successfully employed to eliminate the need for students to travel to seminars and oral examinations.

Whereas the utilisation of new technology for the above mentioned purposes in distance education is straightforward, it is not so obvious to find new ways of allowing students to conduct laboratory projects with practical work from their homes, taking serious cost limitations into account. Here an innovative solution had to be found, since for the understanding of technical subjects such as electrical engineering work on experiments, practical problems, and examples is indispensable.

Therefore, up to now, two approaches are taken. One possibility is to arrange practicals in laboratories on-site a university, that require the local presence of the students. In order to save time and travel costs, it is essential to schedule these practicals close together and to minimise their number. The other approach is to carry out experiments at home. To this end, Fernuniversität used to send out experimentation kits such as microprocessor boards. Their disadvantage is that they have to be returned together with the results obtained. This method has many drawbacks such as limited kit size, damages during shipment, and high costs for inspection, repair, replacement, and handling.

The above considerations establish the need for a new approach to conduct technical experimentation under the conditions of distance teaching. The requirements to be fulfilled by a new system at the students' side are minimum initial costs and as low as possible costs for using telecommunication services, no need for travel, and provision of a generic environment allowing for great flexibility in experimentation. The selection of the time for the latter ought to be fully at the student's discretion, and not limited to the working hours of the laboratory supervisor.

In this paper a novel idea for meeting this need under the given requirements is presented. The concept is called *Distance Laboratory*. Assuming that students have a personal computer equipped with a WWW browser and access to the Internet, it does not require any further investments on the students' side. This assumption is feasible as already more than 98% of Fernuniversität's electrical and computer engineering students have their own computers. For experimentation, the students work with particular programs on their computers. In the course of this, data are generated and transmitted via the Internet to the university, where they are loaded into automatically operated experimental facilities. Results are returned showing the students how their experiments ran, and providing feedback for improvements or corrections in case of errors.

For Chinese universities and students the Distance Laboratory is useful for two main reasons. First, although Computer Aided Instruction is already in widespread use in many universities, such as Guangdong University of Technology, accessibility of practicals from students' homes via the Internet would be helpful in reducing waiting times and congestions in laboratory rooms, and would allow each student to practise more extensively according to personal schedules. Then, for large parts of the Chinese population distance education is a necessity as they live very far away from universities in general and the so-called key universities in particular, whose degrees are recognised abroad and which are, therefore, especially interesting when a higher degree is pursued. Here the Distance Laboratory can fulfill the special requirements engineering disciplines impose on distance teaching technology.

In the sequel, the technical concept of the Distance Laboratory is developed, its functionality is compiled, and the concept for its implementation outlined. As an example for its usage details of an exercise on the design of digital circuits are given. It can be carried out via the Internet in its entirety. The practical comprises the design of a digital circuit, its implementation using programmable logic, and also the test of configured, real hardware. There are further applications of this concept in computer programming, programmable logic control, distributed digital control, and process automation.

2. Technical Concept

Software projects can be accomplished by students at their homes in an easy and straightforward manner. After having developed programs locally on their personal computers, the students just need access to a host computer at their distance teaching university to run their programs on unknown data sets and to transmit results. For this purpose, in co-operation with two telecommunication companies Fernuniversität provides access to its internal network FUNet from all over Germany at local telephone rates. If a student has no private personal computer, he or she can also use the computer facilities at one of the 67 regional study centres in Austria, Germany, Hungary, and Switzerland.

Obviously, it is more difficult to deal in a similar way with laboratory experiments that involve practical work with hardware. Such experiments cannot be performed via the Internet, since they require manual set-up locally. For a laboratory on the design of digital circuits, for instance, this means to assemble circuits from discrete logic using plug-in boards, wire-wrapping, or other methods. With the advent of programmable logic, however, these techniques have become obsolete. By using RAM-based reconfigurable field-programmable gate arrays (FPGA), complete laboratory projects can be carried out via a network and based on software, only.

A similar observation can be made with respect to process automation, where the emphasis in engineering work and, hence, the educational needs have shifted towards the software side. At the Technical University of Vienna this observation gave rise to a new laboratory concept as described in [2,3]. Here students develop process control software on individual workstations. When a program is ready, it is sent via a LAN to a host where it is queued until a corresponding testbed in form of a process model becomes available. Then this process is run under control of the student program. The students can observe their experiments, but they may not even touch the models as these are encapsulated in transparent boxes.

For the Distance Laboratory we extend this concept by two main features:

(1) After debugging, the student programs are first subjected to process simulators running on the personal computers of the students to avoid unsuccessful experimental runs and the costs of the corresponding data transmissions as well as possible damages to the experimental rigs.
(2) The LAN is replaced by wide area connectivity, in general the Internet.

On their personal computers at home, with tools provided by their university the students develop control software for their experiments, which are first simulated. When this step is successfully completed, the control software is transmitted to a host at the university via the Internet using different services — in the simplest case electronic mail. The corresponding host queues the incoming requests, simulates the experimental runs once more for safety reasons and, then, down-loads each control program to a specific rig for carrying out an experiment. During the experimental run the host samples status data, which are processed and returned to the student to provide information on the outcome of the experiment.

The Chair of Computer Engineering at Fernuniversität is offering the following practicals in the framework of the Distance Laboratory:

- programming and emulation of the first freely programmable digital computer Zuse Z3,
- programming and emulation of a hypothetical computer with RISC

and stack architecture,
- development and test of digital circuits on the basis of field-programmable gate arrays,
- programming of process automation software in the real-time language PEARL to be executed on a single board computer,
- programming of a microcontroller for discrete control applications,
- configuration of a multifunction controller for regulation tasks,
- configuration of a distributed control system by means of function block diagrams to carry out tasks in process automation.

The first two of the above applications only require the server itself, whereas for the other ones the devices mentioned are connected via serial interfaces to the server. With the process automation devices thus connected then suitable process models are controlled.

3. Functionality

The three user groups have the following requirements.

(1) *Students:* For their information the practicals offered are presented in the Internet. Based on this, they register for one or more experiments. After studying additional material and preparatory texts, they carry out simulated experiments and send their solutions to the real experimental rigs at Fernuniversität. Finally, they receive the results of the real experiments and write the corresponding experiment reports.

(2) *Laboratory supervisor:* The duty of this person located at Fernuniversität is to maintain and to take care of the virtual and real experiments. He or she answers student questions if technical problems arise.

(3) *Examination office:* When a student registers for a practical, the examination office needs to grant an admission. The successful completion of all practicals required for graduation is to be reported to the examination office for recording.

These requirements lead to a large number of functions to be provided by the Distance Laboratory, which can be grouped as follows:

(1) Presentation and registration:

  (a) Presentation of the practicals offered in the Internet
  (b) Registration of a student for the Distance Laboratory

(2) Preparation of a practical:

   (a) Transfer of documents to prepare the experiments (additional material, descriptions of experiments)
   (b) Transfer of all programs and corresponding documentation required for the experiments
   (c) Submitting answers to the preparatory questions on an experiment
   (d) Sending back sample solutions to these preparatory questions

(3) Virtual experimentation: Providing a model of a real experimental set-up, which can be programmed by the student, allows the latter
- to parameterise,
- to set input data,
- to simulate and
- to visualise output data.

(4) Real experimentation: The parameterisation and input data generated during simulation are sent for real experimentation to the corresponding experimental rig and are evaluated by the following functions:

   (a) Submission of experimental data by the student for real experimentation
   (b) Sending back the results (output data) of real experimentation to the student together with a preliminary credit in case of success or an error description

(5) Experiment report:

   (a) Transfer of the documents required for experiment reporting
   (b) Submitting answers to the questions on experiment evaluation
   (c) Sending back sample solutions to these evaluation questions

(6) Crediting: Upon successful completion of a Distance Laboratory practical a credit is sent to the student.

(7) Organisation of the Distance Laboratory: To carry out the real experiments as well as to co-ordinate and to ensure correct operation of the Distance Laboratory the following functionalities are provided:

   (a) Assigning an identification number to each participant of the practicals after checking the admission requirements
   (b) Administrative registration of each participant with the required data

(c) Management of the real experiments to be run in a waiting queue
(d) Checking and management of the preparatory questions on experiments
(e) Checking and management of the questions to be answered in the course of writing experiment reports
(f) Checking submitted experimental data for validity
(g) Running experiments based on submitted data and parameters
(h) Deleting identification numbers after completion of the participation in practicals (by withdrawal or successful completion)
(i) Notifications to the examination office and to the laboratory supervisor

(8) System administration on the server:

(a) Access control and authentification
(b) User interface for the administration of the computer and the experiments
(c) Generation of protocol files
(d) Generation of statistics

The user's part of the system Distance Laboratory is transferred from the WWW site of Fernuniversität to a student's computer at home after selecting and releasing a practical. Since there are different computer platforms and since provision of multiple programs with equal functionality for these different platforms is to be avoided, it was necessary to write the programs [1] in platform-independent programming and scripting languages (cp. Figure 1). Here platform-independent means that students can access the WWW page using a variety of computer hardware, and that they may employ any operating system and any browser running on their hardware.

4. Implementation Concept

With access to and utilisation of different Internet services the Distance Laboratory constitutes a client-server system with the Internet as its network. The students' computers represent the clients, and the server is a dedicated computer located within the Chair of Computer Engineering at Fernuniversität.

By the necessity to program the user part of the Distance Laboratory in a platform-independent way, i.e., with architecture-independent elements,

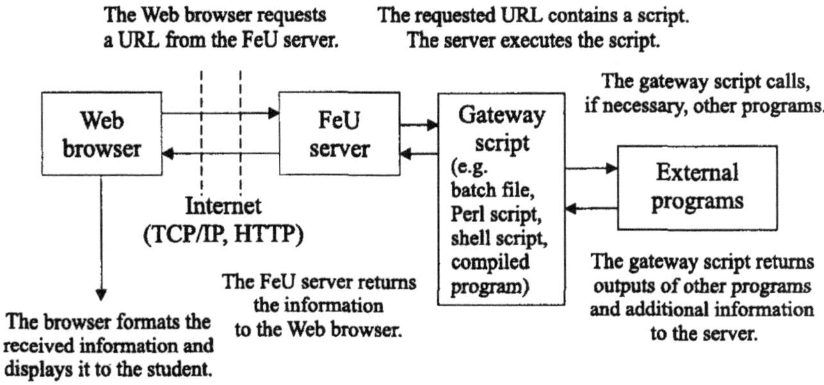

Figure 1. CGI programming and gateway script

the following approach appeared appropriate in connection with publication in the Internet:

- Textual information, e.g., the collection of learning material, the presentation within the WWW page or the experiment descriptions, were written in the description language HTML. These HTML documents have three essential advantages: first, HTML documents are transmitted in the Internet via the HTTP protocol; second, they enable the students to read texts and additional visual information in a non-linear manner and to navigate through them; and third, HTML documents are formatted and presented by a WWW browser only after their transmission to a target system. To achieve a maximum of acceptance and flexibility, respectively, in the layout, but also as wide a support as possible by the various browsers, HTML is utilised in its version 3.2. Browser-specific HTML extensions were excluded.
- Animations and the proper virtual laboratory experiments were written in the object oriented high level language Java. The required architecture-independence is given by the intermediate code produced by the Java interpreter, a binary code for a precisely specified virtual processor. This so-called bytecode is transferred via the same communication path between client and server which is also used by the HTML documents. The virtual processor is emulated on the target systems by a virtual Java Machine (JVM), which interprets the bytecode and executes the Java programs.

  There are two kinds of Java programs. The so-called Java applications are programs of their own, which are runable with a self-sufficient JVM. Java applets, on the other hand, are integrated in a WWW page and can produce animations on this WWW page and provide interactive tools. To execute applets, WWW browsers need to have integrated JVMs. Most WWW browsers support Java applets that were developed using the Java Development Kit (JDK) in its version 1.0.2. This restriction does not hold for Java applications, so that for them JDK in the version 1.2 could be employed.

- The co-operation of user and computer is determined by a graphical user interface. For HTML documents it is inherently given; for Java applications and applets the Abstract Window Toolkit was used.
- The computer at Fernuniversität runs under the operating system Linux. Its functionality as a WWW server was provided by the installation of the Apache HTTP server software. The Distance Laboratory leads to dialogues between students and the server, two kinds of which can be distinguished:
  - On-line dialogue: A student is connected with the server via the Internet. All queries and data transmissions initiated by the student result in a direct acknowledgement by the server. At the time of an acknowledgement the user is connected to the network.

    A registration for laboratory participation is an example for an on-line dialogue. Immediately after transmitting the registration data the registration is confirmed. Furthermore, the registration must be directed to the examination office to check the admission requirements.

    On-line dialogues are processed by Common Gateway Interface (CGI) scripts as they allow for interactive execution of programs on a WWW server. The programming language Perl in its version 5 was used to program the script files. Figure 1 illustrates the rôle of CGI programming for dialogues.
  - Off-line dialogue: A student has transmitted data to execute a real experiment, or has registered for a laboratory experiment; however, the provision of the real experiment's results or of an access identification number cannot be guaranteed for the duration of the student's network connection. The response to such a request or the transfer of the results, respectively, is realised at a later stage with the mail services of the Internet. By utilising the SMTP/POP3 mail service,

the student does not necessarily need to be connected to the Internet for the transmission of replies.

- The programs for the administration of the laboratory data of the various practical participants and for analysing the protocols and statistics generated were written in the scripting language Perl, version 5, as well.
- The server also comprises interfaces to the single experiments, which are carried out after the transmission of the pertaining user data under observation of specific temporal boundary conditions. As the single real laboratory experiments are very heterogeneous, a programmable modular interface was necessary, which allows for the attachment of the real experimental rigs by parametrisation. The modular structure enables the addition of further experiments to the system Distance Laboratory at a later stage.

5. A Simple Use Case: Direct Current and Ohm's Law

Although very basic as an experiment, a simple practical on direct current and Ohm's law exercises the full functionality of the Distance Laboratory. The practical consists of the four following files or programs, respectively.

(1) *Preparation:* The preparation document is an HTML file containing explanations on direct current, the preparatory questions, and instructions for the students on how to format the e-mail messages to be sent to the Distance Laboratory system.

(2) *Virtual experiment:* The proper experiment is provided by a Java application offering the following menu options:

- Initialise experimental parameters with default values
- Load experimental parameters from disk
- Store current experimental parameters on disk
- Start simulation
- Stop simulation
- Request help on the Distance Laboratory
- Request help on this practical
- Terminate the application

In its window, the application shows on top three measuring devices required, in the centre the experimental set-up with active sliding regulators to its left and right, and a scrollable explaining text at the bottom. When the experiment is running, the current in a simple circuit is measured with an Amperemeter. The voltage of the current source and the resistance of the consumer can be adjusted with the active elements. Even a short-circuit can be set, which is acknowledged by the Amperemeter with a special message. The settings and experimental parameters can be initialised, saved and re-loaded. Upon terminating this application, the student has to send the settings and parameters saved by e-mail to the host system.

(3) *Application Interface Module:* This is a small program written in the language C which processes the data contained in the e-mail messages submitted by students.

(4) *Experiment report:* The document for final reporting is another HTML file containing further explanations on direct current, some assignments on the experiment to be worked out, and instructions for the students on how to format this practical's final e-mail message to be sent to the Distance Laboratory system.

6. Case Study: The Distance Laboratory Employed for Digital Circuit Design

Among others, the Distance Laboratory provides a platform for the design of digital circuits. From the university on CD-ROM or to be down-loaded via the Internet, the students receive all necessary documentation, a small design entry tool, and a circuit simulator all running on personal computers. This tool supports design entry either by schematic entry or by using a hardware description language such as VHDL.

Then, the student designs are transferred via the Internet to the host at Fernuniversität, where they are processed by an electronic design automation (EDA) program yielding all data necessary to configure a field-programmable gate array. The host down-loads such configuration data sets to a connected hardware rig containing an FPGA. Then, stimuli specific to the laboratory project and provided by the instructor are applied to the FPGA and, finally, the resulting outputs and events are recorded. After a job is processed, this record is returned to the student for evaluation. The record contains the details of the circuit implementation on the FPGA. In the course of translation, for instance, the EDA tool generates evaluated net-lists. They indicate how the circuit was realised, and whether there are superfluous or wrong signal connections. Since further attributes such as gate propagation time or switching behaviour are part of the model, too, the evaluation can a priori indicate timing bottlenecks. Thus, segments of a formally correct circuit may have such long signal propagation times in an implementation, that certain dependencies between signals or states or certain temporal conditions may never be met. To eliminate such sources of error, further attributes and parameters can be employed to revise a design, which instruct the translator to optimise the pertaining circuit segments for their timing performance. Then, these segments are implemented with shorter data paths or faster switches. Furthermore, simulation files are provided, showing the temporal behaviour of a circuit graphically to allow for an evaluation of critical signals.

7. Didactic Requirements

It is considerably different and often also more difficult to didactically prepare experiments for the Distance Laboratory than for classroom use. Whereas one can respond to the group of students there, distance and asynchronicity require to cater for many possible situations. In particular, the information provided must be sufficient and exhaustive, because it cannot be taken for granted that all participants have an equal level of previous knowledge. Hence, it is difficult to estimate a priori, which details can be left out and where more details are required. Classroom teaching allows to skip chapters, or to repeat them in order to establish firm knowledge. If distance teaching provides too voluminous material, there is the danger of saturation; participants with more substantial previous knowledge receive too much, others too few information, which may result in a loss of motivation in both cases. Since at distance it is not easily possible to explain technical issues using intuitive models, correspondingly elaborate and expensive illustrations need to be provided. The material must be clearly structured to enable students to put a considered issue into a larger context. There need to be possibilities to skip the treatment of known facts, or to obtain more profound information on issues not understood, yet.

References

1. B. Heulmanns, W.A. Halang and J. Düring: Ein netz- und multimediagestütztes Fernpraktikum. In *PEARL 99 — Multimedia und Automatisierung*, P. Holleczek (Ed.), pp. 39 – 48, Reihe Informatik aktuell, Berlin-Heidelberg: Springer-Verlag 2000.
2. U. Schmid, H. Haberstroh and St. Stöckler: *Process Control Education for Computer Science: Facts and Fiction.* Proc. SEFI/TEMPUS JEP 2011 — IMPACT Workshop on Computer Science Topics for Control Engineering Education, pp. 13 – 22, Vienna, September 1993.
3. U. Schmid, W. Kastner and H. Haberstroh: *Process Control Education for Computer Science: From Fiction Back to Facts.* Proc. TEMPUS JEP 07759 — MODIFY Workshop on Automation and Control Engineering in Higher Education, Vienna, July 1995.

AN ADAPTIVE VIRTUAL UNIVERSITY

JOHN GAROFALAKIS[1, 2], EVANGELOS SAKKOPOULOS[1, 2],
SPIROS SIRMAKESSIS[1, 2, 3] AND ATHANASIOS TSAKALIDIS[1, 2]

[1]*Research Academic Computer Technology Institute*
Internet and Multimedia Technologies Research Unit
61 Riga Feraiou Str. 26110 Patras, Greece
http://www.ru5.cti.gr/

[2] *University of Patras*
Computer Engineering & Informatics Department
26500 Patras, Greece
http://mmlab.ceid.upatras.gr/

[3]*Hellenic Open University*
84 K Palama Str.
26442 Patras, Greece
http://www.eap.gr
E-mail: {garofala, syrma, sakkopul, tsak}@cti.gr

We present approaches for the organized design and augmentative development of an adaptive Virtual University. It combines several techniques to provide personalization features to the educational material and the exchanging data streams. In this way it customizes the educational process, served by any virtual university to the learning curve of the user. At first adaptation is performed per activity and then knowledge of the different levels is passed to all of them providing personalization globally. In order to prohibit outdated data to keep loading the user aging of personalization is also included. Furthermore curriculum sequencing provides guidance to the user's learning procedure. Most interesting educational pages for the users are selectively delivered to them. The categorization of incoming data streams is handled by content and property based filtering. For the overall procedure we discuss the methodology followed to cover the needs of system upgrading, code reuse and administration issues.

1 Introduction

In the last few years, there are a number of virtual universities that appeared on the Web [37, 38, 39]. A virtual university is an infrastructure system without a traditional campus, classes or a library; instead there are web-based facilities that provide richer functionality and features than their physical analogs [31]. A typical hypermedia application serves the same pages and the same set of link to all users. In order to improve usability, adaptive web-based applications make it possible to deliver personalized views or versions of a hypermedia document for all the users with diverse needs and knowledge backgrounds gaining access to the system [32, 35]. A virtual university environment that adopted intelligence in content providing is the Electronic Education Environment [3]. However these adaptation techniques are focused to a specific service (e.g. educational content delivery or presentation, document topic filtering) and therefore work completely independently in an environment that is supposed to cover a broad set of needs towards the common target of usability and learning improvement. The fruitful design and successful correlation of adaptation capabilities simultaneously for educational material and accompanying supportive services is a task not as simple as one may guess. In it is a commonplace after several years of web development that they are mostly the result of an implementation ad hoc, growing usually from small to large applications and becoming very soon both complex to use and difficult to maintain [18].

In this paper, we present techniques and approaches for the organized design and augmentative development of an adaptive Virtual University environment that combines several techniques to provide personalization features to the educational material and the exchanging data streams. The Virtual University environment has been implemented to support the postgraduate course in the School of Fine Arts in Greece [40]. The designed hypermedia environment aims to cover the fundamental needs of a student in a virtual university environment, which is wide range of automatically renewable educational material on any subject chosen under the umbrella of a powerful set of supportive tools homogenized with the user's topics of interest.

Special care has been taken in order to fully support incremental scaling, reusability and maintenance of the web-based learning environment both in users' terms and educational volume. The aim is to define a framework that will define well the development procedure of a web-based learning environment. A combined Web engineering methodology (Unified Modeling Language – UML [18] and WebML [11]) has been adopted for the conceptual and presentation model standardization.

The environment at the moment provides courses on web development and advanced graphics and fine arts. Key features included are the curriculum adaptation [8] and the communicational information filtering [30]. The system uses with a range of supportive tools like communication tools and common shared space. The Virtual University environment supports personalization features to the educational topic and the exchanging information flow in order to customize the educational process to the learning curve of the student. This is accomplished by acquiring each user's learning model and activity choices. The educational profile is first developed for each student based on a questionnaire and continuously evolves according to the student's choices and activities within the virtual university framework.

This paper is organized as follows; section 2 presents a overlall description of the virtual university. The adaptive web used in the system is described in section 3. The particular adaptation mechanisms are the theme of section 4. Section 5 outlines intelligent filtering in data. In section 6 we discuss the methodology followed to develop the environment. Results are summarized and future work is presented in section 7.

2 Overall Description of the Environment

The designed adaptive hypermedia environment addresses to users with different knowledge backgrounds and targets. The environment is optimized to include any web-based course that might be available. The courses on all directions are available for every student. In fact it is possible to take any of the courses at every possible combination. However in order to clarify the scale of difficulty for each course there is a short description and a grade (starting from one grading up to four for the most advanced topics) indicating the complexity and the demanding know-how of each one of them. Introductory topics address to novice students and will cover introduction of the Internet, introduction in computer assisted multimedia design etc. Advanced topics cover areas such as advanced web application development, advanced 3-dimensional modeling, etc.

Due to the diversity of the students all courses are personalized and delivered differently to groups of students with common characteristics. An educational profile is developed for each student based on a questionnaire that the student is asked to fulfill after choosing his/her first course to attend. The stereotype of the user evolves while the student performs activities in the Virtual University environment (such activities are the specific course flow that is followed and the students' achievements in tests and projects).

As a sequel the stereotype of the student is used in order to support the system's curriculum adaptation model [8]. In this case adaptation is used in order to perform at first a fundamental pedagogical curriculum sequencing – set by the curricula author -, but, which is most, automatic information pushing of the most appropriate online resources for every student based on its profile. Complementary the technique of link deactivation is used in order to deliver specialized dictionary help for keywords throughout the corpus of a course.

On the other hand an intelligent cognitive filtering is performed, in conjunction with the web based educational material collaborative filtering, to unify the popular communicational (email) and workspace (share space) support within the Virtual University framework, in full parallelism with the fact that every university gives its students an email and some electronic space to utilize with the classes. The communication services in our framework take into consideration the activities of the user in its educational journey within the courses, by deriving some key notions, in order to make a categorization of the information flowing into his/her mailbox. As a result it makes use of the students profile to selectively filter out and categorize its incoming data stream delivering them to proper activity-based topics together with older relative information creating in this way a personal archive. In the virtual university email support feature, the student is assigned an email account or alternatively he/she can choose to use their own account within the system through the web client supplied (IMAP protocol version 4 [16] support for the communication).

All the above environment structure has been presented so as to be an actual paradigm of the adaptation and standardization techniques described in the following sections. Our aim is to present the combination of the well-known educational techniques and outline a design procedure that will maximize the maintenance and reusability of any web-based learning environment. The design has been based on a XML -based profile for the hypermedia domain. Starting from the conceptual model of the application we produced the object oriented basic guidelines for the navigational structure model. In order to support personalization a web based modeling language was used with both declarative concepts and procedural educational rules that compute and store user-specific information.

3 Model of the Adaptive Web Environment

The user profile records information concerning the user and his knowledge state [5], [1]. This information is vital for the system's operation according to the user's needs and preferences. The method used is an implicit collection of user's actions and it requires minimum user involvement [17]. However, such data is quite difficult to gather because it is not easy to represent the user's knowledge abilities. Moreover, the nature of the Web imposes certain constraints on the system's perception of the user. For the time being, it is difficult and time-consuming to record every user action. In the environment at hand it has been chosen to keep track of the users' traversal path for every visit, the courses', topics' and subjects' keywords and analytical scores in tests, projects and all given grades in general (every user- student has a personal history list of achievements and grades just like all students).

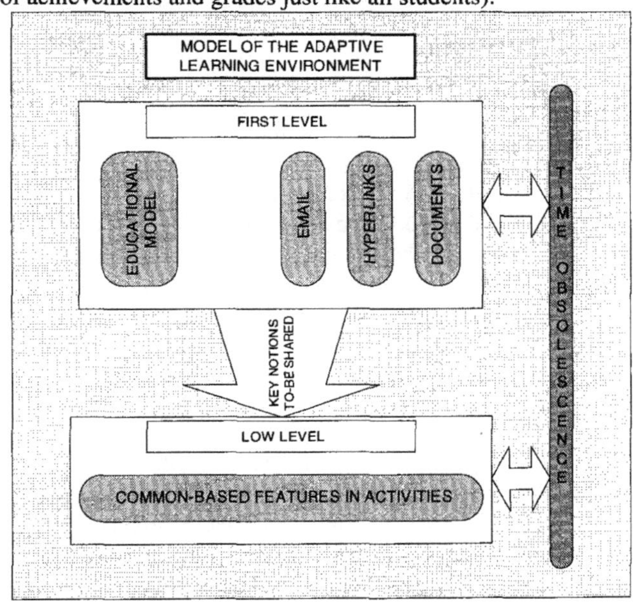

Figure 1. Model of the Adaptive Learning Environment

3.1 Model of the Adaptive Learning Environment

Due to the variety and diversity of the possible activities of a single user in the Virtual University there is a need for differentiation in the model itself. This model contains different levels that represent each environment service and a low level that interconnects the behavior of the user within all the services together. As a result the model of each user is both a learning description for the educational procedure and activity representation for the rest services. Specifically the educational procedure is being monitored for the choices (e.g. courses, topics and key notions selection) and the progress (e.g. tests, questions and project achievements). To the other end information exchange within the whole set of communication tools is also recorded (e.g. topics in emails exchange, titles in file exchange and hyperlink exchange). In this way the method creates a set of characteristics (e.g. keywords) that best describe and therefore represent each user's activity.

In the sequel the profile's higher level members are examined for similarity in the characteristics. Each member of the activity level delivers to the interchange level the properties that describe it. In this common pool best-matched properties are considered interconnected and therefore of common interest. These notions that are found common in more than one profile member in the activity level are stored in the interconnection member of the profile in the lower layer. They are used to improve the usability of the environment by interconnecting the activities that they describe in a dynamic sense personalized per user.

3.2 Aging parameters in the Model

In order to prevent forgotten and obsolete notions to be maintained in the environment's model, it is designed to support time-based distinction of users. The properties that have not been used for a period of time longer than two academic seasons become disabled (though kept in the users model) indicating that perhaps the user has nothing more to do with this keyword. In the third subsequent season these keywords are being deleted as out-dated for the user. The property obsolescence can be easily transformed so as to be based on the hypothesis that a uniform distribution of property appearance over time is more valuable than others [2]. Although this approach has been neither proved nor disproved, the mere influence of time is a subject of high effect.

3.3 Educational Target

A learning model that used quite often in the past by other educational systems and which is used in our frame is the overlay model [9]. In this model, the user's knowledge is considered to be a subset of the knowledge perceived by an expert in the learning field. Using this representation, the system presents the educational material to the user so that in the end his/her knowledge will match the expert's knowledge. Another way of modeling the user's knowledge is to use Bayesian networks [25], [34]. These networks probabilistically reason about the student's knowledge state concerning the various knowledge concepts.

4 Course Personalization Methods

The Virtual University environment consists of an educational model that uses a curricula adaptation based firstly on the stereotypes, created with the registration's questionnaire, and subsequently mixed with personalization features for each user.

It is recommended that a Web-based educational environment should offer some sort of guidance to the user by presenting the next best course units to be learned [33], [26]. The used type of curriculum sequencing involves the selection of the most appropriate section or topic to be presented next. This selection is made according to the concepts learned by the user indicated in his/her profile. If the user has not learned yet all the outcome concepts of the current subsection (section) then the system will select the topic (subsection) with the least unknown prerequisite concepts. This goes on until the user learns the outcome concepts of all sections of the specific course.

The users receive key characterization in the educational profile level according to their interests deriving from their topic accesses. Once a topic (typically a web page) is updated with new material concerning a specific topic, the users who had with certain frequency expressed interest on it in the past are informed about the changes. Thus instead of making the users go after recently updated web pages, it is desirable to have information selectively flowed to them. This is called information filtering [17]. In our case we address the collaborative filtering method, which is the filtering of information based on the advice of others [23]. The users are not only informed of the recently updated topics that they have visited quite often in the past, but also for those topics that have been accessed with certain frequency by other users belonging in the same group of interest with the first ones. In particular, the profile of the users' information needs is captured through their classification in groups of interest.

The classification of the users into subsets according to their path traversal and page accesses will be achieved by using the spectral filtering method developed in [6, 12, 13, 21]. The initial motivation for the development of the method was the discovery of high-quality topical resources in hyperlinked corpora. The full power of the approach is visible when being applied on entities other than hyperlinked documents. In our paradigm we have two kinds of entities: web pages and users accessing them.

5 Filtering on the Interchanging User Data within the Virtual University

Cognitive filtering characterizes the contents of an incoming stream data and the information needs of potential topic specific pools of knowledge, and then using these representations to intelligently match data streams to pools [24]. Our approach is more a combined content-based and property-based filtering under [27] the common umbrella of the lower profile layer. Cognitive filtering in this environment lies in between filtering based on the content of the incoming streams of the communication data and filtering based on the properties that include more than areas of interest of the user. In this way the environment automatically transforms according to the user needs transparently to the user. The Virtual University performs categorization through filtering in a common sense manner by delivering relative information of data streams together in just one most suitable place per different activity.

In this way each educational course and topic is intelligently possible to be accessed from all topic relevant places within the environment. Adaptive presentation of hyperlinks interconnect all relevant resources such as emails (e.g. exchanged among student partners), files (e.g. shared or distributed by course responsible) and all sorts of hyperlinks from all sections of the Virtual University. It is possible to access all sorts of topic-specific knowledge pools from any of them. We imagined this like the best way to access an email from our own mailbox or have a look in a book from the course's library just while we attend a course (without having to look in all the email list or the library's citations).

6 Basing Adaptivity Features on Standards

During the last few years many methods for hypermedia and Web design have been proposed; see [22] for an overview. Most of them are not based on the UML, like RMM (Relationship Management Methodology) [19] and OOHDM (Object-Oriented Hypermedia Design Method) [29]. They utilize entity-relationship diagrams, OMT or their own notation and techniques. Recently, some new approaches propose UML extensions for the hypermedia domain, for instance the development process of Conallen [15], the extension for multimedia applications in [28] and the UML extension of [4].

6.1 Design Approach

The design and development process was addressed as follows, assuming that a number of different kinds of specialists played distinct roles:
1) The data expert designed the structural model;
2) The application architect designed pages and the navigation between them;
3) The style architect designs the presentation styles of pages;
4) The site administrator designs users and personalization options, including business rules.

This is in fact the layout description of the OOHDM (Object-Oriented Hypermedia Design Method) that is an object-oriented evolution of HDM which uses abstraction and composition mechanisms in an object oriented framework to describe complex information items and specify navigation patterns and interface transformations. In OOHDM, a hypermedia application is built in a step-by-step process supporting an incremental or prototype process model. Each step focuses on a particular design concern, and an object-oriented model is built.

6.2 Standardization

All web based learning environment aim to support a large number of different courses and students that evolves continuously and expands rapidly over time. However web application development is a multi-facet activity involving different players with different skills and goals. In that sense there is a need for an educational environment that is not only covering the wide spectrum of different educational services, but it also is based on careful and organized design that facilitates reusability and supports maintenance for a long period of use.

To achieve that, standardized representation was used for the user modeling profile, the courses and the communicational services. The environment at hand did not introduce yet another language for data modeling from scratch, but combined in the best features of a number of classical notations like the E/R model [14], the ODMG object-oriented model [10], and UML class diagrams [7]. To cope with the requirement of expressing redundant and calculated information, a simplified, OQL-like query language was employed, by which it is possible to specify derived information. This synthesis of methods allowed separation of concerns that is a key requirement for any Web modeling procedure.

6.3 Personalization

In order to support personalization, the environment is explicitly modeled in the structure schema in the form of predefined entities called User, Group and Activity. Groups describe sets of users with common characteristics, whereas users denote individuals. Users always belong to at least one group, at first the default one (generic users). Each user or group is described by means of specific Activity properties that form the profile. Activity properties are modeled as special type of entities in the structure schema. As the normal entities, user and group profiles are internally sub-structured into attributes and components, which are used for writing derivation queries. Their features were used to store group-specific or individual content, like course selections, list of topics, and keywords derived from communicational streams of data.

Then, declarative expressions (Object Query Language) were added to the structure schema, which define derived content based on the profile data. This personalized content is used both in the composition of the multiplayer profile and in the definition of presentation specifications for each modeled case. Furthermore XML [36] syntax was used to define in high-level abstraction the reactions of the user profile to site-related events caused by the users, like hyperlink clicks and content updates. These rules provide in detail the adaptation done in all levels of the user model.

The interaction between the users and the environment is proactive in two senses. First the users choose which educational material to see and what activities to perform by clicking on hyperlinks, in response to that the user model autonomously determines which content to render, by anticipating the effect of the user clicks. This feature was modeled, by expressing the filling semantics of pages. In the case that the user accessed a page, which contains an index over an entity pointing to data on that entity, the content of the pointed data is pending, i.e., it depends on the user's choice and the user's profile of one element in the preceding index unit. In order to cope with pending elements are filled using with a default value expressed by means of a declarative query (e.g., the object of a preceding index unit that satisfies a given predicate). Alternatively leaving the pending element empty, so that the user must explicitly perform a selection in one or more preceding units to display the content of the pending unit or filling the pending unit with a predefined default value (e.g., the first element chosen from a preceding index unit) was used in corresponding cases.

Syntactically, the treatment of a pending element is specified by choosing one of the above three options as the value of an ad hoc filling attribute, located in the "pointing" unit. If no value is specified, the pending unit is left empty.

In order to support personalization, declarative expressions (Object Query Language) were added to the structure schema, which define derived content based on the profile data. This personalized content is used both in the composition of the multiplayer profile and in the definition of presentation specifications for each modeled case. Furthermore XML syntax was used to define in high-level abstraction the reactions of the user profile to site-related events caused by the users, like hyperlink clicks and content updates. These rules provide in detail the adaptation done in all levels of the user model.

To publish the above relationships on the web it is fundamental to specify the site view of the environment to be built. In Figure 2 show an excerpt specification of an environment using the WebML graphical notation. Each page, shown as dashed rectangles, consists of units to be displayed together – dynamic in content. The example shows that careful specification of the core elements is helping the web developer to build a consistent and successful set of pages for any web application.

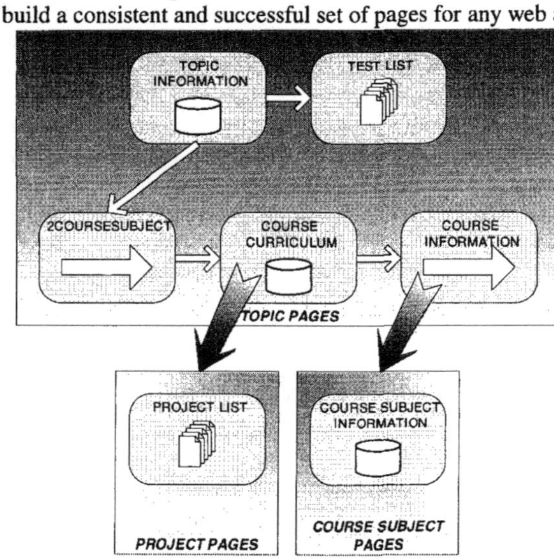

Figure 2. Composition and Navigation example

User Comments and the Next-Generation VU

In this paper we present techniques and approaches for the organized design and augmentative development of an adaptive Virtual University environment. It is an environment that is actually used at full scale to support a number of different postgraduate courses of internet and multimedia technology in a 1500 students' university department. Since the activation of the environments services last semester we have received encouraging comments through the on-site evaluation form. Our choice to combine course material and supportive tools together in a single adaptive environment appears to have improved students' studies and it is as they say "handy in the everyday use" of the system. At the moment we are conducting a second formal evaluation with a fill-in form e-mail to students and also by interviewing the academics responsible for the course material in order to evaluate the traversal paths used by students in their studies.

The VU as any web application development is a multi-facet activity involving different players with different skills and goals. To achieve that, standardized representation was used for the user modeling profile, the courses and the communicational services. Therefore the techniques used for the design and implementation are extensively discussed as they were considered fundamental in order to support system upgrade, code reuse and administration issues.

Our future work aims to personalize even more services for the virtual university users in order to attract different academic community members such as researchers. Finally we believe that an extension of our adaptive user model will try to cover the needs of alumni in a virtual university.

References

1. Anderson, J. (1993). *Rules of the Mind.* Lawrence Erlbaum Associates.
2. Arampatzis, A.T., van der Weide, T.P., Koster, C.H.A. and van Bommel, P.: 2000, *Term selection for filtering based distribution of terms over time, RIAO' 2000 Conference Proceedings, Vol. 2,* April 12-14, Paris, France, 1221-1237
3. Barua, A., Chellappa, R. and Whinston, B., A.: An electronic infrastructure for a virtual university, *Communications of the ACM*, 9/1997/Vol. 40, No 9.
4. Baumeister, H., Koch, N., Mandel L.: Towards a UML extension for hypermedia design. InProceedings «UML»'99, France, R., Rumpe, B. (eds), LNCS, Vol. 1723. Springer-Verlag 614-629, 1999.
5. Beck, Stern, Haugsjaa 1996 Applications of AI in Education, ACM Crossroads.
6. Bharat, K. and Henzinger, M. (1998) Improved algorithms for topic distillation in a hyperlinked environment. In Proceedings of ACM Conf. Res. And Development in Information Retrieval, pp.104-111.
7. Booch, G., Jacobson I., and Rumbaugh, J. (1998): The Unified Modeling Language User Guide, The Addison-Wesley Object Technology Series.
8. Brusilovsky, P. (1998): Adaptive educational systems on the world-wide-web: A review of available technologies. In 4th *International Conference in Intelligent Tutoring Systems,* San Antonio, TX
9. Carr, B. and Goldstein, I. (1977). Overlays: a Theory of Modeling for Computer-aided *Instruction. Technical Report,* AI Lab Memo 406, MIT.
10. Cattell, Barry and Bartels (Eds.) (1997): The Object Database Standard: ODMG 2.0, Morgan-Kaufmann Series in Data Management Systems.
11. Ceri, S., Fraternali, P., Paraboschi, S. (1999): Data-Driven, One-To-One Web Site Generation for Data-Intensive Applications. Proc.VLDB, pp. 615-626.
12. Chakrabarti, S., Dom, B., Gibson, D., Kumar, S., R., Raghavan, P., Rajagopalan, S. and Tomkins, A. Spectral filtering for resource discovery. In *Proceedings of ACM SIGIR Workshop on Hypertext Information Retrieval on the Web,* Melbourne, Australia, 1998.
13. Chakrabarti,Dom,Gibson, Kleinberg, Kumar, Raghavan, Rajagopalan, Tomkins (1999): A. Mining the Web's link structure. *IEEE Computer* 32 (8) pp.60-68.

14. Chen (1976): The Entity-Relationship Model, Towards a Unified View of Data, ACM-Transactions on Database Systems, 1:1, pp. 9-36.
15. Conallen, J. (1999): Building Web Applications with UML. Addison-Wesley.
16. Crispin, M. (1996): Internet Message Access Protocol, Version 4r1 , RFC 2060.
17. Hanani, U., Shapira, B. and Shoval, P. (1999): Information Filtering: Overview of Issues, Research and Systems. User Modeling and User-Adapted Interaction, Kluwer Academic Publishers, Netherlands.
18. Hennicker, Koch, (2001): A UML-based Methodology for Hypermedia Design, *First International Workshop on Web-Oriented Software Technology*, Spain.
19. Isakowitz, Stohr, Balasubramanian (1995): A methodology for the design of structured hypermedia applications. Communications of the ACM, 8(38),34-44.
20. Jacobson I., Booch G., Rumbaugh J. (1999): The Unified Software Development Process. Addison Wesley.
21. Kleinberg, J. (1998): Authoritative sources in a hyperlinked environment. *Proc. ACM-SIAM Symposium on Discrete Algorithms*
22. Lowe D., Hall W. (1999): Hypermedia & the Web: An engineering approach. John Wiley & Sons.
23. Maes, P. and Kozierok, R.: Learning Interface Agents. *Proceedings of AAAI*, 459-465, 1993
24. Malone, T., Grant, K., Turbak, F., Brobst, S. and Cohen, M.: 1987, Intelligent Information Sharing Systems. *Communication of the ACM* 30(5), 390-402.
25. Martin, J. and VanLehn, K. Student assessment using Bayesian nets. International Journal of Human-Computer Studies, Vol. 42.
26. Mac Arthur J. W., Environmental fluctuations and species diversity. In *Ecology and Evolution of Communities*, ed. by M. L. Cody M. L. and J. M. Diammond J. M. (Belknap, Cambridge, 1975) pp. 74–80.
27. Morita, M. and Shinoda, Y.: Information filtering based on user behavior analysis and best match retrieval. *Proceedings of the 17th NNUAL Intl. AACM SIGIR Conference on Research and Development, 272-281,* 1994
28. Sauer, S. and Engels, G.: Extending UML for Modeling of Multimedia Applications. In Proceedings of the IEEE Symposium on Visual Languages VL'99, IEEE Computer Society 80-87, 1999
29. Schwabe and Rossi:, The Object Oriented Hypermedia Design Model, Communication of the ACM, Vol. 38, #8, Aug. 1995
30. Shapira, B., Shoval, P. and Hannani, U.: Stereotypes in information filtering systems, *Information Processing and Management* 33(3), 273-287, 1997
31. Shih, K., T.: Software Systems for Virtual University Operations, *ACM Multimedia Conference*, 2001.
32. Stern, M., Woolf, B. and Kurose, J. (1997). Intelligence on the Web?. Proceedings of the 8th World Conference of the AIED Society, Kobe, Japan.
33. Stern and Woolf. (1998) Curriculum sequencing in a Web-based tutor. In B. P. Goettl, H. M. Halff, C. L. Redfield, and V. J. Shute, editors, *Intelligence Tutoring System (Proc. 4th Int'l Conf. ITS'98)*, pages 584-593. Springer.
34. Stern, M., Beck, J. and Woolf, B. Naive Bayes Classifiers for User Modeling. *Proceedings of the Seventh International Conference on User Modeling*, 1999.

35. Woolf, B. (1992). AI in Education. *In Encyclopedia of Artificial Intelligence*, 2nd Edition, S. Shapiro, Ed. NY: Wiley, 434-444.
36. XML, Principles, Tools and Techniques, WWW Journal, Vol II, (4), Fall 1997.
37. The Virtual University Organization , USA. (2002): http://vu.org/
38. Kentucky VU, USA (2002): http://www.kyvu.org/
39. VU Gazette, USA (2002): http://www.geteducated.com/vugaz.htm
40. Athens School of Fine Arts, Greece (2002): http://www.asfa.gr

AMADeUs: A Framework To Support Multi-Dimensional Learner Evaluation

Patrícia Tedesco and Alex Sandro Gomes

Centro de Informática – UFPE - Cx. Postal 7851 Cidade Universitária
CEP:50732-970 Recife-PE Brazil
{pcart, asg}@cin.ufpe.br

Abstract. Brazilian math assessments are an important social problem nationwide. A significant amount of our students score 3/10 at assessments that take place at the end of their secondary school years. The teachers´ skills are one of the most important variables and the use of educational technology significantly contributes to the improvement of students´ achievements. Thus, teachers´ continuous education is essential. Also, by providing distant formation courses, we can reach a broader range of teachers. AMADeUs, our project, is based on the principle that multi-dimensional learner evaluation is very important to build a better picture of students' development and participation. Our design decisions were taken based on experiences with matematica.net. Furthermore, pilot studies are been conducted to orient the design processes and a methodology for this type of courses.

Introduction

Nowadays, computational environments for Distance Education (e.g. BlackBoard, WebCT) are mostly generic tools that allow for course creation without any link to the domain in question. Furthermore, they do not offer any specific support for neither the student nor the teacher.

Another common way of designing and implementing environments is based on instructionism, which considers that good presentations of knowledge are enough to guarantee learning. This suffers from a serious limitation: little or no consideration for the student's learner model. Works in AIED (Artificial Intelligence in Education) have been striving to solve this problem (amongst others) for a long time now.

As far as distance learning goes, there is a gap to be fulfilled with the application of higher-level educational environments, which, not only provide better tools for the teacher, but also that provide adequate support for the learning process. As far as teaching is concerned, we should aim at providing support not only for the teacher to follow the learning of specific concepts, but also for him/her to follow the evolution of competencies such as organisation, group interest, discipline, level of communication. Thus, methodologies for multi-level evaluations are of great interest.

The computational system we are proposing not only incorporates evaluation techniques, but also, in doing so, it caters for the processes of negotiation (amongst

learners, and learners and teacher) and mediation. This is achieve by the use of intelligent support agents that will help users perform this activities. In its first application, our platform will be used for teacher formation.
The AMADeUs solution emerged from the necessity of implementing an architecture that took the domain specific needs into consideration. The domain was elementary math teacher continuous formation.

Motivation

There are important assessment problems associated with math's learning in elementary levels [Ine2001]. In general, students finish secondary courses with minimal maths knowledge, corresponding to competencies to solve primary maths problems. In the last three years of school, no more knowledge is acquired. The same report indicates that assessments improve significantly when educational technology is used in learning.
In this light, we can see that there is a clear identified necessity to better form maths teachers. Actually, formation courses occur in various forms. The main distinction being the number of teachers and distance from formation centers. In the first case, if the number of teachers is too large, administration prefers to organize single, short-duration events. Those meetings are like conferences, in which teachers have little opportunity to interact with their peers and instructors. On the other extreme of the spectrum, there are teachers living far from formations centers. In this case, they are frequently trained by private consultants societies. The interventions are brief and non-systematic. Graduate professionals, with short pos-graduate formation, conduct those courses. In both cases, teacher participate in short time courses without continued evaluation.
Many authors indicate that teacher's formation should be organized as a continuous process. Information technology can be an alternative solution to make it feasible. We are investigating this solution with many schoolteachers. In our solution, teachers are engaged in communities of practices and were accompanied with mixed methodology. Virtual and classroom activities are combined and distributed in a long-term formation program. Pos graduate tutors assisted the teachers. In a complementary way, teachers work and challenge peers from the same school and far from those work place.

Some Possible Solutions

The socio-constructivist approach to learning [Vygotsky 1998] suggests that the learner is part of a social group, and, as such, should be able to question, discover and understand the world in which he/she is inserted. The boom of communication technologies [Paiva 1997] has made it possible for us to implement computer environments that take advantage (and enconurage) group interaction. This kind of environment is generally known as *Computer Supported Collaborative Learning* (CSCL).

Amongst the various possibilities in CSCL, we want to focus on the tecnology based on projects. The idea is to teach based on discovering solutions for real life problems. According to Dewey (1933), knowledge and ideas emerge from situations where we need to learn from experiences that mean something for us. Boud, Keogh e Walker [1985] define reflection as bein the act of mulling things over, and trying to understand our own experiences. This is a fundamental skill in learning, and is also the one we lack most. Thus the need for intelligent facilitators.

When talking about reflection, we cannot leave out the process of articulation. Self, Karakirik, Kor, Tedesco e Dimitrova [2000] define articulation as being the act of verbalising our thought processes. Amongst the main benefits of this are the fact that verbalising might help us develop our thought processes; articulating something brings its weaknesses to light, and may generate interesting discussions on the topic. As a general rule, collaborative learning is more productive when participants are engaged into open-ended problem solving. A possible way for constructing this learning situations is to propose projects involving learner groups and to provide intelligent support that reinforces the ideas of reflection and articulation.

A project can be defined as a process that is divided into stages, related to one another, forming a flow. Each stage can be evaluated through the execution of one (or more) tasks that should show some results. Figure 1 shows an example of a workflow. The environment we are building is based on the idea of workflows – which allow us to visualise and evaluate the work being done in the different stages of the project. The idea is to provide tools for evaluating tasks, monitoring group interaction and evaluating the learning process.

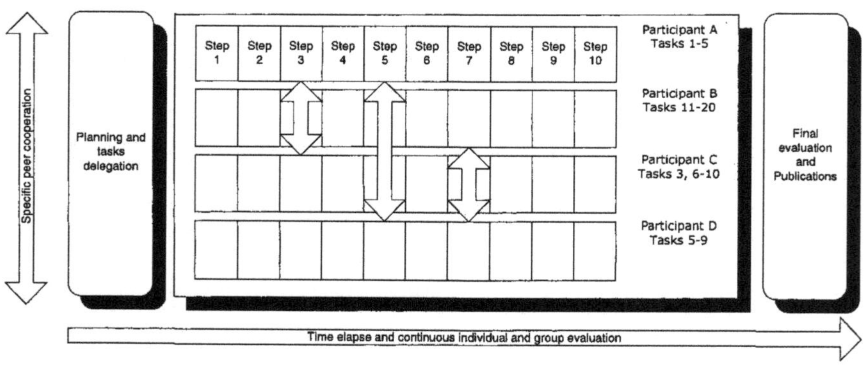

Fig. 1. A Workflow

Collaborative Learning Support

Aiming at supporting more effective colaboration, AIED research has been trying to better understand the collaboration process and to build system that supports it. This is stems from the fact that the computer provides an excellent context for group interactions [Littleton e Häkkinen 1999]. Learning collaboratively implies achieving solutions that would not be found otherwise and negotiating shared knowledge [Crook 1994]. Dillenbourg [1999] argues that we can support collaboration by (1) fixing initial conditions; (2) constructing scenarios; (3) supporting productive interactions, by structuring the dialogue and (4) monitoring and regulating the learning process. In our plaform, we intend to support collaboration in these four levels. The idea is to follow Dillenbourg´s guidelines and structuring the ineraction (via the use of tools that facilitate communication and agents that monitor the dialogue) and through the presence of mediators (either the teacher or artificial ones).

The AMADeUs´Architecture

Our project involves creating a general framework for adaptive learning environments. To start with, due to the serious problem with maths´ learning in Brazil, we intend to implement a prototype directed to mathematics.
Technically speaking, one of the main novelties about our project lies on our use of constructivism to allow for the implementation of an assessment system that allows for a continous, diagnostic evaluation of the learning process, differently from most on-the-market learning environments. Furthermore, we also intend to promote effective collaboration by organising participants´groups in project teams, and guiding their interaction [Jermann et al. 2001] in accordance with the guidelines for effective collaboration defined in [Tedesco 2001]. We have also taken special care while designing the interface – we have used user centered design techniques and taken users´ awareness into consideration.

AMADeUs first prototype has mathematics as its domain (we have discussed the need for further materials of this sort earlier on in the paper), and we have established a partnership with the State Secretary for Education in Pernambuco (a state in the Brazilian Northeast).

Our initial model consists of several agents, three of them being directly concerned with intelligent support. The idea is to evaluate the entities performance during construction of the first prototype. The results obtained then will indicate to us wheter we need to include, remove or alter agents funcionalities. It should be noted that we are taking into consideration issues of reusabilitly, maintainability, scalability and portability across platforms while designing our agents. The system´s architecture is shown in Figure 2.

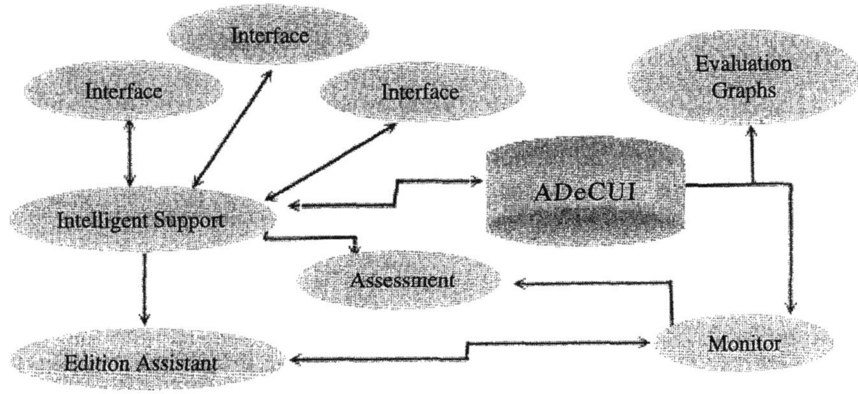

Fig. 2. The AMADeUS Architecture.

Since we want AMADeUs to be as generic as possible, we have been also thinking about a way of using its core with computer science applications. To us, one of the best ways to do it is to build a tool for collaboratively carrying out projects. According to Santoro [2001] such environments must provide tools for: defining processes to account for collaborative process; selecting and implementing tools for performing project-related tasks; storing and retrieving information about past projects; using the internet as its basic platform. Thus, we will be incorporating tools for guiding the collaborative process in the AMADEUS framework [Gomes 2001]. One of the most effective ways of doing so is to incorporate intelligent support agents, that will help participants interact, reflect on the interaction, and thus reach more refined solutions.

Intelligent Support

As far as intelligent support goes, we have several agents working on different levels. In the following, we present each of them in turn. In fact, in order to account for a multi-level evaluation and (subsequent) support, the student modelling component our system consists of a multi-agent society, whose members are described below.

A_1 – Action Modelling Agent

This agent is initialised every time a new student logs onto the system, and follows him/her until the end of the interaction. A_1 is basically responsible for collecting (and analysing) students´actions.

When the agent finds out that the learner is having some difficulties with the syllabus, it sends the teacher a notification. A_1 reasons about the actions following 3 criteria: (1) possible misconceptions; (2) correct actions and (3) strategies used for solving the current problem

A_1 can also learn tutor´s actions, and is able to take the initiative with the tutor´s permition. That obviously includes suggesting new learning situations, interacting with other learners, and so on and so forth.

A_2 - Student´s Production Agent

This agent analyses students´ records (their production and teacher/instructor´s evaluations) in order to suggest the strengths and weaknesses of each student. It also uses information from A_1. As we determine students´ competencies, A_2 accumulates a learner model. Besides performance and quality of production, the following parameters are also included (as suggested in [Hoppe and Plotzner 1999]) : (1) can help in topic; (2) needs help in topic.

When it deems necessary, A_2 asks A_3 (described in detail later on) to form groups based on the contents needed by learner x.

A_4 - Rithm Monitoring Agent

Sometimes, students in distance learner courses indicate their lack of motivation/ understanding by not doing their activities, and not logging on the system. Thus, A_4 uses this information to try to assess whether there are problems and where they are, and thus inform the learner models. It can try to solve it by forming groups, sending communications to the leaners and informing the tutor that there are problems.

A_5 – Interface Agents

This agent analyses users activities in the microworlds interfaces, and will try to help its charge by taking local decisions (which situation to present now? Does the interface need to be adapted?) It will base its decisions on a library of past situations faced by previous students of the system. A_5 also provides feedback for the learning monitoring system A.De.C.U.I.. It also has functionalities to interpret situations and feedbacks provided by A.De.C.U.I.

The agent that monitors the microworld interfaces is responsible for monitoring whether the student has already seen all the available situations. It also helps the tutor to identify and propose new problem situations for the students and to reinforce learning by assessing what has been done in each microworld.

A6 – Editoring helper

This is responsible by helping the teacher to create new learning situations for the students. The teacher consults the production knowledge base and conceptual maps graph in order to assess what would be most beneficial for the student. The teacher can also see other teacher´s work for similar situations.

A7 – ADeCUI´s data Analyser
This agent will analyse the data present in A.De.C.U.I. in order to give feedback to the interface agents about what the learners know and what are their weaknesses. Data mining techniques are being applied here in order to guarantee that the relevant information will be available to the agent or to the teacher in due time.

Group Agents

A_3 - Group Monitoring Agent
This agent works with information from A_1 and A_2 in order to form groups to learn given topics. When A_3 needs to form a group, it asks the agents A_2 to inform which learners could fit the profile, and sends them messages inviting them to join a group. Agents A_1 and A_3 then negotiate in order to find activities that are beneficial for all the group members. Agent A_3 also monitors the group interactiong, trying to keep the group motivated and collaborating effectively.In order to do so, A_3 keeps track of the social roles played by group members, identifying the following: collaborator, tutor, competitor, leader, reflective, shy and idea generator.

A_3 also has the following responsibilities: a) motivate members that are not participating as much, and trying to reinforce the guidelines for consensual decision making [Tedesco 2001]; b) mediating possible conflicts; c) reminding participant of options not explored yet. A_3 also keeps a group model, which includes a detailed log of the interaction, not only for users to see and reflect upon but also for the teacher to consult.
Having described the agents provided for intelligent support, we will now focus on another support level: The one present at the interfaces.

About the Other Components

In AMADeUs, there are several environments students (and teachers) can interact in. We have provided environments for individual learning (interfaces, email box, pigeonhole), for group interaction (lists, chats, foruns, evaluation central, common workspaces) and so forth. We have paid special attention to group formation and negotiation issues (below we describe our findings about awareness interfaces) and evaluation.

It is worth noting that we have also provided space for the teachers to interact with one another and to find better ways to perform their activities (planning of courses, tutoring, evaluation) . In fact, we (together with our project team) working on finding out a methodology to design tools for the teacher to use.

Awareness Interfaces

The first results obtained during a pilot study have indicated that asynchronous user component web interfacse are too complicate for use. Users models of same processes are inappropriate and conduct to many difficulties in utilization. Besides, maths teachers, as a significant number of teachers in elementary education, are not familiar with information technology. Our main intention concerning the interface is, however, to create extremely simple web interfaces that approximate, as much as possible, users' models concerning cooperative learning to teach. Another principle adopted in web design was that signaling co-presence could improve cooperative initiatives and facilitate the users´ conceptualizing process (Erickson T. and Kellogg, 2000).
The interface design is centered on users´ actual practices. Our aim is to create, through the interface, awareness of social participation, as a group constituent, with specific roles and objectives, but interdependent with each other through social contracts.
The group's coordination, as promoted by expert tutors, intends to facilitate group conscience emergence. As we have already mentioned, the intelligent support provided will aim at reinforcing good collaboration – and that certainly involves group participation from all members. The main semiotic principle is the limited number of elements and signs in the web interface. The interface is also used to communicate co-presence in the web site. Participants can follows peers and tutors navigation through little signs on the pages.

About Multi-Level Evaluation

Evaluation in e-learning is organized according to different strategies. Systems' design is typically guided by *a priori* effectiveness comparisons of different evaluation strategies. In this platform, our aim is to coordinate the positive contributions of specific evaluation strategies, take advantage of the best features of each of them.
Our design principle is that comparing and combining different actors' points of view can substantiate evaluation results better that using single strategies. The idea is to take different strategies that focus on single actor's (students, tutors or graders) points of view on its own and combine their results in order to produce a better picture of our users.
In this light, we have proposed a combination of four strategies, which refer to those actors' evaluations of students´ progress. The four strategies are: open-end evaluation (the traditional evaluation of production, exams or papers by tutor and assistants), continuous participation evaluation (grades, tutors and staff continually evaluating contributions on chats rooms, forums and e-mail list services; interface agents following and grade students activities, and intervening in the interaction), auto-evaluation (students point of view – including the possibility of the student negotiating his/her evaluation with the system) and peer-evaluation (peers point of view – where we allow peers to evaluate and negotiate each other's evaluation).

For each strategy, we have designed specific environments and support agents. All those points of view are integrated, processed and represented in simple reports and graphs. Results from different sources are compared and combined to produce a coherent and usable student evaluation. In this way, we seem to be able to produce more agreeable and consistent results. This strategy is expressed in the design through a completely distributed evaluation dependant architecture. Active and passive units and environments compose this specific architecture.
Student's participations are monitored in chat rooms, discussion forums, e-mail lists, individual e-mail to tutors and teachers. Intelligent interfaces in user software components are responsible for modeling and evaluating students learning in action. Teacher's points of view are constructed by themselves through students production analyses in a traditional way. This point of view in complemented by participation evaluation. Peer point of view is captured in specific environments into where peers are invited to evaluate colleagues and judge colleague's production.

The AMADeUs Design

The initial proposal for the AMADeUs architecture was based mainly on a literature review together with the participants experiences in various areas. The AMADeUs team is multi-disciplinary, taking onboard teachers, Educational specialists, Psychologists, Computer Scientists and so forth.
As the design stage went on, we incorporated tools for intelligent support and group monitoring and formation. Part of our new insights came from the case studies we have carried out – as described below.

Case studies

We have carried out a first formation course to observe the parameters that could orient the interface and architecture conceptualizing processes. The focus of the course syllabus was maths teaching and learning with educational software.
Ten (10) teachers from a public school in Recife composed the groups of participants. The teachers were invited and they presented as volunteers in the study. All those professional were mathematic teachers.
The course was conducted focused specially the use of educational technology in mathematical education. We organized interlaced modules sequences of theoretical expositive meetings and experimental classes with educational software sessions. Both were conducted at the school. The overall course had six modules distributed as follows: introduction to educational technology in mathematical education, additive structures teaching and learning, multiplicative structures teaching and learning, fraction teaching and learning, function structures teaching and learning
We adopted a mixed methodology encompassing local and distant seminars. The course was programmed last for one whole year. The local meetings were conducted twice a month, lasting three (03) hours at a time. The total local meetings time

duration was 68 hours. Those meetings were interleaved with virtual discussions through both synchronous and asynchronous communication tools. The discussions were sensed anticipate the next local meeting discussion.

Observing the activity in a discussion list environment, we have:

This first experience was a very difficult one. Teachers were really septic about distance learning.

- dropbox – collect learner's production and contributions
- messages – the frequency and quality

Chat sections were those where participants engagement were modest. Discussions were difficultly mediated and anonymous contributions confounded participants.

Conclusion and further work

In this paper, we have briefly presented AMADeUs, our project of a computational distance learning platform that tries to address the deficiencies found in most on-the-market distance learning platforms: we provide mechanisms for multi-level evaluation; intelligent support that addresses not only the needs of the learner but also the needs of the teacher (in dire neglection these days); we take issues like motivation and effective collaboration into consideration.

We also have members working on methodologies to design environments that are adequate for the teachers´ pedagogical activities; we are working on group formation and negotiation and so on and so forth. Even though our project was conceived with maths in mind, we have already seen that it can be used in other domains. Our next idea is to adapt it to be used in computer science education. The idea of collaborative projects can be widely used in computer science (for designing software, for example).

In the very near future we intend to carry out a couple more case studies to validate our design methodology. We also intend, as soon as we can, to put the system to good use, in order to evaluate it, and modify it accordingly.

References

Boud, D., Keogh, R. and Walker, D.: "What is Reflection in Learning?". In Boud, D., Keogh, R. and Walker, D.(eds.) *Reflection: Turning Experience into Learning*, Kogan Page, 7-17, 1985a;

Boud, D., Keogh, R. and Walker, D., (1985). "Promoting Reflection in Learning: a Model". In Boud, D., Keogh, R. and Walker, D.(eds.) *Reflection: Turning Experience into Learning*, Kogan Page, 18-40, 1985b;

[Choren2000] R. Choren, H. Fuks e C. J. P. Lucena. *"Using Group Support System to Meet Educational Objetives*", em Sixth International Workshop on Groupware. Portugal. Outubro 2000.

Crook, C.: *Computers and the Collaborative Experience of Learning*, Routledge, 1994;

Dewey, J.: *How we Think: a restatement of the relation of reflective thinking to the educative process*, Heath, 1933.

Dillenbourg P.: Introduction: What do you mean by Collaborative Learning? In Dillenbourg, P. (ed.) *Collaborative Learning: Cognitive and Computational Approaches*. Bennet, N., DeCorte, E., Vosniadou, S. and Mandl, H. (eds), Advances in Learning and Instruction Series. Elsevier Science, 1-19, 1999;

Dillenbourg P.: *Virtual Learning Environments*. Workshop on Virtual Learning Environments, EUN Conference 2000: "Learning in the New Millennium: Building New Education Strategies for Schools", 2000;

Groove Networks.: *Groove Product Backgrounder*. White Paper. URL: www.groove.com;

Hoppe, H. U. and Ploetzner R.: Can Analytic Models Support Learning In Groups?. In Dillenbourg, P. (ed.) *Collaborative Learning: Cognitive and Computational Approaches"*. Bennett, N., DeCorte, E. Vosniadou, S. and Mandl, H. (eds.) *Advances in Learning and Instruction Series*. Pergamon Press, 103-121, 1999;

INEP, Relatório SAEB 2001: novas perspectivas. Dezembro 2001, 97 p.;

Jermann, P., Soller, A. and Mühlenbrock, M..: From Mirroring to Guiding: a Review of the State of the Art Technology for Supporting Collaborative Learning", to be presented at the Euro-CSCL'2001, 22nd-24th of March, Maastrich, Holland, 2001;

Littleton, K. and Häkkinen, P.: "Learning Together: Understanding the Processes of Computer-Based Collaborative Learning" in Dillenbourg, P. (ed.) *Collaborative Learning: Cognitive and Computational Approaches*. Bennet, N., DeCorte, E., Vosniadou, S. and Mandl, H. (eds), Advances, 1999

Nunes C. R., Ribeiro J. N. G. and Ferraz C. A. G. *Investigando Educação a Distância e o Projeto Virtus na UFPE*, Simpósio Brasileiro de Informática Educativa.

RecifeATM, "*REDE RECIFE ATM*" URL: http://www.di.ufpe.br/~recifeatm.

Self, J., Karakirik, E., Kor, A., Tedesco, P. and Dimitrova, V.: "Computer-Based Strategies for Articulate Reflection (and Reflective Articulation)". In Young, S. S., Greer. J., Maurer, H. and Chee, Y. S. (eds.) *Proceedings of the International Conference on Computers in Education/International Conference on Computer Assisted Instruction*, National Tsing Ha University, Taiwan, 3-12, 2000;

Soller, A., Goodman, B., Linton, F. and Gaimari, R.: "Promoting Effective Peer Interaction in an Intelligent Collaborative Learning System". In Goettl. B.P., Halff, H.M., Redfield, C.L., and Shutte, V.J. (eds.), *Proceedings of the 4th International Conference on Intelligent Tutoring Systems, ITS'98*, Lecture Notes in Computer Science 1452, Springer Verlag, 186-195, 1998

Tedesco, P.: *Mediating Meta-Cognitive Conflicts in Group Planning Situations*. Unpublished Doctoral Dissertation, Computer Based Learning Unit, The University of Leeds, 2001;

Tiessen E. L. and Ward D. R.: *Developing a Technology of Use for Collaborative Project-Based Learning*". Proceedings of Computer Supported on Collaborative Learning. Stanford, EUA, 1999.

Erickson T. and Kellogg W. A., Social translucence - an approach to designing systems that support social processes, *ACM Transactions on Computer-Human Interaction*, Vol. 7, No. 1, March 2000, 59–83.

Vygotsky S. L.: *A formação social da mente: o desenvolvimento dos processos psicológicos superiores*. 6ª ed. São Paulo: Martins Fontes, 1998.

[WT97] Ward D. R. and Tiessen E. L.. *"Supporting Collaborative Project-Based Learning on the WWW"*. Proceedings of Computer Support for Collaborative Learning. Toronto, Canada. 1997

ARSAC Gilbert et BALACHEFF Nicolas et MANTE Michel (1992) Teacher's role and reproducibility of didactical situations, *Educational Studies in Mathematics*, vol. 23, n° 1, 5-29;

Hoyles C. and Noss R.: A pedagogy for mathematical microworlds, *Educational Studies in Mathematics*, **23** (1992), n° 1, 31-57;

ISO2000, *International Organisation for Standardization HomePage.* URL: http://www.isso.ch/

Moll L. C. (1990), Vygotsky and education: Instructional implications of sociohistorical psychology. New York: Cambridge University Press.

THE EFFECTIVENESS OF USING COMPUTER-MEDIATED INSTRUCTION IN DISTANCE MATHEMATICS EDUCATION

MAY, S.C. CHAN

The Open University of Hong Kong
30 Good Shepherd Street,
Homantin, Kowloon, Hong Kong,
SAR, China
E-mail: mchan@ouhk.edu.hk

This paper will report work in progress on an investigation of the effectiveness of using computer-mediated instruction on learning of mathematics at the Open University of Hong Kong (OUHK). Based on the statistics generated from the WebCT system in 1999 and 2000 showed that it only about 6% of foundation pure mathematics students actively involved in the discussion board and the others browsed the page only. The aim of this study is to investigate whether WebCT is an appropriate electronic tool to enhance OUHK mathematics students' learning. This study consists of two phases which include distribution of questionnaire and focus group interviews. The paper identifies the variables from literature for designing the instruments.

1. Introduction

OUHK is the only university offering degrees to part-time adult learners in distance learning mode in Hong Kong. A communication on-line system (WebCT) was introduced four years ago to provide an additional communication channel for students. WebCT is a Web-based course tool to the higher education marketplace [1]. It integrates communication tools, including a discussion board, chat room and e-mail etc. [2]. Owing to the successful experience of the use of WebCT in higher education institutions in the USA and Canada, OUHK has been adapted WebCT since 1999 as a teaching and learning enhancement tool.

WebCT was used not only as a 'mandatory' communication tool for computing and information technology courses, but also as an 'enhancement' communication tool for mathematics, engineering, language, business and nursing courses, etc. For mandatory courses, some marks of the final grade will usually be assigned to participation in WebCT. Students are therefore required to access and participate in discussions in WebCT during the academic year. For enhancement courses, WebCT is an optional tool. Students have a choice to access and participate in WebCT. All mathematics courses have been used WebCT as an enhanced learning component in the 2001 academic year.

2. Purpose of study

On average in 1999 and 2000 about 800 students enrolled in the course: M121 A Foundation in Pure Mathematics. Statistics obtained from the records of the WebCT system shows that around 2000 messages were posted in each of these two academic years. Upon further examination, it was found that more than 88% of students had accessed the WebCT page, but only about 6% (52 of 866) of them were actively[1] involved in the discussion board in 2000 academic year. It means that the majority of M121 students browsed the page only. To explore the effectiveness of using WebCT, it is necessary to investigate whether using WebCT is an effective tool for OUHK mathematics students to enhance their learning.

The aim of this study is therefore to investigate whether WebCT is an appropriate tool to enhance students' learning of mathematics. This study is to examine OUHK mathematics students' attitudes to the use of WebCT in collaboration with their learning of mathematics, to investigate the factors that encourage and discourage these students from participating in discussion in WebCT, and to evaluate these students' perceptions of the effect of using WebCT in learning mathematics. To achieve this study, the following research questions will be served as guidelines:

1. What are distance mathematics students' attitudes to the use of WebCT in collaboration with their learning of mathematics?
2. What are the factors that encourage and discourage distance mathematics students in participating in discussions in WebCT?
3. According to distance mathematics students' perceptions, what is the effectiveness of using WebCT in the learning of mathematics?
4. What is the relationship between attitudes, factors, and perceived effectiveness obtained from the last three questions and distance mathematics students' background?

However, this is a two-year research study and it is still at the beginning stage. This paper will therefore identify the variables from previous research findings about the positive and negative feedback related to students' attitudes to using computers, factors that influence participating in discussions, the effectiveness of using computers in learning, and the relationship between the above issues and students' background to design the instruments for this study.

3. Factors identification

3.1 *Using technology in mathematics education*

Examples of the use of computers to enhance the teaching of mathematics have been in existence for at least two decades. In a study of examining the effects of use of problem-solving software [3], 120 elementary students were taught problem-solving strategies and regularly used computer problem-solving software (Bounce, Ponds, Safari Search, and Puzzle Tanks) for 15 weeks. Analysis of students' journals and classroom interview data indicated that students learned to monitor their learning and improved their problem-solving skills.

Another example also shows a study using e-mail communication to promote problem-solving skills, where the cognitive approach has been applied. This study was to evaluate the authenticity of a specific email activity that linked

---

[1] Students who posted more than ten messages in discussion board for discussion and searching for help were considered as active students.

preservice teachers to elementary students in a mathematical problem solving activity at a large Midwestern university in the U.S.A [4]. The results showed that the email activity helped the preservice teachers to develop a sense of the mathematical and problem solving skills of students at certain grade levels as well as provided them with an additional opportunity to learn about teaching mathematics so that it had a significant impact on their preparations to teach mathematics. Therefore the use of computers not only enhances students' learning of mathematics but also helps them understand the teaching and learning process from a constructivist approach.

A change in the use of a Computer Algebra System (CAS) with a group of first year undergraduate mathematics students at the University of Ballarat was documented by [5]. The use of CAS in a computer laboratory exercise was increased from an hour per week in 1995-96 to two hours per week in 1997-98. In a survey to monitor students' response to the changes in teaching and organization in 1997-98, the results showed that more than 70% of students either agreed or strongly agreed that the use of CAS had helped them increasing their understanding of mathematics. Additionally, there was some improvement in learning when comparing students' exam results obtained in 1996-97 with the results obtained in 1997-98. The results revealed that CAS was helpful to the first-year undergraduate mathematics students at the university of Ballarart.

The above examples show that computers not only play an increasingly significant role in mathematics teaching and learning but also provide a positive effect on mathematics students' learning for first year university students. Additional, the results show that the use of computers promotes better understanding, problem-solving skills, and participation in discussion. The consequence is that the use of computers reinforces constructivism in mathematics education. Therefore the use of technology is a very helpful and appropriate strategy to apply for mathematics education.

3.2 *Difficulties in learning mathematics*

Literature suggests that an inadequate mathematics background and too many demands on time are two major factors influencing first year students' learning of mathematics. The following examples demonstrate this. A study identifying factors that influence first-year students' success in mathematics [6] consisted of three phases – an open-ended questionnaire, five point Likert type questionnaire and interview. The results suggested that self-motivation was the major factor to affect students' success. On the other hand, difficult lectures, inadequate mathematics background and too many demands on time were very influential factors for unsuccessful students.

Another study predicting mathematical preparedness of first-year undergraduates to engineering and mathematics programmes at Aston University [7] also found that there was sufficient correlation between the mean performance and the prior qualification grade of the first year entrants. Similar to first-year mathematics students in Massey University and in Aston University, OUHK students also have a high time pressure in studying and a variety of academic background. Therefore these two factors are highly applicable to

OUHK students because OUHK adopts the open entry policy so that those with any qualification background are admitted, and the adult part-time students at OUHK have to commit themselves to their work and family as well as their studies.

Gender has also been revealed as one of the most important factors affecting mathematics learning [8][9][10]. For example, a cross-national study of the affective and cognitive dimensions of math anxiety [9] examined 671 sixth-grade boys and girls who came from China, Taiwan and the United States (U.S.). The results of both mathematics-achievement and the math-anxiety measures showed the existence of gender differences in mean levels of math anxiety in the Taiwanese sample and the U.S. sample. The girls in Taiwan and the U.S. had higher levels of math anxiety than boys. A meta-analysis synthesized the findings of 151 students which were mainly from journal articles, ERIC, and doctoral dissertations concerned with the nature, effects, and belief of mathematics anxiety [8]. Collectively the research surveyed suggested that females at each grade level (K-12 and post secondary) reported higher mathematics anxiety levels than males. The results also suggested that mathematics anxiety depressed performance in mathematics.

Besides gender, age was suggested to be another important factor to affect learning in mathematics. A study has been made to determine how effectively the investigative and interactive approaches of Mathematics 1[2] moderated students' beliefs and built their mathematics confidence and facility in investigating mathematical situations [11]. The results revealed that age moderated the level of mathematical confidence in Mathematics 1 students. More older (i.e., aged 30 or over) than younger (aged less than 30) students indicated that mathematical confidence has improved after studying Mathematics 1.

Overall, studies in the literature suggest constructivism is a very important theory to mathematics education. The use of technology is appropriate to apply to the teaching and learning of mathematics because the cognitive learning approach can be promoted. Moreover, the use of technology motivates first year undergraduate students. On the other hand, inadequate mathematics background, time pressure, gender and age are factors affecting students' learning of mathematics. These factors will be potential factors to affect OUHK students' learning of mathematics, so these factors are the guidelines for this research.

3.3 *Distance teaching with computers*

The increased use of computers as means of communication has meant that computers have become an ideal communication channel in distance education today. The use of computers in both distance and face-to-face education will of course have both advantages and disadvantages. The following examples show the use of computers and the results in the field of distance education.

A study reports how learners moved from an independent learning focus and engaged themselves in interactive learning experiences within the Web-based

---

[2] A new course was designed for older students and students with weak mathematics background offered by University of Auckland.

educational context [12]. An online unit was offered as part of Master of Online Education Program at the University of Southern Queensland (USQ) to provide some practical examples of strategies designed to promote learner engagement and accommodate different models of student learning. The unit electronic discussion area and personal contact though e-mail were maintained throughout the teaching event. The feedback from students was positive. Student commented "I appreciate the support, flexibility and assistance, which has motivated me to take a deep approach to learning". The feedback also indicated that the rapid response from instructors and peers motivated their participation in online communication and stimulated students' continuities in their studies. Therefore the use of computers in this Online Education Program not only provides a constructivist learning environment but also motivates students' learning.

Literature also suggests that another advantage of using computers in distance education is to overcome isolation. At Murdoch University there was a withdrawal rate of 43%, which was an unacceptably high figure. A study describes an attempt to overcome isolation for distance students through an on-line introductory unit so that they could keep on studying [13]. The study, as a pilot group, selected five on-campus students who were so depressed by their lack of academic progress they decided to withdraw from their studies. All the students were provided a range of powerful on-line capabilities such as e-mail, html pages, cgi forms, and discussion groups for accessing materials from the Web, communicating privately with each other, interacting simultaneously with all other members of the tutorial, responding to specific questions posed by the tutor, and handling the assignments electronically. All students gave positive feedback on their experiences during the course, but more importantly passed all the subjects they enrolled in, and continued their enrolment in the following semester with a confident and positive attitude, which was a different attitude to when they had commenced the first unit. Again, the interactions between students themselves and with tutors enabled distance students to experience feedback from peers so that the feeling of isolation was decreased. Consequently, it increased students' motivation to continue the course.

As a whole, using computers in distance education is inevitable today because of the rapid development of the Information Age. Literature shows a lot of positive impacts such as motivating learning, increasing confidence, enhancing communication and overcoming isolation, etc. on distance education. The use of computers reinforces two-way communication between tutor and students and overcomes psychological barriers to learning as distance students. Therefore the application of computers as one of the communication channels seems to be an appropriate way to enhance OUHK students' learning.

3.4 *Feedback on using WebCT in education*

WebCT provides three asynchronous and real-time communication channels for students, these should increase "the comfort level of students who might not participate in class", which could reduce any shyness problem [14]. The possible application of WebCT in Computer Assisted Language Learning (CALL) helped the students who were in a Second Language Class at Idaho State University [14].

The results from this practice showed that e-mail messages were generally informal so that students did not feel much pressure on their level of grammatical correctness, and they were willing to participate in e-mail communication. A similar discussion and conclusion arose from a study using a threaded discussion group by ten faculty members at a southeastern university in USA [15]. Faculty members using discussion groups within undergraduate and graduate classes from various colleges were contacted via e-mail. The qualitative data was collected through e-mail response from the faculty and a professor expressed "Students who do not feel comfortable talking in class, especially when expressing ideas they think will differ from others, often become more involved". A survey of a trial delivery of freshmen English using WebCT for a total of 76 students at Cambrian College [16] also commented that "students who did not feel comfortable talking in class often became more involved". These results suggest that using computer-mediated instruction not only encourages students' participation but also breaks through shyness.

A report at Saint Louis University evaluates the use of WebCT in classes of social work students [17]. A total of 80 social work students from two sections (one undergraduate level and the other graduated level) were studied. A comparison was made between traditional (undergraduate, age category of 0-30) and nontraditional (graduate, age category of 31 or older) students in which nontraditional students attributed their improved course performance to specific course tools (course syllabus, course calendar, hyperlinks, etc.) in WebCT. Moreover, the feedback showed that the use of WebCT was of greatest benefit to graduate students because WebCT could promote communication with students, created greater impact on students' engagement and course performance.

More than 60% of respondents said 'strongly agree' or 'agree' when students were asked to rate "the bulletin board was useful in communication with my fellow students" in a study of the use of WebCT to support face-to-face lectures for a large class of first year statistics students at the University of Wollongong [18]. In similar studies positive feedback was collected from an investigation of students' comments on the use of WebCT as a supplement to the ordinary lectures at the City University of Hong Kong [19]. More than 53% of students gave 'strongly agree' or 'agree' when answering "I think the 'Private Mail', 'Bulletin Board' and/or 'On-line Chat' on WebCT is/are effective way(s) to communicate". A majority of the respondents for the survey of a trial delivery of freshmen English using WebCT [16] found the experience in using WebCT to be a positive one. Student commented "it was a very effective medium of communication". Overall, students found that WebCT was a very helpful tool for communication.

Another advantage to stimulate the use of WebCT in education is to improve students' course performance. A Canadian study reported the use of WebCT to foster authentic communication for Second Language students from the United Arab Emirates (UAE) [20] in that Asian students can have unlimited time to construct their meaning when inputting, to read, and to respond to the items that are of maximal interest. Thus, using the bulletin board for communication was an effective way to help Asian students to read and write English comprehensively. It is not surprising to see similar feedback obtained from other study. A Learn

Online project was conducted for the students who studied a distance course in the Health and Community Studies division at Grant MacEwan Community College [21]. The course was converted to a Web-based format using TopClass and WebCT courseware and a collaborative design-team approach. Feedback showed that students liked the flexibility of the online courses as well as the feeling of connection to other peers and to the instructor. This research suggests that similar results to the above factors may arise for OUHK foundation mathematics students in that they will increase their personal skills on using the technologies, improve their course performance though the motivation from the provision of WebCT, and reduce the feeling of isolation through the use of e-mail communication.

As a whole, the literature review revealed that there were a number of reasons for users to use WebCT in education. Two of the most common factors to encourage students to use WebCT in learning based on students' perspectives include motivation and communication. The other popular factors were to overcome psychological problems such as isolation and shyness. These are the important guidelines for this study.

3.5 *Negative feedback on using WebCT and other computer channels in education*

On the other hand, the use of new technology may frighten the mature distance students who cannot keep up with the rapid development of a new era. The results of other studies have revealed that the use of computers in education has not always served to enhance learning and in some instances educators have been hesitant to introduce it into their classes [2]. A study of educational benefits and burdens to students when using WebCT as an adjunct to traditional classroom learning environment in 1997 and 1998 at Creighton University [2] indicated that less than half of respondents (44%) agreed that using WebCT helped to keep their interest in the classes and only 37% answered that using WebCT helped them learn quicker. In an overall sense, students did not provide the clear-cur preferences of using WebCT to teaching with 29.7% of responses expressing preferences for WebCT but 30.8% preferring the traditional approach. These results were not encouraging.

The literature also suggests other factors influencing students' learning when using technology in education. The following examples reveal the negative feedback on the use of computer-mediated instruction in teaching and learning. The findings of a study into the use of computer-mediated conference [22] showed some negative results with 80% of students reportedly having difficulty in connecting to the university computers. Some students solved their problems by trial and error when they could not get the notes or were unable to abort messages. One of the findings from a study identifying deterrents to the participation in Web-based Continuing Professional Education (CPE) by Certified Public Accountants (CPAs) [23] was in contrast with the positive response to electronic communication in that the accountants preferred face-to-face interaction with instructors and peers. These accountants also worried about the quality of a Web-based course and the lack of immediate feedback. Therefore these results revealed that negative feelings and technical challenges were the major barriers to the students.

Another important factor that discourages students from using new technologies is lack of technical support. A study of the effects of the Internet on the research activities of Australian academic psychologists [24] found that 71% of psychologists relied on trial and error to learn how to use Internet in research activities and reported that "they do not satisfy with the existing technical support" and "they were frustrated by unhelpful technicians". Additionally, Internet students from another study [25] felt that they had gained valuable experience in the use of the Internet, but they had to tolerate the technical problems such as limited 'out-of-hours' support. Another study of an empirical perspective in students' use of the Internet [26] used focus group interviews with 77 students in two UK universities. It found that students lacked adequate introductory and continued support so that students decreased their interest in exploring the Internet. A lack of technical support may also be a barrier to OUHK students to access to WebCT because the provision of a Helpdesk hotline from 8.45am to 5.45pm, Monday to Friday every week and 8.45am to 1pm on Saturdays may not be enough for thousands of part-time students at OUHK.

3.6 *Attitudes toward computers and the use of computers*

A study categorizing computer use and its relationship with attitudes toward computers for undergraduate students at Wake Forest University found that there were significant correlations between the attitude items and the categories of use including the use of networks for task-based purposes, the use of networks for non-task purposes, for data-management operations, and for mathematical computations [27]. Other results revealed that low users of computers used computers for task purposes because they were forced to but were not interested in computers. This is evidence that attitudes towards computers are important issues to impact students' participation in the use of computers.

Another study on the effects of an educational computing course on preservice and inservice teachers related to attitudes toward computers (anxiety, confidence and liking) and the use of computers found that teachers did change their attitudes toward computers after studying a mandated educational computing course at California State University in Los Angeles [28]. Twenty students voluntarily participated in the follow-up questionnaire survey and semi-structured interviews and the results showed that the course changed their attitudes toward computers so that they had confidence and were not afraid any more of integrated use of computers into classroom learning. Consequently these students' interests in the use of computers were motivated. Once again, this result revealed that there was a strong relationship between attitudes toward computers and the use of computers.

Another research study found that the level of anxiety was negatively related to computer experience for Hong Kong Students. In a study measuring the computer anxiety and PC involvement of a number of different cultural groups of computer-using students from China, Hong Kong, Malaysia, New Zealand, Tanzania and Thailand [29]; however, the overall conclusion drawn from six groups of students showed that experience of computer use could reduce computer anxiety, the statistics data revealed an interesting result that Hong Kong university students claimed the highest level of computer experience, but this group contained the highest mean level of computer anxiety, so it appeared that experience did not tend to alleviate anxiety for Hong Kong students. These research studies suggest that the computer experience is either positively or negatively related to attitudes toward computers. Once again, the relationship between prior computer experience and attitudes toward computers should be examined in this study.

As suggested in earlier, age, gender, prior computer experience are three common demographic factors always to be investigated in the study of using computers or learning mathematics with computers. Owing to the open entry policy, adults aged 17 or over and hold a Hong Kong Identity card can be admitted as OUHK students. The characteristics of OUHK students are therefore wide with a variety of previous educational backgrounds and working experiences. The statistics shown in the booklet of facts and figures published in December 2001 [30] indicates that 13.8% of them hold a university degree or better, 29.4% of them acquired a sub-degree or diploma, etc., 10.6% completing HK A-level or GCE A-level, 31.9% finished HKALE (Hong Kong Advanced Level Examination) or HKCEE (Hong Kong Certificate for Education Examination), more than 44% of them were managers or professionals, 24% were clerical or secretarial, 10% were technical personnal, 20% were communications, transport and others, and about 3% were unemployed. Computer experience will be obtained from the different educational backgrounds and different occupations. Therefore educational background and occupations are another important demographic factors to be examined in this study.

As a whole, the literature suggests that the common issues that affect students' participation in the use of computers include attitudes toward computers, technical challenges, a lack of technical support, gender, age and prior computer experience, etc. The following main variables (Figure 1) will serve as the guidelines to design the questionnaire for this research.

4. Conclusion

To synthesis all the feedback on the use of technology including WebCT in mathematics education, distance education and other applications in education, some common factors are identified as shown in Figure 1. These factors will be the guidelines to design the questionnaire. The questionnaire will be in a form of statements and students will be asked to select the scale which can be describe their feeling and situation best. The primary questionnaire is in progress and a pilot will be undertaken in July 2002, the results of the pilot will be reported in August 2002. The focus group interviews will then be followed by further investigation into the reasons for the important issues identified from the results of questionnaire.

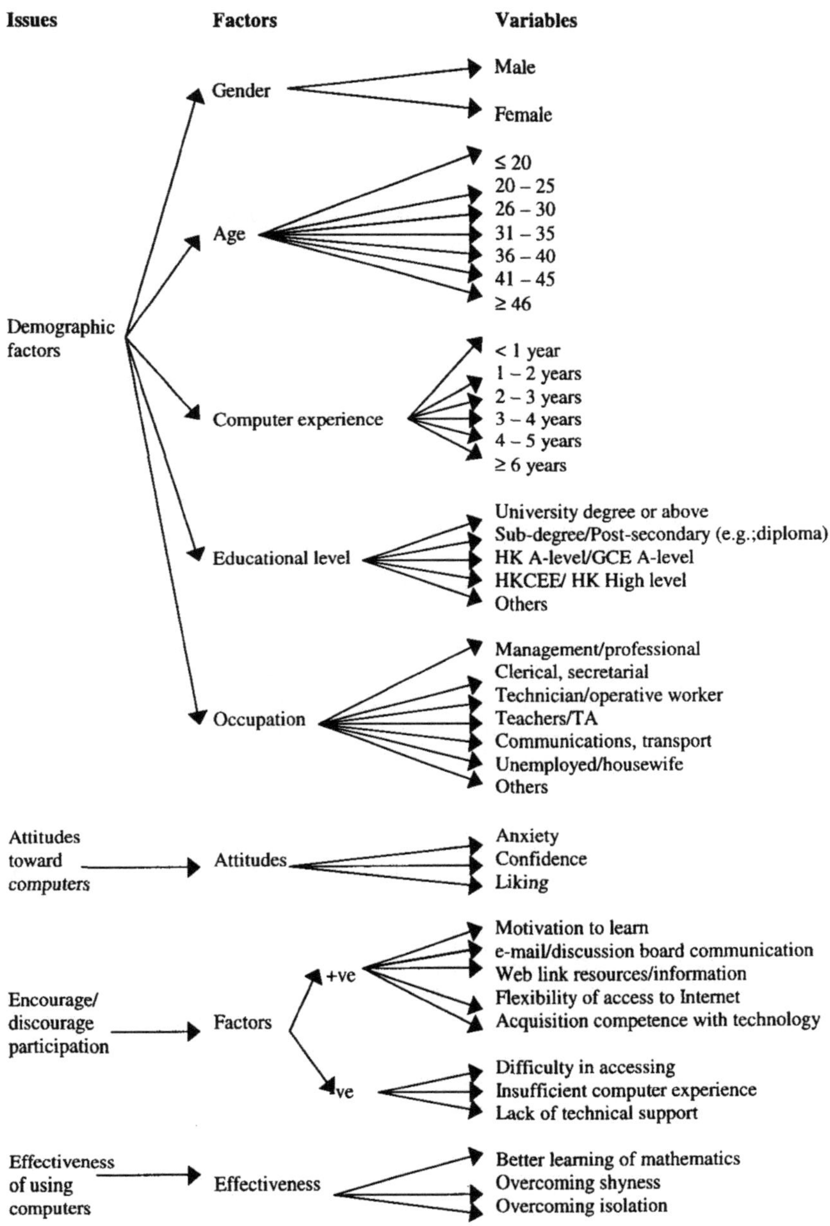

Figure 1. Variables used in the questionnaire

References

1. C.Vallone: Internet Education. *FDCH Congressional Testimony*, on the Internet, Distance Learning & the Future of the Research University, Subcommittee on Basic Research, Committee on Science, U.S. House of Representatives (2000).
2. D.A.Morss: A study of student perspectives on Web-based learning: WebCT in the classroom. *Internet Research*, **9**, 5, 393–408 (1999).
3. M.Cardelle-Elawar, K.Wetzel: Students and computers as partners in developing students' problem-solving skills. *Journal of Research on Computing in Education*, **27**, 4, 387–401 (1995).
4. D.M.Poole: An email activity: Preservice teacher's perceptions of authenticity. *Journal of Technology and Teacher Education*, **8**, 1, 13–28 (2000).
5. R.Pierce, K.Stacey: Reflections on the changing pedagogical use of Computer Algebra Systems: Assistance for doing or learning mathematics? *The Journal of Computers in Mathematics and Science Teaching*, **20**, 2, 143–161 (2001).
6. G.Anthony: Factors influencing first-year students' success in mathematics. *International Journal of Mathematical Education in Science and Technology*, **31**, 2, 3–14 (2000).
7. W.Cox: Predicting the mathematical preparedness of first-year undergraduates for teaching and learning purposes. *International Journal of Mathematical Education in Science and Technology*, **31**, 2, 227–248 (2000).
8. R.Hembree: The nature, effects, and relief of mathematics anxiety. *Journal of Research in Mathematics Education*, **21**, 33–46 (1990).
9. H-Z,Ho, D.Senturk, A.G.Lam, J.M.Zimmer, S.Hong, Y.Okamoto, S-Y.Chiu, Y.Nakazawa, C-P.Wang: The affective and cognitive dimensions of math anxiety: A cross-national study. *Journal for Research in Mathematics Education*, **31**, 3, 362–379 (2000).
10. D.B.McLeod: Research on affect in mathematics education : A reconceptualization. In D.A. Grouws (Ed.), *Handbook of Research on Mathematics Teaching and Learning: A Project of the National Council of Teachers of Mathematics*. New York: MaCmillan Publishing Co. (1992).
11. B.J.Miller-Reilly: Exploration and modeling in a university mathematics course: Perceptions of adult learners. In D. Coben, J. O'Donoghue & G.E. Fitzsimons (Eds.), *Perspectives on Adults Learning Mathematics*. Netherlands: Kluwer Academic Publishers. (2000).
12. J.McDonald, S.Reushle: Engagement in Web-based Education: Designing for Models of Student Learning. *Indian Journal of Open Learning*, **9**, 3, 287–297 (2000).
13. D.Lake, Reducing isolation for distance students: An on-line initiative. *Open Learning*, **14**, 3, 14–23 (1999).
14. S.Siekmann: To integrate your language Web tools – call WebCT. *Paper presented at the Natural Language Processing and Industrial Application*, New Brunswick, Canada. *ED422899*. (1998).

15. Y.S.Bailey, V.H.Wright: Innovative uses of threaded discussion groups. *Paper presented at the Annual Meeting of the Mid South Educational Research Association. ED446716.* (2000).
16. R.Mende: Learner reactions to college English on WebCT. *ED437997.* (1999).
17. S.P.Wernet, R.H.Olliges, T.A.Delicath: Postcourse evaluations of WebCT (Web Course Tools) classes by social work students. *Research on Social Work Practice*, **10**, 4, 487–504 (2000).
18. R.M.Corderoy, A.Porter, G.Lefoe: Supporting large classes using WebCT: A case study. *Indian Journal of Open Learning*, **9**, 3, 403–413 (2000).
19. A.Y.S.Cheng, S.K.C.Wong, S.K.C. An experience of implementing the Web-based instruction project at City University of Hong Kong. In *Proceedings at the Conference on Integrating IT & Teaching Development* at Lingnan University, Hong Kong (1999).
20. S.Carey, E.Crittenden: Using technology to foster authentic communication for second language students. *In Proceedings of the Technological Education and National Development Conference. ED447277* (2000).
21. C.White: Learn Online. *T H E Journal*, **27**, 9, 66–69 (2000).
22. J.A.Ross, C.A.Crane, D.Robertson: Equity of access to computer-mediated distance education. *Journal of Distance Education*, **X**, 2,17–32 (1995).
23. K.J.Perdue, T.Valentine: Deterrents to participation in Web-based continuing professional education. *The American Journal of Distance Education*, **14**, 1, 7–26 (2000).
24. S.R.Sharifabadi: Effects of the Internet on research activities, information seeking and communication behaviour of Australian academic psychologists. *Ph.D. thesis, University of New South Wales, Sydney* (1996).
25. L.Carswell, P.Thomas, M.Petre, B.Price, M.RichardsDistance education via the Internet: The student experience. British Journal of Educational Technology, **31**, 129–46 (2000).
26. N.Selwyn, N.Marriott, P.Marriott: Net gains or net pains? Business students' use of the internet. *Higher Education Quarterly*, **54**, 2, 166-186 (2000).
27. A.Mitra: Categories of computer use and their relationships with attitudes toward computers. *Journal of Research on Computing in Education*, **30**, 3, 281–295 (1998).
28. S.Yildirim: Effects of an educational computing course on preservice and inservice teachers: A discussion and analysis of attitudes and use. *Journal of Research on Computing in Education*, **32**, 4, 479–496 (2000).
29. R.Harris, R.Davison: Anxiety and involvement: Cultural dimensions of attitudes toward computers in developing societies. Journal of Global Information Management, **7**, 1, 26–38 (1999).
30. The Open University of Hong Kong: *Facts & Figures December 2001*. The Open University of Hong Kong, Planning Unit, 7 (2001).

Author Index

www.ingramcontent.com/pod-product-compliance
Ingram Content Group UK Ltd.
Pitfield, Milton Keynes, MK11 3LW, UK
UKHW020312150926
8624IPUK00014B/526

9 789812 381262